T3-BEA-241

Sept 04   Allee Chrestiansen

A Puppy Owner's
SURVIVAL Manual

Julia Barnes and Dr. Matthew Brash

BARNES
& NOBLE
BOOKS
NEW YORK

This edition published by Barnes & Noble, Inc.,
by arrangement with Ringpress Books Ltd., a division of Interpet Publishing.

© 2004 Barnes & Noble Books

M 10 9 8 7 6 5 4 3 2 1

ISBN 1-7607-5303-2

GENDER
Throughout this text, dogs have been referred to as 'he' instead of 'it' –
but no gender bias is intended.

ACKNOWLEDGEMENTS
Cartoons: Russell Jones

Printed in Singapore

THE TEN-PART SURVIVAL GUIDE

Puppy Owner's Survival Manual has been divided into 10 parts so that you can find your way around with ease, learning as much as possible about your canine companion.

CONTENTS IN DETAIL

PART FOUR: *GETTING READY*

PART FIVE: *HOME SWEET HOME*

Being consistent; Providing rewards; Clicker training.

PART NINE: *GROWING PAINS*

PART TEN: *HEALTH CARE*

Part I
Man's Best Friend

The Wolf In Your Home

When you see dogs parading in a show ring, or performing fabulous feats of obedience for their human owners, it is hard to remember that these animals are the descendants of wolves. They may not look very wild, but, in fact, every dog you see, whether it is a tiny Chihuahua or a massive St Bernard, is the product of his wolf ancestry, and a lot of canine behavior can be traced back to these far-off roots.

THE PACK MENTALITY

Animals organize themselves into groups in order to increase their chances of success in the battle for survival. A group will be better able to defend itself against enemies, it will be more efficient at finding food, and, perhaps most importantly of all, a group provides the best environment for reproduction and for rearing offspring, which ensures the survival of the species.

In order for group-living to be successful, there must be a hierarchy, or the group members will waste all their strength fighting amongst each other. Roles must be designated so that the strongest and fittest go out hunting and bring back food for the females who are caring for their young.

There may be changes in status from time to time, as challenges are made to usurp the more senior members as they become older and less able to cope with the rigors of leadership. However, it is in the group's interests to accept the established hierarchy and to concentrate on the business of day-to-day living.

Dogs have been living with men for hundreds of thousands of years, yet despite the huge adaptations they have made to end up as 'man's best friend', they still retain the pack mentality inherited from their wolf ancestors. The 'wolf' in your home sees his human family as the pack. In his eyes, the pack must have a leader, and the status of all pack members must be clearly defined.

This outlook on life is a great bonus to the dog owner, as he has an animal who is ready to accept leadership. It is our duty to take on this role – not as a grim, authoritarian figure, that is crushing all the individuality and enthusiasm out of the inferior members – but as a firm, fair and consistent leader who does not shrink from making decisions and taking action when it is needed.

EARLY DOMESTICATION

Why did the wolf and his descendants decide to abandon their independence and throw in their lot with man? In the earliest times, man and wolf would have competed with each other, hunting for the same food. Man could supplement his diet by growing crops, and, if times were lean, the wolf would have turned scavenger, living off the food discarded by humans.

It may have been that an orphan wolf cub occasionally joined the human settlement and was raised by the children. This type of animal may have proved himself a successful hunting companion, or he may have been valued as a guard, barking to give an early warning if strangers from other tribes were approaching.

Inevitably, the story of the dog's domestication is based mostly on conjecture. The first concrete evidence comes from a grave that was excavated in Germany, dated around 14,000 BC. By this time, men were hunting with more sophisticated weapons. They had graduated from using stone axes to making use of arrows with stone blades. This obviously increased the range from which an animal could be attacked, and the companion wolf would have been invaluable for bringing down the prey when it was wounded, and either killing it, or holding it at bay until human help arrived.

At this time, there would have been many different types of wolf, varying in size, build and coat. We can only assume that man discovered the concept of breeding animals to produce a similar type. Therefore, the puppies produced by a bold, strong hunter would be valued in the hope that they would inherit similar skills. If more guard dogs were needed to protect the settlement, the best guard dog would be mated to a bitch who shared similar qualities. In this way, man produced dogs with different skills who were happy to work alongside him.

In 1979, a Russian fur farmer wrote of his experiment to selectively breed for silver foxes with a placid temperament. The aim was to produce foxes that were easier to handle in their cages on fox farms. Over a period of 20 years, he worked on a breeding programme using over 10,000 foxes from different farms. The result was not only the production of foxes that were friendly and amenable, they also wagged their tails! Interestingly, they also developed physical changes: some were born with drop ears, some with black and white coat, and some with curly tails.

CHANGING TIMES

Some dogs breeds have a very ancient history that we can trace back over thousands of years; others have been developed in more recent times, and their lineage dates back for just a hundred years or so. There are some enthusiasts who put forward great claims for their breed's distinguished past, but, in fact, the history of dogs can be traced back to five main types. The evidence for this comes from fossils dating back to the Bronze Age. The types were as follows.

MASTIFFS

Mastiff-type dogs have been recorded in word, and in illustrations, from ancient times. The Ninevah bas-reliefs of 850 BC, in the British Museum, show a powerfully built dog with a big head and loose skin, which is reminiscent of many of the Mastiff breeds.

The English Mastiff became a favorite of the Romans. Hundreds of dogs were exported to Rome, either to fight in the arena or to be used as war dogs. Special suits of armor were made for these dogs, and they would have gone into battle wearing collars with knives attached to injure the enemy and the enemies' horses.

GREYHOUNDS

This group includes the fast, athletic hounds that hunted by sight. There are archaeological remains of a dog that strongly resembles a Greyhound which were found in the Middle East, dating back 4,000 years. It is thought that this was the rootstock for breeds such as the Whippet, the Saluki and the Afghan Hound.

SHEEPDOGS

Dogs were also needed to assist farmers, and the Collie breeds evolved as the perfect workmates, herding livestock so that it could be moved from place to place. Some of the bigger dogs were also used to defend livestock against predators, and breeds such as German Shepherd Dogs and Pyrenean Mountain Dogs were bred as guardians of the flock.

SPITZ-TYPE DOGS

This covers a big group of dogs coming from a wide geographical area. They tend to be tough dogs, with great powers of endurance, that could be used as sled dogs or hunters in the more remote regions. The husky-type dogs – the Siberian Husky, the Alaskan Malamute, and the Samoyed – represent this type.

POINTERS AND SETTERS

Many different types of dog were used for hunting, but this type was selectively bred to hunt small game. It is thought that the Spanish Pointing Hound was the rootstock of the many Pointer breeds that have developed throughout Europe, such as the German Shorthaired Pointer, the Hungarian Vizsla and English Pointer. The Setter breeds (Irish, English, Gordon, and Red and White) also come within this group.

COMPANION DOGS

Hundreds of breeds developed from these five main groups, but, alongside the dogs that were bred to work, there is a long history of small dogs, bred down from larger animals, who were highly prized as companions.

A number of Roman writers, including Pliny the Elder (23-709 AD) wrote of the virtues of pet dogs. Pliny wrote that "they were the most faithful of all animals, bar none".

The Pekingese was adopted as the preferred pet of Chinese Emperors. In fact, there is a record of a Chinese Emperor, living in 1680 AD, who decided that dogs were much more intelligent than humans, and so all his dogs were given exalted ranks and were dressed in the appropriate regalia. Apparently the females were dressed to match their husbands' ranks!

The Lhasa Apso and the Shih Tzu, with their origins in Tibet, also have a distinguished history. The Buddhists believed that when a monk transgressed during his life, he was reincarnated into the body of a small dog. As a result, the Shih Tzu and the Lhasa Apso lived in temples and were revered as 'holy dogs'.

THE MODERN ERA

As long as there has been work to do, the dog has found a place at man's side, and, showing remarkable powers of adaptability, he has survived through thousands of years, even though he may have lost his original working purpose.

A number of breeds are still used in their traditional roles, such as the Border Collie, who continues to provide the most efficient means of herding and moving livestock, and sporting enthusiasts still make use of the dogs who were bred to find game and retrieve it. However, many other breeds have had to reinvent themselves to find a place in modern-day society.

Fortunately, for the dog, this has coincided with a huge increase in the demand for companion dogs. In previous centuries, keeping a dog purely as a pet was considered the height of luxury, and that is why many of the small Toy breeds, such as the Pug and the Cavalier King Charles Spaniel were the favorites of royalty. Now most people keep dogs first and foremost as companions, and this is a role they have excelled at.

But this is not the end of the dog's story of survival. Working instincts from bygone days have been harnessed to the changing needs of society, and there are now a number of dogs who have found new careers in a modern world.

SECURITY DOGS

The dog's ability to guard and protect has been used from the very beginning of domestication. Today, it would be highly unsuitable, not to say dangerous, to have a fierce guard dog to protect the family home. However, the instinct to guard and protect has proved of great value to the security services.

German Shepherds have always been the preferred police dog throughout the world, but increasingly a wider range of breeds is being used to cope with changing work demands. Although dogs are still needed to guard, patrol, and sometimes even to attack criminals, they are also needed for tracking – using their sense of smell to follow a trail which may be many hours old. Dogs are also used to sniff out explosives, and their work detecting drugs has become of increasing importance. The Labrador Retriever and the English Springer Spaniel are popular choices for this type of work.

SEARCH AND RESCUE

The traditional search and rescue breed was the St Bernard who trudged his way across mountain passes to find travelers who were lost in the snow. Today, the St Bernard's role has largely been replaced by helicopter, but a number of different breeds are still used for this type of work.

Despite modern technology, a dog with a good nose is still the best way of finding people who get into difficulty when they are in remote and desolate areas. A number of mountain climbers, potholers, and even backpackers, can truthfully say they owe their lives to a dog's sense of smell.

When a large-scale disaster occurs, such as an earthquake that turns hundreds of buildings to rubble, search and rescue dogs will play a leading role. A number of breeds are used for this work; Border Collies are widely used, but Spaniels, Retrievers, German Shepherds and Pointers have all been successful.

ASSISTANCE DOGS

This is probably the biggest growth area for career dogs, and the type of work they do is expanding all the time. The first assistance dogs were used as guides for the blind. From small beginnings, this has grown into a worldwide phenomenon, giving independence to thousands of blind people. The first guide dogs were German Shepherds, and although this breed is still used, it is the Retriever breeds, particularly Labrador Retrievers and Golden Retrievers, that are most commonly used.

In fairly recent times, dogs have been used to help the physically disabled. They work mostly within the home, opening doors, switching on lights, and retrieving articles for their disabled owner. They can also act as a steadier when their owner is getting up from a chair, and they are trained to bark to raise an alarm. Again, it is the Retriever breeds that have proved the most successful.

In contrast, a wide variety of breeds are used as hearing dogs, alerting their owners to the doorbell, the telephone (deaf people use specially adapted telephones or minicoms), to a cooker timer, or to a baby alarm. They can also be trained to fetch their deaf owner when he or she is required, and to indicate an emergency, such as the burglar alarm or the fire alarm going off, by alerting their owner and then dropping to the floor.

The size of a hearing dog is unimportant, and so this widens the choice of suitable dogs. The most successful are dogs that bond closely with their human owner, and those without strong hunting, guarding or herding instincts. Interestingly, a number of Toy breeds, such as the Chihuahua and the Papillon, have made excellent hearing dogs.

RACING DOGS

As we have seen, the Greyhound has an ancient lineage, and the breed's amazing ability to run at speed has become big business in today's society. Track racing, where Greyhounds chase an artificial lure around an oval-shaped circuit, is a big spectator sport in the United Kingdom, the United States, and in Australia, where people enjoy the thrill of watching dogs racing, as well as betting on the result.

COMPETITION DOGS

With the increased leisure time available to many people, there is a growing interest in training dogs for competition. At one time, this was largely restricted to Competitive Obedience, but now there is wonderful selection of sports that dogs and owners can get involved with, adding a new dimension to their partnership.

Agility is the fastest-growing discipline, but Flyball and Canine Freestyle (Heelwork to Music) have a growing band of enthusiasts. There are also many working tests available so breeds can show off their inherited skills. These include Herding Trials for the pastoral breeds, Hunting Tests for the hounds, Earthdog Tests for terriers and Dachshunds, and Field Trials for the sporting/gundog breeds. The sighthounds are not forgotten, and artificial lure coursing is a popular leisure sport for many owners.

THE FUTURE

It is impossible to predict the future with any degree of accuracy, but, looking at the dog's history to date, you can be pretty sure that he will be among the survivors going into the next millennium. Any animal who can transform himself from a rival hunter to man's all-round helpmate and companion, deserves a place at anyone's hearthside.

Chapter 2

Forming A Partnership

There are many different aspects to choosing a puppy, as will be discussed in later chapters. However, one of the most vital areas to research is often the most neglected. When you are looking at different breeds, the first question you should ask is, what was this type of dog bred to do?

You may like the way a dog looks, or it may seem to be a convenient size, but if you do not understand the inherited behavior and temperament of the breed, you may end up with a dog that is totally unsuitable for your lifestyle.

It is therefore important to look at the main breed groups, and highlight inherited characteristics.

GUNDOGS/SPORTING DOGS

The hallmark of breeds in this group is their trainability. They were developed to work alongside their owners in the field, and so a biddable nature and an eagerness to work was all-important.

The group can be subdivided, depending on the task the dog was expected to carry out. The Retrievers (Labradors, Goldens, Flat-Coats, Chesapeakes, etc.) were expected to retrieve game both on land and in water. Today's Retrievers tend to be energetic dogs with a strong instinct to retrieve. They are characterized by a soft mouth (which means they will carry without damaging), and a love of swimming. Most Retrievers tend to be happy-go-lucky types with a great enthusiasm for life.

Spaniels were used to flush out game as well as to retrieve. Some of the Spaniel breeds, such as the English Springer, retain strong working instincts, whereas in other breeds such as the American Cocker and the English Cocker, inherited behavior of this type has become more diluted. Generally, Spaniels are busy dogs with an outgoing, fun-loving temperament.

Pointers and Setters were first used to find and point or set game so that it could be driven forward into the nets. With the introduction of the gun, the Pointers or Setters

would find game and hold it on point, or drop, in the case of the Setters, until the hunter arrived with his gun. Both breeds are still used in the field, but the Setters (particularly the Irish, with his glorious chestnut coloring) have become popular companion dogs. These breeds have a tendency to range and they require plenty of exercise, but they also enjoy their creature comforts.

There are a number of all-round gundogs, which were mostly developed in Europe. This category, which includes the German Shorthaired Pointer, the Hungarian Vizsla and the Weimaraner, are active, intelligent dogs who love having a job of work to do.

HOUNDS

Hounds can be divided into two main sub-groups: sighthounds and scenthounds. Sighthounds were used to hunt by sight, and they include the canine athletes – Greyhounds, Whippets, Afghans and Salukis – who were developed to run at tremendous speeds. In fact, they make remarkably good companion dogs, as, although they enjoy their exercise, they are almost equally keen on lying on the sofa. The instinct to chase remains high, and this should be considered before taking on a sighthound breed.

The Scenthounds vary in size from the Bloodhound to the Dachshund, so there is plenty to choose from in this group. As their name suggests, they hunted by following a trail, and all the breeds are characterized by a formidable sense of smell. Generally, these are dogs with considerable stamina who need a fair amount of exercise. They are reasonably easy to train, but inclined to turn a deaf ear when they get on a scent!

TERRIERS

Most of the terriers were bred to go to ground after foxes and rabbits, and to catch rats. They are feisty little dogs with great spirit and determination. Breeds such as the Jack Russell, the Cairn and the Border may be small in size, but they more than make up for it in terms of character. They share a liking for digging, and need to lead an active life.

There is another type of terrier that was bred for bull-baiting and dog fighting, as well as for catching rats. The Bull Terrier, the Staffordshire Bull Terrier and the American Staffordshire Bull Terrier are all representatives of this type. Fortunately, the barbaric sports that these dogs were used for have long since been outlawed, and, for the most part, these breeds make good companions. They are loyal and loving, and have a great sense of fun. However, the instinct to fight is not completely dead and buried, and these breeds can be tricky to mix with other dogs.

PASTORAL

This group includes all the breeds that were used to work with livestock. Some of the breeds were used to guard the flock, and these tend to be larger, heavier types such as the Pyrenean Mountain Dog and the Maremma Sheepdog. These tend to be gentle dogs, but can be quite formidable when roused. The German Shepherd is rarely thought of for his original role of guarding and herding, and most people associate the breed with security work. This is a highly intelligent breed that requires plenty of mental stimulation.

The Collie breeds (Rough, Smooth, Bearded, Border) plus the smaller Shetland Sheepdog were used for herding livestock. They vary considerably in temperament, and so each should be researched separately. The Border Collie retains a very strong herding instinct, and, in a domestic situation, this is often translated into a strong desire to chase things that move, such as joggers or bicycles. Most Border Collies are often ball-obsessed, and will spend hours chasing and retrieving a ball. The true workaholic of the canine world, the Border Collie is a breed that needs a great deal of mental stimulation, and should only be considered by those who have lots of time to devote to training and competing.

The Australian Shepherd shares the same versatility and is becoming popular in the United States.

WORKING

This is a big group that covers the breeds that are not associated with herding. The dogs with strong guarding instincts, such as the Rottweiler, the Boxer, the Mastiff and the Bullmastiff, are included. These big, strong breeds need experienced handling, but in the right hands they can become first-class companions.

Newcomers to the dog world are often attracted to the sled dogs from the North such as the Alaskan Malamute and the Siberian Husky. These breeds are stunning to look at – it is almost like having a wolf in your home – but they do not make suitable pets if you are simply looking for a companion dog. These breeds have a strong work ethic and will not be happy unless they have a strenuous routine of mental and physical exercise. However, if you want to take up sled racing, these are the breeds to go for!

TOY DOGS

Breeds that were developed to be lapdogs have got the skills of companionship down to a fine art. There is a wide variety of breeds, all with their individual characteristics, but they share a love of people and will become very attuned to their owners.

If you want a slightly bigger dog, the Cavalier King Charles Spaniel is an excellent choice as he combines a sweet and loving temperament with a bright, intelligent outlook on life, and he will be ready to have a go at anything. Some of the other Toy breeds are quite demanding in terms of grooming, as many, such as the Pekingese, the Maltese and the Yorkshire Terrier, have splendid long coats.

NON-SPORTING/UTILITY

As the name suggests, this is the group for breeds that don't fit into any other category. Breeds as diverse as the Dalmatian, the Akita, and the Shih Tzu are included, and they have absolutely nothing in common with each other.

If you have an interest in any of the breeds within this group, you will need to do your homework and find out all you can about the breed in question.

MIXED BREEDS

There is no necessity to buy a purebred dog, and you may decide that a pup of mixed breeds will suit you best. There are two types that fall into this category. A cross-bred dog has two different purebred parents, such as a Golden Retriever mated to a Labrador Retriever, or a Border Collie mated to a German Shepherd Dog. The resulting puppies will inherit characteristics from both parents, and so you can make a rough guess at size, temperament and coat type.

If two dogs of mongrel or mixed breeding are mated, when neither parent is from known breeding, you can only guess how the resulting puppies will turn out. While the mystery may appeal to some people, it is far safer to make a more informed choice so that you know what you are going to end up with.

For a full list of AKC and UK registered breeds, see Appendix II, page 251.

Part II
The Right Choice

Chapter 3

The Commitment

You may feel very committed to the idea of owning a dog, but before you make your final decision, think long and hard about the responsibilities of caring for a living creature for the next 12-14 years. This may seem very obvious, but, unfortunately, hundreds and hundreds of dogs end up in rescue shelters because their owners failed to understand what was involved in owning a dog.

RESPONSIBILITIES OF DOG OWNERSHIP

Put the picture of an appealing puppy right out of your mind, and get down to the realities of dog ownership. Ask yourself the following questions:

- Do you feel confident that you can provide a home for your dog for the duration of his life?
- Are all the members of your family equally committed to the idea of owning a dog?
- If you plan to start a family at some point in the future, will your dog still have a place in your home?
- What is your working routine? No dog should be left on his own for longer than four hours maximum.
- Can you afford to pay feeding bills and veterinary bills?
- Do you have the time to exercise your dog on a regular basis?
- If you plan to have a longcoated breed, do you have the time for grooming?
- Can you afford the services of a professional groomer if you are planning to buy a Poodle, or a wirecoated breed that needs its coat stripping? (See page 78.)
- Are you prepared to spend the time training your dog?
- Will you take your dog on holiday with you, or will you need to pay for boarding kennels?

Nobody can foresee the future, and sometimes circumstances change dramatically due to illness or some other misfortune. However, when you are embarking on dog ownership, you must be confident that you can fulfil your responsibilities.

DIFFERENT DEMANDS

The most rewarding and successful relationships between dogs and their owners are not the result of a lucky chance. Like all relationships, the human-canine relationship has to be worked at, and the most important single factor is choosing the type of dog that is most likely to fit in with your lifestyle.

You may love the idea of taking on an energetic Border Collie, but if you do not have the time to give to training and stimulating this highly intelligent breed, or providing sufficient exercise, think again. You would probably be much better opting for a less demanding breed.

Many owners love grooming – and it can be a bonding, therapeutic experience for both dog and owner, but no one likes a smelly, tangled uncared-for animal. If you do not have the time or patience for grooming, choose a low-maintenance, shortcoated breed.

Some breeds are much more demanding in terms of training than others. If you have a Toy dog, a few simple training exercises will suffice. But if you take on a Rottweiler or a German Shepherd Dog, for example, you must be prepared to work hard at establishing your authority and bringing out the best in these strong, intelligent dogs.

DIFFERENT LIFESTYLES

Just as there are many different types of dog, there are also many different types of owner. There is no bar to owning a dog: you can be young or old; you can live on your own or have a large family; you can go out to work part-time or stay in all day. However, you must choose a dog that will adapt to your lifestyle.

Elderly owners: Generally, elderly owners are better suited to the smaller breeds, which tend to be less demanding in terms of exercise. Toy dogs are also less boisterous, which can be an important consideration.

Family owners: A sense of mutual respect must be established between dogs and children, but, if this is achieved, a dog makes a wonderful addition to the family. It is better to choose a friendly, outgoing and tolerant breed, such as a Labrador Retriever or a Golden Retriever, as they are more likely to enjoy the hurly-burly of family life.

Working owners: You can go out to work and own a dog, but only if you are employed for part-time hours. You cannot leave a dog on its own for longer than four hours maximum. This is equally true for all breeds, regardless of their size or temperament. When you get home, you must be prepared to take your dog out, or play with him, so that he receives some undivided attention.

If you have to work longer hours, you can employ the services of a dog-sitter or a dog-walker, but if this is needed five days a week, you are probably being unrealistic about your own ability to care for a dog. If work has to take priority, it is better to choose another pet, such as a cat, or delay owning a dog until your circumstances change.

SIZE MATTERS

Size is an obvious consideration. There are few, if any, owners who have problems because their dog is too small, but big dogs can cause big problems. Consider the following points before opting for a canine giant.
- Big dogs are more expensive to keep. Feeding bills will be considerably higher.
- Big dogs need a large sleeping area. If you buy a bed or a crate, there must be enough space for a fully-grown dog to stretch out in comfort.
- You will need a car that is big enough to accommodate a large dog.
- If you have small children, you will need to supervise all interactions, particularly when the dog is young and boisterous.
- You need to be fit and strong so that you can control a big dog at all times.
- Generally, big dogs have a shorter life-expectancy than the smaller breeds.

COAT CONCERNS

All dogs need to be brushed and examined once a week as a minimum requirement (see pages 120-125). But there is a vast difference in the grooming needs of different breeds, so this must rate as a very important consideration. There is a wide range of different coat types, each with their own specific grooming requirements (see Chapter 15: Coat Care). However, the following categories give an indication of the workload that is involved.

Shortcoated: If you are not a fan of grooming and your time is limited, choose a low-maintenance shortcoated breed. Boxers, Beagles, Labrador Retrievers and Weimaraners fall into this category.

Longcoated: Beautiful to look at, but hard work to maintain. Daily brushing is essential, and bathing is often needed more frequently to keep the dog clean and fresh-smelling. The workload within this group varies from Setters and Spaniels, which take a reasonable amount of looking after, to the luxuriant long coats of breeds such as Rough Collies and Yorkshire Terriers, which demand total dedication. You will also have your work cut out with a number of the shaggy sheepdog breeds, such as the Old English Sheepdog and the Bearded Collie.

Non-shedding: A dog that does not shed its coat sounds great, but the reality bears closer examination. A Poodle or a Bedlington Terrier will need regular trips to a groomer, approximately every six to eight weeks, so that the coat can be clipped. The Komondor and the Hungarian Puli have long, corded coats that are left to grow into spectacular 'dreadlocks', which can reach all the way to the ground.

Wirecoated: Terriers such as the Airedale Terrier and the West Highland White Terrier have a harsh outer coat that needs to be stripped at least twice a year. Unless you are showing your dog, and therefore managing the coat on a continuous basis, you will need the services of a groomer. This also applies to some other breeds, such as the Schnauzer breeds.

HEALTH ISSUES

Everyone hopes to buy a healthy puppy that will live a long life, suffering few health problems. Good breeding, followed by careful management and preventative health care (see Chapter 25: Health Care Programs) will play a large part in achieving this goal. However, there are some inherited disorders, such as eye conditions and bone disorders, that are more likely to affect specific breeds. It is important to be aware of relevant health issues when making your choice.

The average life-expectancy of a dog is between 12-14 years. But the bigger, heavyweight breeds, such as Mastiffs and Great Danes, may not reach double figures. In contrast, a Toy dog, such as a Maltese, is blessed with longevity and may well live to 15 or even 16 years of age.

Chapter 4

Top Dogs

Some people have a very firm idea about the breed they want – perhaps they were brought up with a Boxer for example, or perhaps they have friends that keep English Springer Spaniels, and so they have had the opportunity to get to know the breed. For others, it is a matter of looking at the breeds, and then narrowing down the choice. The aim of a prospective owner is to find the dog that is most likely to fit in with their lifestyle.

The popularity of certain breeds rises and falls according to fashion, and there are other breeds that remain as constant favorites. We have compiled profiles of the 50 most popular breeds, to help you make your choice. The grooming and exercise requirements are given for adult dogs so that you can see the workload involved. For more information on these topics see Chapter 15: Coat Care, and Chapter 16: Exercise. Many of the breeds have health issues that need to be checked out; these are indicated, but for more information on health problems see Chapter 27: A-Z of Canine Disorders And Diseases.

There is sometimes a slight variation in the size of a breed, depending on the governing kennel club. We have therefore given an average size, which will give a good idea of what you are letting yourself in for!

AKITA

Roots: Developed in Japan as a guard and a hunter.
Character: Aloof with strangers, but very loyal to his family.
Training: There is no doubting his intelligence, but the Akita also has a streak of independence which makes him quite difficult to train.
Grooming: The outer coat is coarse and straight and is relatively easy to care for. The coat sheds spectacularly twice a year.
Exercise: A large, powerful dog that needs plenty of exercise.
Health check: Eye testing and hip scoring (to assess for hip dysplasia) is required.
Average size: Dogs 26-28 ins (66-71 cms), bitches 24-26 ins (61-66 cms).

One of the delights of the dog world is that it is full of extremes. If you want a small dog, you can go for the tiny Chihuahua – the world's smallest breed – which measures just 5 ins (11 cms) at the shoulder, or you can go for the mighty Irish Wolfhound, the tallest dog breed, which can be as big as 34 ins (86 cms).

ALASKAN MALAMUTE

Roots: A sled dog from Western Alaska.

Character: Affectionate, with a strong sense of hierarchy, so you must establish your leadership early on.

Training: Needs to have his mind occupied, and responds well to all mental activity.

Grooming: Regular attention, particularly when the coat is shedding.

Exercise: A true workhorse, strenuous physical exercise is essential.

Health check: Hip scoring is required for breeding stock.

Average size: Dogs 25 ins (64 cms), bitches 23 ins (58 cms).

AMERICAN COCKER SPANIEL

Roots: A North American speciality, developed from the English Cocker Spaniel. The breed was originally used to retrieve quail, but is now better known as a glamorous companion.

Character: An even-tempered dog with an obvious enjoyment of life.

Training: Quick to catch on, eager to please.

Grooming: A demanding breed that needs daily grooming, plus specialized trimming.

Exercise: Moderate.

Health check: Eye testing for hereditary cataract.

Average size: Dogs 14-15 ins, bitches 13-14 ins.

AUSTRALIAN SHEPHERD

Roots: Developed in the Basque region of Spain to guard and herd sheep, and then taken by migrants to Australia.

Character: A devoted family dog, but can be protective. Reserved with strangers.

Training: A very high work drive that needs to be channeled. Excels in all the canine sports.

Grooming: Regular grooming is needed to keep the coat in good order and the feathering tangle-free.

Exercise: Requires extensive daily exercise.

Health check: Eye testing and hip scoring is required.

Average size: Dogs 20-23 ins (51-58 cms), bitches 18-21 ins (46-53 cms).

BEAGLE

Roots: A scenthound from Britain that was used to hunt in packs.

Character: Amenable and easy to live with.

Training: A quick-witted dog, who can go 'deaf' when he picks up a scent.

Grooming: Low-maintenance.

Exercise: Active and energetic, the Beagle loves his exercise.

Health check: No testing required.

Average size: Both sexes 13-16 ins (33-40 cms). In the US, the breed is divided into two sizes – under 13 ins (33 cms), and 13-15 ins (33-37.5 cms).

All dogs have an amazing sense of smell – in Beagles it has been estimated at 100 times greater than in humans. In North America, and in Australia, Quarantine Beagle Brigades work in airports detecting meat (raw and processed), fresh fruit and vegetables, foliage and eggs.

BERNESE MOUNTAIN DOG

Roots: A general farm-worker from Switzerland, guarding the flock and pulling carts full of dairy produce to market.

Character: Kind, devoted to his family.

Training: Intelligent, but a slight tendency to be stubborn.

Grooming: A soft, silky coat, with abundant feathering. Daily grooming is needed.

Exercise: A steady routine of regular outings.

Health check: Hip scoring and elbow scoring is required for breeding stock. Osteochondrosis – OCD – (see page 231) can be a problem.

Average size: Dogs 25-27.5 ins (64-70 cms), bitches 23-26 ins (58-66 cms).

BICHON FRISE

Roots: Comes from the Mediterranean area, and became a favorite in the royal courts.

Character: Lively and playful.

Training: Bright, quick to learn.

Grooming: The distinctive white coat with corkscrew curls demands a huge amount of work to keep it in order.

Exercise: This can be moderate, but should not be neglected.

Health check: Incidence of Legge-Perthes disease (a condition affecting the hip) and patella luxation (see page 233) in the breed.

Average size: Both sexes 9-11 ins (23-28 cms).

BORDER COLLIE

Roots: Comes from the borders of England, Scotland and Wales, and is known worldwide for his herding skills.

Character: A canine workaholic who must have his mind occupied.

Training: The most versatile of all breeds, the Border Collie is superb at all the canine sports.

Grooming: The moderately long coat, with feathering, must be kept tangle-free. The smoothcoated variety is low-maintenance.

Exercise: An extensive and varied routine is required for this high-energy breed.

Health check: Eye testing is required.

Average size: Dogs 21 ins (53 cms), bitches slightly less.

BORDER TERRIER

Roots: Comes from the borders of Scotland and England and was developed to go to ground after foxes.

Character: Happy and adaptable.

Training: Bright and willing, particularly when motivated.

Grooming: The harsh coat is low-maintenance, but it will need to be stripped twice a year.

Exercise: Enjoys the stimulation of going out and about, but does not need extensive exercise.

Health check: Currently no inherited conditions to test for.

Average size: Dogs 13-15lbs, bitches 11-14 lbs.

BOSTON TERRIER

Roots: Born and bred in the USA, the breed resulted from crossing a Bulldog and a white English Terrier.

Character: Well-mannered, friendly.

Training: Responsive.

Grooming: A shortcoated breed that is easy to care for.

Exercise: Moderate needs, but loves to be part of family activities.

Health check: Can be prone to eye injuries.

Average size: Comes in three different categories – lightweight is under 15 lbs, (6.8 kgs), middleweight 15-20 lbs (6.8-9.1 kgs), and heavyweight 20-25 lbs (9.1-11.4 kgs).

BOXER

Roots: Created in Germany to be an all-round, guard, working and companion dog.

Character: Extrovert and lively, with a great sense of loyalty.

Training: Can be trained to a high standard.

Grooming: Easy to care for.

Exercise: A muscular and energetic dog who needs plenty of exercise.

Health check: Heart tests for breeding stock. Deafness may occur in white Boxers.

Average size: Dogs 22-25 ins (57-63 cms), bitches 21-23 ins (53-59 cms).

BULLMASTIFF

Roots: Known as the gamekeeper's dog, the Bullmastiff was developed from interbreeding the Bulldog with the Old English Mastiff. He was used to patrol country estates, and to be on the lookout for poachers.

Character: A formidable guard, who needs experienced handling. Loving and loyal to his family.

Training: It is important to establish leadership early on as this breed has dominant tendencies.

Grooming: A short coat that requires minimal work.

Exercise: Regular walking is required, but only allow free-running in a completely controlled environment.

Health check: Guard against gastric dilation and torsion of the stomach (see page 223).

Average size: Dogs 25-27 ins (63.5-68.5 cms), bitches 24-26 ins (61-66 cms).

BULL TERRIER

Roots: A British-bred fighting dog, but now highly valued as a family companion.

Character: Amiable and easy-going, loves his family, but this breed can be difficult to handle with other dogs.

Training: Not obedience-orientated, and inclined to be stubborn, but he will accept basic training.

Grooming: Low-maintenance.

Exercise: Regular walks are required or the breed can become obese.

Health check: Hearing should be tested, check for incidence of liver and kidney disease.

Average size: No size is stipulated, but, generally, males weigh 55-70 lbs (25-32 kgs), and bitches range from 45-60 lbs (20-27 kgs).

CAVALIER KING CHARLES SPANIEL

Roots: Developed from the Toy Spaniel of Europe; they became a great favorites of Charles II of England, and the breed was named after him.

Character: Gay and affectionate.

Training: Responsive, does well in Obedience and Mini-agility.

Grooming: The long, silky coat needs daily attention.

Exercise: An adaptable breed that can adapt to the amount of exercise he is given.

Health check: Eye testing and heart testing is required.

Average size: Both sexes 12-13 ins (30.5-33 cms).

Charles II was so fond of his dogs that he sometimes found it hard to concentrate on affairs of state. Diarist Samuel Pepys blamed him for "playing with his dogs all the while, and not minding his business."

CHIHUAHUA

Roots: The name comes from the Mexican state of Chihuahua, but the breed probably originated in the Mediterranean area, and was taken to its adopted home by Conquistadors.

Character: Friendly and inquisitive.

Training: Smart as a button, the Chihuahua loves being given things to do.

Grooming: The smoothcoated variety requires minimal grooming; the longcoated Chihuahua needs daily attention.

Exercise: The tiny Chihuahua, the smallest dog in the world, will have sufficient exercise pottering around his home and garden/yard.

Health check: Patella luxation can be a problem (see page 233).

Average size: Not to exceed 6 lbs (2.7 kgs).

CHOW CHOW

Roots: A guard dog and hunter from China.

Character: Reserved, but very loyal towards his family.

Training: The Chow does not see the point of Obedience exercises, but he will respect house rules.

Grooming: The coat may be rough, which requires daily grooming, or smooth, which is easier to deal with.

Exercise: Not high in energy, but thrives on variety, so be imaginative in your choice of outings.

Health check: Entropion, a condition where the eyelids turn inwards, occurs in the breed (see page 221).

Average size: Dogs 18-21 ins, bitches 17-20 ins.

COCKER SPANIEL (English)

Roots: Like all the spaniel breeds, the Cocker's origins are in Spain, but he was developed in England to flush game birds, particularly woodcock – hence his name.

Character: Happy, merry.

Training: Eager to please, loves working with his owner.

Grooming: The flat, silky coat has extensive feathering, so daily attention is needed to keep it tangle-free.

Exercise: Regular walks are a must for this active dog.

Health check: Eye testing is required for breeding stock.

Average size: Dogs 16 ins, bitches 15 ins.

COLLIE (Rough)

Roots: A native shepherd dog from Scotland.

Character: Loving and affectionate, bonds strongly with his family.

Training: Give the Rough Collie a chance and he will surprise you, doing well in a number of canine disciplines.

Grooming: A wonderful coat that demands total dedication from the owner to keep it in good order.

Exercise: Rain or shine, the Rough Collie enjoys his exercise, and doesn't mind if he spoils his coat!

Health check: Eye testing is required.

Average size: Dogs 24 ins (61 cms), bitches 22 ins (56 cms).

DACHSHUND

Roots: A German breed that was used to go to earth after badger.

Character: Bold and surprisingly courageous for their size. The longcoated variety tends to be a little more docile than the wirecoated and the smoothcoated varieties.

Training: An intelligent little dog, the Dachshund can develop his own agenda if you give him the opportunity.

Grooming: This differs depending on the variety. The smoothcoated is low-maintainace, the wirecoated is easy to care for on a routine basis, but will need stripping twice-yearly, and the longcoated requires daily attention.

Exercise: The Dachshund's working roots are often forgotten, and so his exercise needs can be neglected. Walks should be moderate in length, but they will be much appreciated.

Health check: Eye testing is required. Spinal problems can occur.

Average size: Dachshunds come in a standard size – 20-26 lbs (9-12 kgs), and a miniature size – under 11 lbs (5 kgs).

DALMATIAN

Roots: Developed in Europe, but became more widely known in England in the 1800s when they were used as carriage dogs, running alongside horse-drawn coaches and guarding the occupants.

Character: Extrovert and lively.

Training: Some Dalmatians enjoy Agility, but they are not the easiest dogs to train unless they are strongly motivated.

Grooming: A spectacular-looking coat that requires very little work.

Exercise: Athletic in build, and bred for endurance, this is a breed that loves to run.

Health check: Ear testing is essential as deafness does occur in the breed.

Average size: Dogs 23-24 ins (58.5-61 cms), bitches 22-23 ins (56-58 cms).

Spotted dogs have a long and distinguished history. They were first depicted on a fresco dated 1700 BC, which now hangs in the National Archaeological Museum in Athens.

ENGLISH SPRINGER SPANIEL

Roots: An English-bred Spaniel; the name Springer comes from the ability to 'spring' game.

Character: Friendly and biddable.

Training: The Springer loves to work, and is one of the most popular of the gundog breeds that are still used in the field. He also does well in Agility, and has excelled as a 'sniffer' dog, detecting drugs and explosives.

Grooming: The coat demands daily attention, as the extensive feathering easily becomes matted and tangled.

Exercise: The more the better, particularly in a country environment where there are plenty of interesting scents.

Health check: Eye testing is required.

Average size: Both sexes 20 ins (51 cms).

GERMAN SHEPHERD DOG

Roots: A German breed that was originally used to herd and guard sheep. It has been adopted worldwide as a police dog.

Character: Watchful and loyal, often showing particular devotion to one person.

Training: A brilliant worker that is successful in Working Trials, Herding Tests and Obedience. However, experience is needed to train this breed.

Grooming: Basic grooming care is required for the straight, harsh coat. Longhaired German Shepherds are popular as pets, even though they do not have the correct coat for the show ring. This obviously requires more thorough grooming on a daily basis.

Exercise: A working breed that thrives on strenuous exercise.

Health check: Hip scoring is essential.

Average size: Dogs 24-26 ins (60-65 cms), bitches 22-24 ins (55-60 cms).

GERMAN SHORTHAIRED POINTER

Roots: A gundog from Germany, bred to hunt, point and retrieve.

Character: Even-tempered, biddable and affectionate.

Training: A versatile breed that thrives on mental stimulation. A successful competitor in most of the canine sports.

Grooming: Low-maintenance.

Exercise: High-maintenance – the German Shorthaired Pointer is used to working all day in the field, and needs a rigorous program of exercise.

Health check: Breeding stock should be hip-scored.

Average size: Dogs 23-25 ins (58-64 cms), bitches 21-23 ins (53-58 cms).

GOLDEN RETRIEVER

Roots: Bred in Scotland to be an all-round retriever, tailor-made for large shooting estates.

Character: Trustworthy, outgoing, reliable. Loves his family.

Training: A true all-rounder who is valued as a gundog, a guide dog for the blind, and as an assistance dog working for the disabled. He is also a highly successful competitor in all the canine sports. Watch out for a slightly stubborn streak, and be prepared to think your way around problems that arise, rather than becoming confrontational.

Grooming: The wavy topcoat, with extensive feathering, is a feature of the breed. It demands daily attention.

Exercise: The Golden loves to run, and he is also a very enthusiastic swimmer.

Health check: Breeding stock must be hip-scored and eye-tested.

Average size: Dogs 22-24 ins (56-61 cms), bitches 20-22 ins (51-56 cms).

GREAT DANE

Roots: This majestic-looking breed originated in Germany where it was used to hunt packs of wild boar.

Character: Gentle, loyal, dependable.

Training: The Dane is responsive, and can reach a reasonable standard in a number of the canine sports.

Grooming: Very little work required.

Exercise: A chance to run is appreciated, but the Dane is happy to take life at a reasonably leisurely pace.

Health check: Hip-scoring for breeding stock. Osteochondrosis – OCD – (see page 231) can be a problem in this giant breed.

Average size: Minimum height given is dogs 30 ins (76 cms), bitches 28 ins (71 cms). However, the average male Dane in the show ring probably makes 35 ins, with females around 33 ins.

The Great Dane comes in a variety of colours, including the spectacular harlequin, which is unique in the dog world. The body coat is white with black or blue 'torn' patches distributed over the coat.

IRISH SETTER

Roots: An Irish-bred dog that dates back to the 14th century. The breed was used to set games, first for the nets, and then for the gun.

Character: Loyal and loving, can be a little boisterous.

Training: Responsive to his owner, but always capable of doing the unexpected.

Grooming: The body coat is flat, and this contrasts with the luxuriant feathering. Regular brushing and combing is needed to keep this tangle-free.

Exercise: A breed that has a real love of running and galloping, but he also likes quality time on the sofa!

Health check: Eye testing for progressive retinal atrophy (see page 233) is required.

Average size: Dogs 27 ins (68.5 cms), bitches 25 ins (63.5 cms).

JACK RUSSELL TERRIER (Parson Russell Terrier)

Roots: Developed in Britain's West Country by a parson – the Reverend John Russell. The breed was used to run with the hounds, and then go to earth after fox.

Character: Bold, friendly, courageous.

Training: A highly intelligent dog, but he needs a lot of motivation.

Grooming: The smoothcoated variety is very easy to care for. Broken and roughcoated dogs will need stripping twice a year.

Exercise: A busy, active breed, the Jack Russell loves to explore, but watch out that he doesn't disappear down the nearest hole!

Health check: Eye tests for breeding stock.

Average size: Dogs 14 ins (35 cms), bitches 13 ins (33 cms).

LABRADOR RETRIEVER

Roots: Originated on the east coast of Canada, where they were used by fisherman to drag out nets from the boats and to retrieve fish that had fallen overboard. When the breed reached England, it was developed as a shooting companion, retrieving game over land and in water.

Character: Cheerful, optimistic, eager to please, the Labrador is an ideal family companion.

Training: A biddable dog that will enjoy all training challenges that comes his way. Excels in competitive sports, as well as being highly valued as an assistance dog and as a sniffer dog.

Grooming: Low-maintenance.

Exercise: Regular, varied exercise is essential. Swimming is considered a major bonus!

Health check: Breeding stock must be hip-scored. Puppies and parents should be eye-tested.

Average size: Dogs 22 ins (56 cms). Bitches 21 ins (54 cms).

The Labrador was expected to work in all weathers, often having to enter the water in icy conditions. Fortunately, he developed the coat to go with the job — a straight, harsh topcoat, with a soft, weather-resistant undercoat — which meant that he did not get soaked to the skin.

LHASA APSO

Roots: Comes from Tibet where he was kept as a watch dog in Buddhist monasteries.

Character: Gay and inquisitive, the Lhasa is loving with his family but can be wary of strangers.

Training: A breed with an independent streak, so training can be a matter of compromise!

Grooming: A wonderful, long coat that requires a great deal of work to keep it in good order. A puppy trim is an option if you want to cut down on the workload.

Exercise: Small and adaptable, the Lhasa will enjoy the exercise he is given, but will not make big demands.

Health check: Breeding stock should be eye-tested.

Average size: Dogs 10 ins (25.4 cms), bitches slightly less.

MASTIFF

Roots: One of the oldest known breeds, his origins go back to Roman times. In the 15th century, Mastiffs were used as dogs of war.

Character: Loving and docile, but can be formidable when roused.

Training: An intelligent breed that can be trained to a high standard. However, do not expect lightning-fast precision work from this easy-going canine giant

Grooming: A short, dense coat that is easy to care for.

Exercise: Great care must be taken to limit exercise

The record weight for a male Mastiff, recorded in the Guinness Book Of Records, is a mighty 315 lbs (143 kgs).

during the growing period. In adulthood, the Mastiff is content with steady, regular exercise.

Health check: Breeding stock must be hip-scored. Guard against gastric torsion (see page 223).

Average size: Dogs 30 ins (76 cms), bitches 27.5 ins (70 cms).

MINIATURE SCHNAUZER

Roots: Developed in Germany, bred down from the Schnauzer and the Affenpinscher.

Character: Steady, alert and reliable.

Training: Quick to learn, enjoys Obedience and Agility.

Grooming: A harsh, wire coat that needs stripping twice a year, plus regular routine care.

Exercise: Adaptable, but generally moderate in demand.

Health check: Breeding stock must be eye-tested.

Average size: Dogs 14 ins (35.6 cms), bitches 13 ins (33 cms).

NEWFOUNDLAND

Roots: Worked with fishermen in Newfoundland, swimming out from the boats to spread the fishing nets.

Character: Loving, affectionate and docile.

Training: Eager to please, enjoys being given a task to perform.

Grooming: A daily routine is needed to keep the coat tangle-free. Coat-shedding is dramatic!

Exercise: Likes to be included in outings, loves swimming.

The Newfoundland truly is the water dog of the canine world – he even has webbed feet!

Health check: Breeding stock must be hip-scored. Osteochondrosis (OCD) can be a problem (see page 232).

Average size: Dogs 28 ins (71 cms), bitches 26 ins (66 cms). Weight is a major consideration, with dogs weighing 140-150 lbs (64-69 kgs), and bitches 110-120 lbs (50-54 kgs).

OLD ENGLISH SHEEPDOG

Roots: Originally used for driving and minding sheep, but rarely used in this capacity any more.

Character: Gentle and kindly, good with children.

Training: Intelligent, but not always the most co-operative.

Grooming: The shaggy coat needs constant attention to keep it clean and tangle-free. Clipping the coat is a sensible option for pet owners.

Exercise: Bred to work in the fields all day, the Old English Sheepdog thrives on a routine of regular exercise.

Health check: Breeding stock should be eye-tested.

Average size: Dogs 24 ins (61 cms), bitches 22 ins (56 cms).

PEKINGESE

Roots: An ancient breed that was kept as the royal favorite of Chinese emperors.

Character: Loyal and courageous.

Training: A born aristocrat, the Pekingese can be stubborn when it comes to training, so patience is required.

Grooming: A long, straight coat is a feature of the breed; it requires extensive, daily grooming.

Exercise: Lively and curious, the Peke needs little exercise, but enjoys the stimulation of going out and about.

Health check: Check out eye problems and back problems.

Average size: Dogs 11 lbs (5 kgs), bitches 12 lbs (5.5 kgs).

POODLE

Roots: In Germany, dogs of Poodle-type were used to retrieve game from water. The Poodle comes in three sizes: Standard, Miniature and Toy.

Character: Good-natured, fun-loving and affectionate.

Training: Intelligent and eager to please, Poodles relish the opportunity to show off, and love performing tricks.

Grooming: A non-shedding coat that needs daily grooming, but the major consideration is clipping, which needs to be carried out every 6-8 weeks. You can choose a number of different styles of Poodle clip.

Exercise: The amount of exercise required depends on the size, but all Poodles are active and energetic.

Health check: The smaller varieties should be eye-tested before breeding.

Average size: Standard over 15 ins (38 cms), Miniature 11-15 ins (28-38 cms), Toy up to 11 ins (28 cms).

PUG

Roots: Originally from China, but adopted as a favorite in the royal courts of Europe.

Character: Even-tempered, thrives on companionship.

Training: Alert and intelligent, the Pug responds well to training.

Grooming: Low-maintenance.

Exercise: Enjoys a game and likes to be included in outings, but otherwise very moderate requirements.

Health check: Patella luxation can be a problem (see page 233).

Average size: 14-18 lbs (6.3-8.1 kgs).

PYRENEAN MOUNTAIN DOG (GREAT PYRENEES)

Roots: Used to guard the flock, working in the Pyrenean Mountains in France.

Character: Calm, confident and loyal, can be wary with strangers.

Training: It is important to work hard at training and socializing this large, powerful dog. Most will respond well, though not quickly!

Grooming: Daily grooming is a must, especially when the coat is shedding. Keeping a white dog clean requires some dedication.

Exercise: The Pyrenean is built for stamina rather than speed, and will enjoy long, interesting walks at a steady pace.

Health check: Breeding stock must be hip-scored.

Average size: Dogs 28 ins (70 cms), bitches 26 ins (65 cms).

RHODESIAN RIDGEBACK

Roots: A hunting dog from southern Africa that was used to track lion and other big game. Also used as a guard.

Character: Loyal to his family, but wary of strangers. A natural guard, but shows no aggression towards people.

Training: A highly intelligent dog that needs experienced handling to bring out the best in him.

Grooming: A sleek, glossy coat that is easy to care for.

Exercise: Agile and athletic, the Ridgeback thrives on extensive exercise.

Health check: Puppies must be tested for dermoid sinus which is an inherited condition.

Average size: Dogs 25-27 ins (63-67 cms), bitches 24-26 ins 61-66 cms).

The Rhodesian Ridgeback is characterized by his ridge — a symmetrical formation of hair that grows in the opposite direction to the main coat on the back.

ROTTWEILER

Roots: Used as a herding and droving dog in Germany, taking cattle to market. The Rottweiller has a strong guarding instinct, and has been used by security forces throughout the world.

Character: Bold, confident, and self-possessed; may be aloof with strangers, but there should be no hint of unprovoked aggression.

Training: Mental stimulation is essential for this intelligent breed. Start training early, and your Rottie will respond to all challenges. He excels at Working Trials and Tracking.

Grooming: Basic routine care is all that is required.

Exercise: A big, powerful dog that needs strenuous exercise.

Health check: Breeding stock must be hip-scored and eye-tested. Watch out for Osteochondrosis (OCD) (see page 231).

Average size: Dogs 25-27 ins (63-67 cms), bitches 23-25 ins (58-63.5 cms).

SAMOYED

Roots: Comes from northern Russia where the breed was used to herd reindeer.
Character: Extrovert, cheerful, affectionate.
Training: Eager to please, but can be a little stubborn.
Grooming: Daily grooming is essential to keep the white coat clean and tangle-free.
Exercise: A strong, active dog that needs a program of regular, varied exercise.
Health check: Breeding stock should be hip-scored.
Average size: Dogs 20-22 ins (51-56 cms), bitches 18-20 ins (46-51 cms).

SHETLAND SHEEPDOG

Roots: Originally used for herding sheep on the Shetland Isles in north-east Scotland.
Character: Alert and vigilant, affectionate with his family, slightly wary of strangers.
Training: Quick-thinking and intelligent, the Sheltie is a bright little dog who loves having something to do.
Grooming: The profuse feathering on the mane, legs and tail needs daily attention. Coat-shedding is prodigious.
Exercise: Reasonably adaptable, but it is important to remember that this is a working breed, and exercise should not be neglected.
Health check: Breeding stock should be eye-tested.
Average size: Dogs and bitches approximately 14 ins (35 cms).

SHIH TZU

Roots: China, with origins also in Tibet. Developed from the Lhasa Apso, and revered as a holy dog by Buddhist monks.
Character: An extrovert dog with a decidedly mischievous streak.
Training: The Shih Tzu loves being the center of attention and can learn any trick with ease. However, he also enjoys the game of 'forgetting' what he has learnt...
Grooming: Daily brushing is needed to keep the long coat clean and tangle-free. A pet trim is preferred by some pet owners.
Exercise: Moderate, but loves to be included on all expeditions.
Health check: Breathing problems can occur in this snub-nosed breed.
Average size: Dogs and bitches 10.5 ins (26.7 cms).

SIBERIAN HUSKY

Roots: A sled-pulling dog that was developed in north-eastern Asia.
Character: Sweet-tempered and friendly, but has a strong hunting instinct.
Training: Adapts well to all training challenges.
Grooming: A dense coat, but surprisingly easy to care for. Extra grooming is needed when the coat is shedding.
Exercise: Extensive exercise is essential, but this presents a problem as the Sibe's strong

hunting instinct means that he cannot be exercised off the lead. Sibe owners have to find safe places to run their dogs in harness.

Health check: Breeding stock should be hip-scored and eye-tested.

Average size: Dogs 21-23 ins (53-58.5 cms), bitches 20-22 ins (51-56 cms).

STAFFORDSHIRE BULL TERRIER

Roots: Bred in England by crossing a Bulldog with a native English Terrier to produce a small, tenacious breed for the sport of dog fighting. He is now highly valued as a companion dog.

Character: Devoted to his family and loves children. Tends to see other dogs as a challenge.

Training: Early socialization with other dogs is essential. The Staffie is bright and intelligent, but needs to be motivated.

Grooming: Low-maintenance.

Exercise: Regular outings are appreciated, but the Staffie will happily get his exercise through playing games.

Health check: Parents and puppies should be eye-tested.

Average size: Dogs and bitches 14-16 ins (35.5-40.5 cms).

ST BERNARD

Roots: The first mountain rescue dog, used by the monks of the Hospice of the Great St Bernard in Switzerland to rescue travelers who were lost in the snow.

Character: Trustworthy and dependable, an ideal family dog.

Training: Saints are easy-going dogs who are not famous for lightning responses. However, it is important to work at basic exercises so you have control over this giant breed.

Grooming: The smoothcoated Saint is easy to care for. The feathering on the roughcoated variety demands more attention.

Exercise: This should be limited during the growing period, and then planned on a regular basis. The St Bernard does not need strenuous free running, but he enjoys a long, steady ramble.

Health check: Breeding stock should be hip-scored.

Average size: Dogs over 27.5 ins (70 cms), bitches over 25.5 ins (65 cms).

The most famous of the early St Bernards who worked in the Swiss Alps was Barry, who was born in 1800. He had an instinct for danger and would insist on being let out of the hospice when snowstorms threatened. He would go in search of lost travelers, and if he needed help, he would return to the hospice to alert the monks.

WEIMARANER

Roots: An all-round gundog, developed in Germany to hunt wild boar and deer, plus small game.

Character: Alert, intelligent, fearless.

Training: A highly intelligent breed that will relish all training opportunities.

Grooming: The shorthaired Weimaraner, which is the most popular variety, is low-maintenance. The longcoated variety has extensive feathering which needs daily brushing.

Exercise: The more the better, for this athletic breed.

Health check: Breeding stock must be hip-scored.

Average size: Dogs 24-27 ins (61-69 cms), bitches 22-25 ins (56-64 cms).

The pale eyes and distinctive silver–gray colour of the Weimaraner led to the breed's nickname – 'the gray ghost'.

WELSH CORGI (PEMBROKE)

Roots: A cattle drover, developed in South Wales, but now valued as a companion dog.

Character: Bold and extrovert, tends to be bossy.

Training: A quick-witted dog who loves being given a job of work. In the US, the breed competes in Obedience and Tracking, as well as in herding tests.

Grooming: A medium-length coat that is easy to care for, but watch out for the seasonal shedding.

Exercise: Moderate, but it should not be neglected as obesity is a problem in the breed.

Health check: No specific inherited conditions.

Average size: Dogs and bitches 10-12 ins (25.5-30.5 cms).

WEST HIGHLAND WHITE TERRIER

Roots: This small terrier comes from the north-west of Scotland where it was used for hunting fox, badger, and otter.

Character: Friendly, outgoing, adaptable.

Training: The Westie likes having things to do and will enjoy training sessions, although he does have a will of his own.

Grooming: Regular routine grooming will keep the coat clean, but professional trimming is needed at least three times a year.

Exercise: This does not need to be strenuous, but the Westie will enjoy a variety of outings.

Health check: Legge Perthes can occur in the breed.

Average size: Dogs and bitches 11 ins (28 cms).

WHIPPET

Roots: Developed in England from his larger cousin, the Greyhound. The Whippet was used for rabbit coursing, and is still used for artificial lure coursing.

Character: Gentle, affectionate, playful.

Training: A kind but firm approach is called for to curb the youthful exuberance of the Whippet. He will quickly learn the rules, but is not interested in Obedience exercises for their own sake.

Grooming: A fine, short coat that requires minimal attention.

Exercise: Active and energetic, the Whippet loves to run and play. Some retain a strong chasing instinct, so be careful where you exercise.

Health check: No specific inherited conditions.

Average size: Dogs 18.5-20 ins (47-51cms), bitches 17-18.5 ins (44-47 cms).

YORKSHIRE TERRIER

Roots: Despite his glamorous appearance, the Yorkshire Terrier was developed by mineworkers in England to keep rats at bay, and to compete in rat pits in public houses.

Character: A spirited little dog, who acts as a very efficient guard, warning when strangers are approaching.

Training: Keenly intelligent and loves to learn.

Grooming: The long, straight, silky coat requires a formidable amount of work if it is kept at full length. Many pet owners opt to have the coat clipped.

Exercise: Moderate, but Yorkies enjoy the opportunity to go out and investigate.

Health check: Patella luxation can occur in the breed (see page 233).

Average size: Dogs and bitches 7lbs (3.1kgs), but most pet Yorkies will be bigger than this.

In the mid 1800s, competitions were held to see how many rats a terrier could kill in a rat pit. A Yorkie, weighing around 6lbs, held the record for killing 20 large rats in just three minutes — not bad for a Toy dog!

Part 3

Tracking Down Your Puppy

Chapter 5

Puppy Outlets

Now you have decided on your choice of breed, the next step is to track down a puppy. It is very tempting to rush out and buy the first pup you can find, but try to curb your impatience. Having worked so hard to find the best breed for you and your family, you want to get off to a good start by finding a puppy from sound and reliable breeding.

WHAT ARE YOU LOOKING FOR?

Before you even start looking for puppies, you should decide what role your dog is going to play in your life.

Do you want your dog purely as a companion?

Obviously you want a quality dog that is typical of the breed, but, if you have no plans to compete in the show ring, you will not be so concerned with specific breed points.

Do you want to show your dog?

If you are planning a career in the show ring for your dog, you will need to evaluate colour, markings, and conformation. A puppy can only be assessed for breed potential; there is no guarantee that a pup of eight weeks will mature into a Champion. However, an experienced breeder will know the key points to look for.

Do you want to compete with your dog?

There are lots of canine activities to compete in, ranging from Competitive Obedience to Canine Freestyle (Heelwork To Music). If you have ambitions to train your dog for competition, you will be looking for a certain type of temperament.

The breeder will help you to choose an outgoing, confident puppy that is very responsive to people. A puppy with good training prospects will enjoy playing games and will often retrieve without being taught what to do.

For more information, see Temperament Testing page 54.

Do you want to work with your dog?

Some sporting owners want a dog that will work as a shooting companion. If this is the case, the best plan is to go to a breeder that specializes in producing working stock. Hopefully, this type of a dog will have a strong desire to work, a good retrieve, and will tolerate loud noises i.e. not gun-shy. Obviously, the dog must be a sound and healthy representative of his breed, but he does not need to be of show quality.

Do you want a male or a female?

There is a difference in temperament between the male and female in all breeds, but this may be more exaggerated in some cases. Talk to people in the breed of your choice, so that you can find out the pros and cons. A male may be slightly more assertive, particularly as he matures, and so, with the larger breeds, first-time owners are usually recommended to choose a female.

If you opt for a female, you will have to cope with her seasonal cycle. This occurs every six to nine months, and the bitch will need to be kept away from male dogs for around three weeks during this time. If you do not plan to breed from your dogs, neutering is a sensible option for both male and female. For further information on neutering, see Chapter 23: The Question of Neutering.

Your decision may also depend on whether you already have a dog at home. With some breeds, it is better to go for a male and a female combination (as long as provision is made for when the bitch is in season), in other breeds two bitches may be a good option. Two males living in the same house can be compatible, but you could face a struggle over hierarchy. Seek the advice of the breeder who will have experience in keeping mixed sexes, and will know what is the best combination.

Do you have a preference for a particular color?

Obviously, this depends on the breed you are choosing. If you have decided on an Irish Setter, for example, you will have no options, but you will be more than happy with the glorious, rich, chestnut coat, which is the outstanding feature of the breed. However, if you are planning to get a Border Collie, for example, you can choose from black and white, red and white, blue and white, tricolor, blue merle or red merle, plus a whole host of different white markings.

Some prospective owners have a fixed idea on color – perhaps they are following a family tradition, or perhaps they want to get a dog that looks completely different from one they previously owned. If you are planning to show or breed from your dog, color and markings will be highly significant and you will need to seek expert advice (see page 53).

Depending on the breed, what are your thoughts on docking?

Traditionally, a number of breeds have docked tails. This is a simple procedure which is usually carried out around three days after birth. The practice started for purely practical reasons. For example, a Spaniel working in dense undergrowth could well be trapped by, or injure, a full-length, feathered tail. This is why many of the gundog/sporting breeds have docked tails. In other breeds, docking has been dictated by fashion, and the Boxer, for example, was developed with a docked tail to give the characteristic, symmetrical appearance.

Times have changed, and there are now a number of countries that ban docking. In the UK and the USA, the breeds in question are always shown with a docked tail in the show ring, but some pet owners prefer to have a dog with a full tail. If you are planning to buy a breed that is traditionally docked, you must decide if you are happy with this, or whether you want to find a breeder that does not dock tails.

FINDING A BREEDER

Once you have worked out the type of puppy you are looking for, the next task is to find a reputable breeder:

- Contact your national Kennel Club for a list of breed clubs. The breed club secretary will know all the breeders in their area, and many will also know who has puppies available.
- Go to a Championship dog show, and, when judging is over, talk to the exhibitors. They may well know of puppies that are available.
- Buy a specialist dog paper or magazine, and look at the advertisements of puppies for sale.
- Surf the internet, and you will find that many breeders have their own websites. You will be able to find out information about the kennel, and you will probably be able to see photos of the sire and the dam if a litter of puppies is available.

Local newspapers often have a 'Puppies For Sale' section, and you may find that some Kennel Club registered litters are advertised. Steer clear of litters that are not registered, as you have no guarantee that you are buying purebred puppies.

TOP TIP

Do not put too high a priority on geographical convenience. It is far more important to get the puppy you want rather than cutting down on fuel bills.

NO-GO AREAS

Unfortunately, there are unscrupulous breeders who mass-produce puppies on puppy farms or puppy mills, purely for financial gain. If you follow the advice given above, you should not get involved with this type of breeder. There are very sound reasons why you should avoid buying from a source where neither breeding stock nor puppies are registered.

- No thought or planning goes into matching the parents of a litter. It is unlikely that either parent will have been checked for hereditary disorders.
- The puppies will probably have been reared in cramped, overcrowded conditions.
- The litter may not have been given the correct, balanced nutrition they need.
- The puppies may not have been wormed.
- Contact with people will usually be limited, so the puppies will not get the handling and socialization that is so vital in the first few weeks (see Chapter 17: The Importance of Socialization).

Inevitably, the result of bad breeding practices coupled with poor rearing is puppies of unsound temperament, with a weakened constitution, and a strong chance of carrying an hereditary disorder.

It is all too easy to give a home to a puppy because you feel sorry for it. This is not a wise move, as the chances are that it will end in heartbreak. Give yourself and your family the best chance of success by going to a reputable source.

QUESTIONS TO ASK

When you make contact with a breeder and establish that they have puppies for sale, there will be a number of questions you should ask:

- What price are the puppies?
- Do any of the puppies have show potential?
- If relevant, what colors are available?
- What age are the puppies now?
- At what age will they be ready to go to their new homes?
- What is the mother like (appearance, temperament, show career, or working/competitive career, if relevant)?
- What is the father like (same factors as above)?
- Is an after-sales advice service provided?
- If a totally unforeseen situation arises and you can no longer look after the dog, will the breeder help?

A responsible breeder will be only too happy to talk to you and to give you as much information as possible. An after-sales advice service should be considered essential, and, although you obviously have no plans to return your puppy, you should expect the breeder to accept responsibility. All reputable breeders pledge that they are responsible for the puppies produced in their kennel for the duration of their lives.

WAITING LIST

Do not expect to find a litter immediately available as soon as you start looking. Some breeds are harder to find than others, and if you are opting for something unusual, like a Finnish Lapphund for example, you will have few breeders to choose from, and you may have to wait until puppies are available.

If you are planning to buy a popular breed, such as a Labrador Retriever, there will probably be plenty of litters around. You may need to go on a waiting list if you have preference with regard to color, particularly if you want a chocolate-colored Labrador which are fewer in numbers.

The hardest puppies to find are those with show potential (see page 53), and, if you are planning to start a show career, you may be in for a long wait. Once you have found the bloodlines you like, you will then have to be on standby until the litter is born. It will then be a matter of assessing the puppies, and seeing if there are any of show quality.

Chapter 6

Assessing Puppies

Breeders have their own procedures when it comes to selling puppies, and you may find that you are given a vigorous vetting before you get as far as visiting the kennel. Do not take this as an insult. A responsible breeder must do everything in their power to find the best possible homes for the puppies they have produced, and so they will need to ask some searching questions. These may include:

• Have you owned dogs before?
• Do you have any experience with the breed?
• Do you go out to work? If so, what arrangements will be made for your puppy?
• Do you have children?
• Do you plan to start a family in the near future?
• Do you have any other dogs?
• Do you keep a cat, or any other small animal?
• How big is your yard?
• Do you plan to show your dog?
• Depending on the breed, do you plan to compete with your dog in one of the canine disciplines?
• Do you plan to breed from your dog?

Be as honest as you can when answering these questions. If the breeder has a picture of your background, it will help when selecting the most suitable puppy. Most breeders will talk to you over the phone, and then invite you to come and see the puppies. Some breeders ask you to visit the kennel before the litter is born. This gives the opportunity to meet adult dogs, and talks can be held without the distraction of puppies.

VISITING THE BREEDER

In most cases, you will go and see the puppies when they are around five to six weeks of age. At this stage you will make your choice, and you will probably be asked to pay a deposit. The breeder will generally keep the puppies until they are eight weeks old. This may differ slightly depending on the breed. Breeders of Toy dogs, such as Pekingese or Maltese, may keep the puppies for slightly longer. If you are trying to buy a puppy with show potential, you may be given several opportunities to view the puppies before making your final choice.

When you make an appointment with the breeder, be as considerate as possible and turn up on time. Breeders lead very busy lives, and there may be a number of people coming to view the litter. Your visit may well be timed to coincide with a time when the pups are most likely to be active, so it is in your interests to be punctual.

TOP TIP

Remember, you are going to visit puppies, so do not come dressed in your best designer clothes. You will almost certainly end up covered in dog hairs, and the breeder may well get a poor impression as to your suitability to own a dog.

PUPPY WATCHING

All puppies are irresistible, and when you see a litter it is very hard to make an objective assessment. As you watch the puppies playing, all sense of judgement vanishes and you feel like taking the whole lot home with you.

To guard against your enthusiasm, it is a good idea to make a list of the key points to look for, and the questions you want to ask the breeder.

HEALTH CHECKS

The top priority is to ensure that the puppies are fit and healthy. There are certain observations you should make before deciding to buy:

- The puppies should be housed in a light, airy environment which smells fresh.
- Droppings should be cleaned up, and there should be no evidence of leftover food.
- The bedding should be clean and comfortable.
- The puppies should be bold and friendly, ready to come forward to meet you.
- Each puppy should be well covered – neither too fat nor too thin.
- The coat should be clean, with no signs of dullness or dandruff. Dirt around the rear may indicate diarrhea.

- The eyes should be bright. There should be no discharge around the eyes or nose.
- The inside of the ears should be pink and clean, with no evidence of foul odor.
- If the puppies' tails have been docked (this is usually done at around three days), the tips should be clean and well healed.

VIEWING ADULTS

It is vital that you see the mother with her puppies. She may not be looking her best – the coat tends to drop when bitches are feeding, and she will not have regained her pre-pregnant figure, but you will get a good idea of temperament. If you like the way the mother behaves towards her puppies, and when she comes up to meet you, there is a fair chance that you will like the puppies she has produced.

It is unlikely that you will see the father (sire) of the litter. In most cases, he will live at another kennel which could be some distance away. However, the breeder will almost certainly have a photograph of him so that you can get some idea of what he looks like.

It is also helpful to meet other adult dogs in the kennel. Not only will this give you an impression of the breed, the dogs could well be close relatives of the puppies, and so you can evaluate the general appearance and temperament which is typical of the kennel.

PUPPY REARING

Some litters are reared in the breeder's home, others are accommodated in kennels. This will depend on the size of the kennel and the facilities that are available. There is a belief that home-reared litters will have had more human contact, and the puppies will be familiar with all the household sights and sounds.

There is certainly some truth in this, but kennel-reared puppies should not be dismissed out of hand.

A conscientious breeder will spend a great deal of time with the puppies, regardless of where they are accommodated, and will make sure they are well socialized.

MAKING YOUR CHOICE

When you first look at a litter of puppies, they will all look the same, particularly if there is no difference in color or markings. But as you watch the pups playing together, you will see their individual characters begin to emerge.

There will be the bold, pushy puppy who always tries to get at a toy first. There will be the 'people puppy' who loves being stroked, and there will be the greedy pup who keeps on licking the bowl long after the food has gone.

The breeder will have watched the puppies since birth and will have a very good idea of their individual temperaments. Try not to get carried away by a whim; you will do much better if you listen to the breeder's advice.

SHOW POTENTIAL

There are some breeders who claim they can spot a puppy with show potential at the very moment it is born, literally when it is still wet. However, many others will agree that it takes time for a puppy to develop, and would not make a judgement until a puppy is at least eight weeks old. Even so, there is absolutely no guarantee that a puppy will fulfil its early potential. For this reason, a breeder often 'runs on' a puppy for a few months to see how it matures.

It takes a very experienced eye to pick out an up-and-coming show puppy, and it is an area where you should rely on expert help, as every breed has its own very specific requirements. Here are a number of key points to look for:

- **Movement:** Watch how a puppy moves, as this can tell you a lot about the way it is put together.
- **Length of body in relation to height:** The general proportions should be correct for the breed.
- **Shoulder angulation:** This is a significant factor in many breeds.
- **Stifle angulation:** This determines the line of the hindquarters.
- **Front legs:** In most breeds, you are looking for straight legs, but there are exceptions such as the Pekingese.

- **Tail carriage:** This may change with age.
- **Head:** One of the most difficult areas to assess, but look for correct proportions of the skull and muzzle. Note the ear-set, and the placing and shape of the eyes.
- **Mouth:** A puppy's dentition is hard to assess before the adult teeth come through, but there are breed requirements as to the bite. Most breeds have a scissor bite, where the upper teeth closely overlap the lower teeth. Some breeds, such as the Bulldog and the Boxer, have an undershot jaw, where the lower jaw slightly overlaps the upper jaw.
- **Coat and color:** The puppy coat will be soft, and the color may well change as the adult coat grows in. The breeder can usually judge what color the puppy will be.
- **Markings:** Usually this refers to white markings, which may become smaller and less distinctive, but you can spot a puppy that is mismarked (incorrect markings for the breed). In some cases, such as in Dalmatians, a large black patch is considered a fault.

PUPPY LOVE

Inevitably, a number of pedigree puppies are born with faults that mean they are not suitable for showing, and it would not be recommended to breed from them.

- The puppy may be mismarked (see above).
- He may have an incorrect tail. For example, a screw tail may appear in a Bullmastiff litter, which is a throwback to their Bulldog ancestry.
- In a Boxer litter, some of the puppies may be born white. (These pups must be ear-tested, as deafness is more likely to occur in white puppies).

If the puppy is completely sound in every other way, he may be sold to a pet home with the stipulation that he will not be shown, and will not be bred from. These dogs make super pets, and, obviously, they are a little less expensive to buy.

Obviously, you as the owner must know and love your puppy for what he is, and not suddenly turn round to the breeder and accuse them of selling faulty stock.

TEMPERAMENT TESTING

A number of breeders use a series of temperament tests so that they can get a detailed picture of each puppy in the litter.

The aim of these temperament tests is to see how a puppy responds to the environment, to handling, to social interaction, and to sound, and then to score the tests on the basis of how the puppy reacts.

The score can then be interpreted to get an idea of the pup's sociability and sensitivity and how he is likely to react to training.

American behaviorist Wendy Volhard has devised a temperament test that is designed for puppies at around eight weeks of age. It is applicable to all breeds.

THE PUPPY APTITUDE TEST

SOCIAL ATTRACTION

Place puppy in test area. From a few feet away, the tester coaxes the puppy to him/her by clapping hands gently and kneeling down. Tester must coax the puppy in a direction away from the point where he entered the testing area.

Degree of social attraction, confidence or dependence.

Came readily, tail up, jumped, bit at hands	1
Came readily, tail up, pawed, licked at hands	2
Came readily, tail up	3
Came readily, tail down	4
Came hesitantly, tail down	5
Didn't come at all	6

FOLLOWING

Stand up and walk away from the puppy in a normal manner. Make sure the puppy sees you walk away.

Degree of following attraction. Not following indicates independence.

Followed readily, tail up, got underfoot, bit at feet	1
Followed readily, tail up, got underfoot	2
Followed readily, tail up	3
Followed readily, tail down	4
Followed hesitantly, tail down	5
Didn't follow, or went away	6

RESTRAINT

Crouch down and gently roll the puppy on his back and hold him with one hand for a full 30 seconds.

Degree of dominant or submissive tendency. How he accepts stress when socially/physically dominated.

Struggled fiercely, flailed, bit	1
Struggled fiercely, flailed	2
Settled, struggled, settled with eye contact	3
Struggled, then settled	4
No struggle	5
No struggle, straining to avoid eye contact	6

SOCIAL DOMINANCE

Let the puppy stand up and gently stroke him from the head to the back, while you crouch beside him. Continue stroking until a recognizable behavior is established.

Degree of acceptance of social dominance. Puppy may try to dominate by jumping and nipping, or is independent and walks away.

Jumped, pawed, bit, growled	1
Jumped, pawed	2
Cuddled up to tester and tried to lick face	3
Squirmed, licked at hands	4
Rolled over, licked at hands	5
Went away and stayed away	6

ELEVATION DOMINANCE

Bend over, cradle the puppy under his belly, fingers interlaced, palms up, and elevate him just off the ground. Hold him there for 30 seconds.

Degree of acceptance dominance while in position of no control.

Struggled fiercely, bit, growled	1
Struggled fiercely	2
No struggle, relaxed	3
Struggled, settled, licked	4
No struggle, licked at hands	5
No struggle, froze	6

INTERPRETING THE SCORES

MOSTLY 1s

A puppy that consistently scores a 1 in the temperament section of the test is an extremely dominant, aggressive puppy who can easily be provoked to bite.

His dominant nature will attempt to resist human leadership, thus requiring only the most experienced of handlers. This puppy is a poor choice for most individuals and will do best in a working situation.

MOSTLY 2s

This puppy is dominant and self-assured. He can be provoked to bite; however, he readily accepts human leadership that is firm, consistent and knowledgeable. This is not a dog for a tentative, indecisive individual. In the right hands, he has the potential to become a fine working or show dog, and could fit into an adult household, provided the owners know what they are doing.

MOSTLY 3s

The puppy is outgoing and friendly, and will adjust well in situations in which he receives regular training and exercise. He has a flexible temperament that adapts well to different types of environment, provided he is handled correctly. May be too much for a family with small children or for an elderly couple who are sedentary.

MOSTLY 4s

A puppy that scores a majority of 4s is an easily controlled, adaptable puppy whose submissive nature will make him continually look to his master for leadership. This puppy is easy to train, reliable with kids, and, though he lacks self-confidence, makes a high-quality family pet. He is usually less outgoing than a puppy scoring in the 3s, but his demeanour is gentle and affectionate.

MOSTLY 5s

This is a puppy who is extremely submissive and lacking in self-confidence. He bonds very closely with his owner and requires regular companionship and encouragement to bring him out of himself. If handled incorrectly, this puppy will grow very shy and fearful. For this reason, he will do best in a predictable, structured lifestyle with owners who are patient and not overly demanding, such as an elderly couple.

MOSTLY 6s

A puppy that scores 6 consistently is independent and uninterested in people. He will mature into a dog who is not demonstrably affectionate and who has a low need for human companionship.

In general, it is rare to see properly socialised puppies test this way; however, there are several breeds that have been bred for specific tasks (such as Basenjis, hounds, and some northern breeds) who exhibit this level of independence. To perform as intended, these dogs require a singularity of purpose that is not compromised by strong attachments to their owner.

For most owners, a good companion dog will score in the 3 to 4 range in this test. Puppies scoring a combination of 1s and 2s require experienced handlers who will be able to draw the best aspects of their potential from them.

THE NAME GAME

Although you have to wait before you can bring your puppy home, you can while away the time by choosing a name for him. This is usually the subject of much debate in the family, and everyone will have their own ideas. There are a few points worth bearing in mind:

- Choose a name that is easy to say. It is best to go for just one or two syllables – such as Sam or Lassie. A name like Bartholomew may sound grand, but it is a bit of a mouthful when you are trying to call your dog across the park.
- Do not choose a joke name – the joke is certain to wear thin over the next decade or so.
- Make sure you come to a decision before your puppy arrives home. There is many a dog called "Puppy" simply because no one could make up their mind!

Part 4
Getting Ready

Chapter 7

Buying Equipment

You will probably have a couple of weeks to wait before your pup is ready to bring home. This may seem like a long wait, but, in fact, you can use the time to advantage getting everything ready for the new arrival.

Fortunately, dogs do not need lots of expensive equipment, but there are a few basic items you will need to buy in order to get your puppy off to the right start.

A PLACE TO SLEEP

Puppies grow at a very fast rate, and rest is essential to their health and wellbeing. There is a huge variety of dog beds on the market, and, to a large extent, it all comes down to personal choice. However, there are a few important points to consider.

INDOOR CRATE

The indoor crate has been a popular option in the US for some time, and it is now readily available worldwide in all big pets stores or by mail order. Initially, some pet owners felt the crate was rather cage-like, and not the type of cozy home they wanted for their dog. However, when a crate is properly used, the benefits for both puppy and owner are tremendous.

- The puppy has a safe 'den' where he can rest undisturbed.
- The owner has a safe place to confine the puppy at night, and when he cannot be supervized.
- You can use the crate in the car, providing a safe place to travel.
- The crate is an aid to house-training (see page 102).
- The puppy learns to be left on his own for short periods, and so is unlikely to suffer from separation anxiety (see page 186) which can become a major behavioral problem.
- If you are going away from home, your pup has a ready-made place to sleep where he will feel secure and can do no damage.

It is vital that the owner understands that the crate is never to be used as a form of punishment, and, apart from night-time, the crate should only be used when you are leaving your dog for short periods (2-3 hours maximum).

Obviously, the size of crate you buy depends on the size of your dog. You might think it is foolish to buy a big crate for a small puppy, but adult dogs love their crates, so it is important to buy one that will still be comfortable for your dog when he is fully grown. Ask the breeder to recommend a size, or the staff in a good pet store will probably be able to help. The following table gives a guide as to the correct size for different breeds.

SIZE GUIDE

Breed	Minimum recommended crate size
	(Measurements in inches: length x width x height)
Irish Wolfhound	54 x 33 x 36
Rottweiler	45 x 33 x 36
Retriever (Labrador/Golden)	42 x 27 x 30
Cocker Spaniel	24 x 18 x 21
Pug	21 x 15 x 18

For further information on crates and crate-training, see page 97

BEDDING

A crate is transformed into a luxury home by using soft bedding to line it with. The best type to use is synthetic, fleece bedding, which can be bought to measure. This provides a cozy bed, and if your pup has an accident, the moisture drains through. It is machine-washable and dries quickly. It is a good idea to buy two pieces of bedding so that you always have one ready to use.

OTHER TYPES OF BED

If you decide against a crate, there are many other types of dog bed to choose from. You may decide that it would be useful to have a dog bed in your sitting room, in addition to the crate, which you will probably keep in the kitchen or the utility room (see page 68).

Cardboard box: This is a perfectly sensible option for your puppy when he first arrives home. Make sure there are no sharp staples in the box, and then cut down the front so your puppy can get in and out easily. Line it with soft bedding (see above) and your pup will think it is a palace! The big advantage is that that you can change the box every couple of weeks as your puppy grows – and it does not matter if he chews it.

When your puppy has grown out of his destructive phase, you can invest in a more permanent dog bed.

Plastic bed: Plastic, kidney-shaped beds are strong, durable, and easy to clean. They may not look comfortable, but a piece of bedding makes all the difference. This type of bed comes in a range of sizes to suit all breeds.

Beanbags: Attractive to look at, but disastrous if chewed – you'll be sweeping up polystyrene beads for months!

Cushions/duvets: Extremely comfortable for your dog, but hard work for you, as covers must be washed regularly.

PUPPY CARRIER

This is optional, and unless you are buying a small breed, your puppy will outgrow a carrier fairly quickly. It is useful in the early stages when your puppy is travelling in the car, although many owners use an indoor crate for this purpose.

FEEDING BOWLS

Your puppy will need two bowls, one for water and one for his meals. A heavy, ceramic bowl can be used for water, but, beware, this type of bowl is breakable. Plastic bowls come in a range of bright colors, but the chewing puppy can soon make a mess of them. The most practical bowls are made of stainless steel. They come in a full range of sizes, and they are virtually indestructible.

FOOD

In most cases, the breeder will provide you with a sample of the diet that has been fed to the puppies, which will last for the first few days after your puppy has arrived in his new home (see page 90). It is important not to introduce any changes in the early stages, so if you want to buy a supply of food, make sure you have instructions from the breeder.

COLLAR

Your puppy will need a soft lightweight collar for early training sessions (see page 169). You can get nylon adjustable collars, and these are ideal when a puppy is growing. When your dog is full-grown, you can choose from the vast range of collars available.

A half-check collar is useful for training, particularly for the larger, more boisterous breeds, but it is probably better to wait until your puppy is a little older before investing in one of these. If your dog is to wear a collar full-time, it is advisable to keep his half-check collar specifically for training. There is a slight risk that the collar could get caught on something, which would cause considerable distress, or could even result in injury.

Full check-chains, often referred to as choke chains, have pretty much gone out of fashion. Fortunately, the era of punitive training, where owners were encouraged to control their dogs by yanking on a choke chain, is behind us. Today, reward-based training is widely accepted as the most effective method of training dogs (see page 150).

LEAD

Lead training (see page 168) will be easier if you have a fairly lightweight lead to begin with. The type of lead you choose as your puppy gets bigger is a matter of personal choice. Generally the smaller breeds suit a narrower lead, and you can get some very attractive matching collar and lead sets. Leather leads are often preferred for the bigger, stronger breeds, as a nylon lead can chafe the hand. Chain leads are uncomfortable to use – unless you always wear gloves! Regardless of the type of lead you choose, it must have a secure, trigger fastening which is 100 per cent reliable.

EXTENDING LEAD

This gives you the opportunity to exercise your pup, while still remaining in control (see page 129). You will not need this while your pup is young and on restricted exercise, but you may find it a worthwhile investment as your pup matures, particularly if you have limited access to areas where you can exercise off-lead.

TRAINING AIDS

When you visit your pet store, you will see a number of different training aids which are designed to help with specific problems. For example, Halti and Gentle Leaders collars are headcollars which are designed as anti-pulling devices. You should only buy this type of equipment if it is specifically recommended by an experienced dog trainer or behaviorist, who will show you how to use it.

TOP TIP

A clicker is the only training aid that you may wish to buy ready for your puppy's arrival home. It is a small, oblong box, fitted with a clicker, which you activate by pressing with your thumb. The 'click' acts a 'yes' marker in training, and has proved an extremely effective method of training (see page 162). Most pet stores now sell clickers, and it is worth buying one in advance as you can start clicker training as soon as your puppy has settled into his new home.

ID

Your dog will need to wear some form of ID. You can buy a disc, engraved with your contact details, which can be attached to the collar. Make sure you have a strong slip-ring, so that the disc stays in place. Many owners are now choosing a permanent form of ID, such as an ear tattoo or a microchip implant. Your vet will carry out these simple procedures.

DOG COATS

If necessary, this purchase can be made at a later stage when your puppy has reached his full size. Strictly speaking, a coat is a luxury item, as most breeds are capable of withstanding the rigors of the weather. However, if you have a fine-coated breed, such as a Whippet or a Greyhound, a waterproof walking-out coat may be appreciated. If you have chosen an exotic hairless breed, such as a Chinese Crested, you will definitely need a coat for outside wear.

GROOMING EQUIPMENT

This will depend on coat type, and your puppy's breeder can give you detailed information on the equipment you may require. However, for basic puppy grooming, a bristle brush is ideal. This can be used to accustom the puppy to the grooming routine. You can then add a comb when your puppy is happy with being handled.

Shortcoated: This is the easiest coat to maintain, and you will need no more than a brush (which can be made of bristle or wire) and a metal comb with medium or wide teeth. A rubber handmitt (sometimes called a curry comb) is useful for general grooming, particularly if the coat is shedding. For detailed information on grooming shortcoated breeds, see page 122.

Longcoated: Seek breed-specific advice. A pin brush, which has metal pins with rounded ends, is generally used on long coats. A wide-toothed comb will be needed, plus a fine-toothed comb for teasing out tangles. It is a good idea to buy a pair of hair-cutting scissors, as long hair can grow in the wrong places (such as between the pads on the feet) and will need to be trimmed. For detailed information on grooming longcoated breeds, see page 122.

Poodles: The equipment you need depends on the type of trim you choose. Generally, a bristle brush should be used where the coat has been clipped, and a wire brush is used on the longer coat. A wide-toothed steel comb is recommended. You will need to find a reputable grooming parlor when the coat needs to be trimmed. For information on grooming parlors, see page 124.

Wirecoated: Many of the terrier breeds have a harsh topcoat, and this needs to be clipped or stripped at regular intervals. Ask your puppy's breeder for detailed information. Routine care is straightforward, and most terrier owners opt for a wire brush, or a rubber curry comb to keep the coat in good order. For information on grooming wirecoated breeds see page 124.

NAIL-CLIPPERS

If your dog does not wear down his nails naturally, they will need to be trimmed (see page 118). The best type of nail-clipper to buy is the guillotine type, although some people prefer to work with a nail file.

TOOTHBRUSH/TOOTHPASTE

Teeth must be kept clean, and some dogs need help from their human owners. For information on teeth-cleaning, see pages 108-110. You can buy a long-handled toothbrush, or a small finger brush, made specially for dogs. You will also need some canine toothpaste, which comes in a variety of meaty flavors!

CLEANING UP

Cleaning up after your puppy is not the most attractive side of dog ownership, but it is absolutely essential if you go out in public places. Pet stores sell a variety of clean-up bags, and pooper-scoops, and so it is simply a matter of never leaving home without the means of cleaning up.

TOYS

This is the fun part of shopping for your puppy! There is a huge selection of toys available, and, for the most part, it is a matter of personal choice. However, there are a few safeguards to be aware of:

- Take care with squeaky toys. A determined puppy is quite capable of chewing the toy and then swallowing the squeaker.
- Avoid toys that have bits that can be chewed off, as these can easily be swallowed.
- Make sure the size of toy suits your dog. Obviously, this does not apply in the first few months, but it is a consideration as a dog reaches maturity. A small energetic breed, such as the Shih Tzu, will love playing with something small that he can easily carry, whereas a big, powerful Rottweiler needs something much more substantial.

Choose toys that are made from hard rubber, or go for the cotton, ragger-type toys, which can be used for tug and retrieve games. You can also buy boredom-busting toys, which are useful if you want to give your dog some occupation when he is left alone. These toys can conceal treats, and your dog has to work out how to get them – a game that appeals strongly to most canine minds!

Chapter 8

Puppy-proofing Your Home

When you went to choose your puppy, what were your first impressions? You were probably entranced by the antics of the pups, and overwhelmed by how sweet and cheeky they were. Did you think that having a puppy in your home might mean that you would be harboring a potential home-wrecker? Almost certainly not – but if you are to survive rearing a puppy, this is the best way to view your puppy's arrival.

A PUPPY'S PERSPECTIVE

Puppies are bright and energetic, but, above all, they are inquisitive. Once your puppy has got used to his new surroundings, he will want to investigate everything that looks interesting. Your pup has no idea of what may be dangerous or what may be valuable – so you must protect him from himself.

Before you collect your puppy, try to see your house from a puppy's perspective. Some new owners have been known to crawl around in a bid to find out what is within a puppy's reach – but this is not entirely necessary! However, it is a good idea to go into each room where your puppy is to be allowed, perhaps sit on the floor for a few minutes, and try to work out what may be potential hazards.

DOMESTIC DANGERS

Every home is different, but here are a few hazards to watch out for:

- Trailing electrical cables. The kitchen is an obvious source of trouble, but watch out for cables from lights, televisions, CD players and computers.
- A tablecloth that hangs within a puppy's reach could lead to disaster.
- Household cleaners, which could be highly toxic to a puppy, are often kept in a ground-level cupboard under the kitchen sink. It is far better to move the cleaners than to risk a fatal accident.
- Some household plants (including spider plants, amaryllis, poinsettia, and

cyclamen) are poisonous to puppies, so, again, remove them from your puppy's reach.
- Children's toys are always a great temptation, and they are very often left on the floor. Not only will children lose a valued toy, the pup may well swallow something that is harmful.

PROTECTING YOUR HOME

Obviously the first priority is to make sure your puppy is safe. But you also want to protect your home from attack! Here are a few guidelines:

- Place all valuable ornaments well out of reach.
- Watch out for the fringes on upholstered furniture and on rugs. They are irresistible to chewing puppies.
- If you have a bookshelf at floor level, remove the books until your puppy has passed the chewing stage.

Above all, try to spread the message of tidiness. If shoes are put away, they cannot be chewed. If toys are placed out of reach, they cannot be a temptation. Remember, your puppy is not hell-bent on destroying your home; he is simply investigating everything that comes his way.

TOP TIP

It is impossible to protect all your furniture from a determined chewer; table legs and chair legs, for example, are an easy target. Your puppy will not do much damage while he has his baby (milk) teeth, but this will change with the onset of teething, which usually starts at around four months.

If you notice that your puppy keeps trying to chew a piece of furniture, you can prevent this from happening by using a deterrent spray, which is available from most pet stores. The bitter apple spray is completely harmless, but it has an unpleasant taste. This will quickly deter your puppy from attempting to chew.

SETTING LIMITS

You will want your puppy to be with you in your house, but you may well decide that there are rooms where he should be excluded. It is important to work out where your puppy is allowed to go well in advance of his arrival. Make sure all members of the family know the rules – and stick to them.

STAIRGATE/CHILDGATE

A stairgate (also known as a childgate) is a worthwhile investment if you want to ensure your puppy stays within his permitted limits. The gate can be placed as a barrier to the lounge for example, or it can be placed at the foot of the stairs to prevent your puppy venturing upstairs. In most cases, a puppy will soon learn the house rules, and you will probably be able to dispense with the gate when your puppy reaches adulthood.

LOCATING THE BED

Before you go to collect your puppy, it is important to decide where he is going to sleep, and then you can set up his crate, or get his bed in position. From the puppy's point of view, he needs to sleep in a place that is warm and free from draughts. Although he will want to be part of the hurly-burly of family life, he will also appreciate a place where he can sleep undisturbed.

Obviously, you will have your own ideas, but many owners find that the kitchen or utility room serves the purpose. Make sure you choose a place that is easily accessible for cleaning. Not only is this essential for the prevention of doggy odors, it is also important when you take preventative measures to control fleas (see page 201).

SUMMARY

All new puppy owners should accept that their home will suffer to some extent when a new puppy arrives. But it all comes down to damage limitation.

TOP TIP

- *Work at puppy-proofing your home, so your pup is safe, with limited opportunities for chewing household items.*
- *Try to be tidy, putting toys, books, and newspapers out of reach.*
- *Work out a routine so that your puppy can be supervised during his wakeful periods.*
- *Invest in a crate so that you know your puppy is out of harm's way at night, and at times when you cannot supervise him.*

MOVING OUTSIDE

The garden will be an important part of your puppy's home territory, so you must ensure that it is both safe and secure.

FENCING

A well-fenced garden is a must for every dog owner, regardless of breed or size. It is rare for a dog to have an in-built desire to escape, but if a cat appears on the horizon, or interesting noises are coming from next door, most self-respecting dogs will want to investigate.

Ideally, the fence should be at least 5ft in height, although this is obviously not so important with smaller breeds. It is also helpful if the fencing is solid (made from wood, brick or stone) as next-door distractions are much more of a temptation if they can be seen. This is particularly true if your neighbor has a dog – the game of running the fence and barking is a canine favorite.

SECURITY

Before your puppy arrives home, go round all the fencing to check that it is in good order. A small pup can squeeze through a tiny hole, and the consequences would be disastrous. Also check that your gate has a secure latch, and train all family members, friends and visitors to keep it closed.

You can put a courtesy sign on the gate requesting this. Many pet stores make specially designed signs, such as *Shih Tzu Lives Here*, which will alert allcomers to your new acquisition.

TOILET AREA

You will need to designate a part of your garden to be used as the toilet area. There are several reasons for this:

- Your puppy will soon learn what is expected when he is taken to this spot, so house-training will be made easier.
- Only one area of your garden will be soiled, so you will know where to clean up.
- If you have children, they can be excluded from this area.
- The urine from dogs can cause yellow patches on the lawn, so a toilet area will limit the damage.

The toilet area must be cleaned every time it is used, so make sure you keep the necessary equipment to hand.

DIG IT!

Most puppies love to dig, and there are some breeds, such as Jack Russell Terriers and Dachshunds, that are addicted to it! There are two ways of tackling this situation. You can put up with a garden that looks like a battlefield, or you can provide a specially-made digging pit.

A digging pit is rather like the canine equivalent of a children's sand pit. Dig out an area approximately 4ft by 3ft, and about 1ft deep, and fill it with sand. You can persuade your pup that this is *the* place to dig, by burying some toys or food treats in the sand, and encouraging him to find them, using the command "Dig". If you catch your puppy red-handed digging up a prize rose bush, you can take him to the pit and give the command "Dig".

GARDEN HAZARDS

Obviously, you will need to supervise your puppy in the garden to begin with, so that you can teach him what is allowed. However, there will certainly be times, particularly as the pup gets older, when he will be let out alone, so you must eliminate any potential dangers.

Some shrubs and flowers are toxic to dogs, so you may need to revise your planting plan, or make sure your puppy is always supervised. Remember to check all insecticides (such as slug pellets) and weedkillers, before use.

These are often highly toxic to animals. Pesticides, such as mice pellets, must be abandoned as a means of rodent control. If your dog eats the pellets, it could be fatal. It is also important to check that all garden chemicals are stored in a secure place.

POISONOUS PLANTS

This list includes the more common plants that are toxic to dogs. For further information, contact your local garden center, particularly if you are choosing new plants.

- Azalea
- Daffodil
- Dumb cane (dieffenbachia)
- Elderberry
- Foxglove
- Holly
- Hyacinth
- Iris
- Laurel
- Lily of the Valley
- Milkweed
- Mistletoe
- Nightshade
- Oleander
- Philodendron
- Primrose
- Ragwort
- Rhododendron
- Stinging nettle
- Wisteria
- Yew

POND LIFE

A garden pond makes a very attractive feature in a garden, but your puppy will be straight in, disturbing the fish and wrecking the plants, within minutes of arriving home. Depending on the depth, a pond could also prove very hazardous to a puppy. So, if you have a pond, you must ensure that it is either enclosed within its own fenced area, or put a cover over it so that your puppy cannot get in.

SWIMMING POOL

Puppies and pools are definitely not a good mix. If you have a swimming pool, it will need to be fenced off so there is no possibility of your puppy getting anywhere near it.

REFUSE COLLECTION

All areas have different methods of refuse collection, but most people end up with garbage bins in the back garden. Make sure these are fenced off so that your puppy cannot get at them. A small pup may not have such ambitious plans, but the enticing smell may prove too much as he gets bigger and stronger.

The problem with household garbage is that it is not only discarded food and packaging that finds its way in there. Discarded toiletries and cleaning agents are thrown out, and if a dog gets his teeth into these, he could end up in serious trouble.

THE OUTDOOR LIFE

The vast majority of dog owners plan to keep their puppy in the house, but there are some circumstances where you might consider an outdoor kennel and run.

REASONS FOR KENNELING

- If you want to keep a number of dogs of different ages, sexes and temperaments.
- If you are keeping a male and a female and do not want either of them neutered, a kennel and run would help you to cope with the bitch's seasonal cycle.
- If you live in a hot climate, a kennel and run would be a healthier option.
- A kennel would allow you to keep a dog even if a family member has an allergy.

REASONS AGAINST KENNELING

- Dogs thrive on human companionship, and, unless they are given times in the house, they will be lonely.
- Kennels are unsuitable for very young or elderly dogs.
- A single dog (without human or canine company) will pine.
- House-training may break down.
- Not ideal for all breeds, particularly those with a short, fine coat, or if you live in a cold climate.

KENNEL CONSTRUCTION AND MAINTENANCE

Visit some of the major dog shows to view various kennel designs and the materials they are made with. Kennels can be made of wood, metal or even fibreglass. Some say wood will not last as long as the more modern materials, but, generally, commercial kennels use only very high-quality timber. Kennels vary tremendously in cost, but it does not pay to skimp and you should aim for quality.

MAIN CONSIDERATIONS

The kennel should be:
- Large enough for your dog to stretch out fully, and to turn around in comfort.

TOP TIP

A pair of dogs who are good friends can share a kennel and run, but if you have a number of dogs that need to be kenneled separately, you can still allow them to enjoy canine company by positioning the kennels and runs alongside each other. Of course, you must be careful to check any tendency to bark at fellow occupants, or you will set up an untenable situation.

- Dry, draught-free and acceptably warm. Some commercially-built kennels include built-in heating systems.
- Easy to clean.

The kennel should have:
- A run area attached, where the dog can relieve himself, obtain a drink of water at all times, and play with suitable toys. Ideally, the run should include a shaded area so the dog can get out of direct sunlight if conditions are hot.
- A raised bed that allows enough room for the dog to stretch out.
- Plenty of light so the dog is not left in darkness.
- Adequate and clean bedding, such as thick wads of newspaper, blankets, etc. Avoid straw – it can harbor mites.
- A door between the kennel and the run that can be closed easily. However, there is no logical reason why it is necessarily harmful for a door to be left open if the climatic conditions allow.
- Padlocked exits to the outside world.

COUNTING THE COST
Providing a good-quality kennel and run is an expensive option, and is only suitable in specific situations. For the majority of dog owners, the fun of having a dog is sharing a home.

Chapter 9

The Professionals

Bringing up a puppy is a family affair, but there are specific times when you need to employ professional services. Firstly, and most importantly, this means finding a veterinarian (vet), but, depending on your breed and your circumstances, you may need to find a boarding kennels; a dog-sitter or a dog-walker may be required, and you may need to take your dog to a professional groomer.

FINDING A VETERINARIAN

It may seem that finding a veterinarian before you have brought your puppy home is a bit like putting the cart before the horse. However, this is an important step, and it is much better to take your time finding the veterinary practice that is most likely to suit your needs, rather than getting in a panic and phoning the first veterinarian you can find when your puppy's vaccinations are due.

TRACKING DOWN A VETERINARY PRACTICE

If you are buying a puppy locally, the breeder may be able to recommend a veterinarian. If the breeder lives outside your area, contact the breed club in your region. The secretary will have details of breeders that live in your area, and you can then ask them for advice. You may have dog-owning friends or neighbors who can put you in touch with a practice, or you may have to look through the local directory and shortlist the veterinarians that are based nearby.

Do not opt for the practice that is closest to you without checking it out. The veterinarian is going to be responsible for your dog's health and wellbeing for the next 12-14 years, so it is an important decision to make.

QUESTIONS TO ASK

It is a good idea to visit the practice so that you can get some idea of how it is run, and what facilities are available. It goes without saying that the premises should be sparkling with cleanliness and should smell fresh. You will want to find out the answers to the following questions:

- Does the practice run an appointment system?
- What provisions are made for emergency cover at night and at weekends?
- What is the basic fee for a consultation?
- What is the fee for a home visit?
- What is the policy on puppy vaccinations and adult boosters?
- Is there a veterinarian in the practice that has experience with your breed?
- What facilities are available (X-ray, ultrasound, etc.)?
- Does the practice make use of alternative therapies such as massage techniques and homeopathy?
- Does the practice hold puppy socialization classes (see page 174)?
- If required, can the practice recommend specialized help, e.g. animal behavior counselors, nutrition counselors, bereavement counselors etc?

TOP TIP

Do not be afraid to ask. In fact, the amount of time that is given to you when you make your initial enquiries will be a good indication of the type of service you are likely to get if you become a client.

MAKING AN APPOINTMENT

Once you are satisfied that you have found a suitable practice, make an appointment for a couple of days after your puppy has arrived home. This will give the veterinarian a chance to give your pup a thorough examination before starting his vaccination program. If you wish, you can also organize a permanent form of ID, such as microchipping or tattooing.

HEALTH INSURANCE

Many insurance companies offer comprehensive health coverage for dogs. It is worth finding out about this, but make sure you read the small print. Routine health care, such as booster vaccinations, worm treatments etc., are excluded from most policies, so you need to find out exactly what you are being offered.

FINDING A BOARDING KENNEL

You will not be needing the services of a boarding kennel straight away, but it is worth making inquiries so you are prepared when holidays come round, or in case something unexpected happens, which means you need temporary care for your dog.

It is easy enough to find a boarding kennel; look in your local telephone directory or a specialist dog paper. The vet may also carry a list of boarding kennels in your area.

Before you rush to make a booking for your dog, find the time to go to the boarding kennel. You can telephone in advance, and ask if someone will show you round the premises.

WHAT TO LOOK FOR

When you visit the boarding kennel, look for the following:

- Clean premises.
- Helpful staff.
- Spacious, draught-free kennels, which should be warm in the winter and cool in the summer.
- Well-fenced, concrete runs, with fresh drinking water available.
- Well-fenced grass, exercise runs, with fresh drinking water available.
- Droppings from runs should be picked up regularly.
- A well-organized kitchen area, where the dogs' food is prepared. It should be clean and smell fresh.

It goes without saying that the kennel must be licensed by the local authority. The relevant paperwork should be available for inspection if required.

QUESTIONS TO ASK

It is important to be familiar with the kennel's routine and general policy, so make a list of questions to ask. These may include:

• What vaccinations does my dog need before entering kennels? (See page 202.)
• Do you need details of recent worming/flea treatments?
• Will you feed the diet my dog is used to getting?
• What is the daily routine of the kennel?
• Will my dog be groomed while he is in kennels?
• Are the dogs allowed free-running exercise?
• Are the dogs given lead-walking exercise?
• Are the dogs kept singly, or are they mixed?
• Can I bring my dog's bed or some bedding from home?
• Can I bring some dog toys?
• What is your scale of charges?
• Do I pay in advance, or when I collect the dog?
• How much notice do you need before booking in my dog?
• If I need to extend or curtail the kennel visit, how much notice do you require?
• Are there any additional charges I should be aware of?
• Do you have a veterinarian on call in case of an emergency?

If you are happy with what you see, and you are confident that the staff is knowledgeable and experienced, you will need to look no further. If you have any doubts in your mind, do not ignore them. There are plenty of well-run boarding kennels available, and if you need to leave your dog you want to be certain that he is receiving the best possible care.

FINDING A DOG-SITTER/DOG-WALKER

Employing dog-sitters and dog-walkers is a relatively recent trend, and if you find the right person, it can certainly enhance your dog's routine.

A dog-sitter may be asked to come in for a couple of hours if the owner has to be away for an extended period (longer than four hours), or some dog-sitters come and live in the house over a weekend, or a for the duration of a holiday so the dog does not have to go into boarding kennels.

Obviously, you must be completely confident that the person you employ is good with dogs, and is entirely trustworthy. Most dog-sitters advertise their services, and so it is a matter of taking up references so that you can vet the individual thoroughly before commencing employment.

A dog-sitter will usually act as a dog-walker as part of the service they provide. There are other people who specialize as dog-walkers. This is a very useful service if you are away for longer than four hours at a time, and it can also be a great help to more elderly owners, or for those suffering from ill health.

It is important to find out how many dogs are walked at a time – there are those who make their money by taking out a 'pack', and this should not be encouraged. One individual cannot hope to control a number of dogs, and so you would be putting your dog in a high-risk situation. However, there are plenty of reliable, experienced dog-walkers who advertise their services in newspapers, specialist dog papers, at pet stores, and at veterinary practices. Again, make sure you take up references before entrusting your dog to someone else's care.

FINDING A PROFESSIONAL GROOMER

If you have chosen a shortcoated breed, you will be feeling very complacent as you will be quite capable of caring for your dog at home (see page 122). It is not difficult to groom a longcoated breed, such as a Rough Collie, although it is certainly time-consuming. Of course, you can keep some longcoated breeds in a so-called 'puppy trim'. A number of breeds, such as the Shih Tzu and the Old English Sheepdog, look very attractive with their coat trimmed, and this may be a sensible option some for pet owners.

There are a number of breeds, such as the Poodle, the Schnauzer breeds, and some of the Terriers, where there is no choice but to employ a professional groomer, and it is important to find someone who is skilled and reliable to look after your dog.

Your puppy's breeder may be able to recommend a groomer. In fact, some breeders are also trained as professional groomers. If you have no luck here, you will need to refer to your local telephone directory, the advertisements in specialist dog papers, or ask if your vet can suggest anyone.

The most important consideration is finding a groomer that has experience with your breed. You may find that someone has specialized in Poodle clipping for example, but has little idea how to make a West Highland White Terrier look smart. Even though you are not aiming for the perfect turn-outs that you see in some dogs exhibited in the ring, you still want your dog to be clean and comfortable and to be a typical representative of the breed.

You will be able to cope with grooming at home while your puppy still has his soft puppy coat, but it is important to find a groomer well in advance of when you need one. It is also a good plan to take your youngster to the groomer before a full grooming or clipping session is needed. Your puppy can meet the groomer, and get used to the surroundings, and this will make him feel more relaxed when he goes in for a full session.

WHAT TO LOOK FOR

When you go to a groomer, you should look for the following signs which indicate a well-run establishment.

- The premises should be scrupulously clean, and smell fresh.
- Staff should clean up the grooming area after each client.
- The bathing area should be purpose-built, with a non-slip rubber mat lining the base of the bath.
- Grooming equipment should be well maintained.
- The staff should be friendly and helpful, and show good handling skills with dogs.
- Certificates to show professional qualifications should be displayed or available for inspection.

If your dog needs regular trips to the groomer, you want to ensure that this is a totally non-traumatic experience. In fact, some dogs positively enjoy their trips to the hairdresser! Make sure you take your time and choose a groomer that is both skilful and sympathetic with their canine clients.

For information on dog trainers, see page 174. For information on dog behaviorists, see page 182.

Part 5

Home Sweet Home

THE BREEDS

One of the most fascinating aspects of the dog world is the tremendous variety of breeds, ranging from giant to toy size, from heavyweight to agile and athletic – all with a stunning array of coat types, colours and markings. If that was not enough, the breeds all have their own unique characteristics and personalities.

Golden Retriever: *A wonderful family dog.*

◀ **Bulldog:** *A natural clown who loves his family.*

▼ **Poodle:** *You can choose the size of Poodle to suit your lifestyle.*

▲ **West Highland White Terrier:** A game little dog, who adapts well to a variety of different lifestyles.

◄ **Rottweiler:** A powerful breed that needs experienced handling. 83

► **Siberian Husky:** A dog that was bred to run and run.

◄ **Lhasa Apso:** The coat is long and luxurious in adult dogs (opposite page).

▼ **Miniature Longhaired Dachshund:** There are six varieties within the breed, depending on size, and coat type.

◄ **Boxer:** An intelligent dog with lots of energy that needs to be channelled.

▼ **Greyhound:** An affectionate and loving companion.

▲ *Cavalier King Charles Spaniel: A lively and intelligent dog who will enjoy mental stimulation.*

► *Miniature Schnauzer: Bright and alert, the Miniature Schnauzer keeps a close watch on everything that is going on.*

German Shepherd Dog: A dog with tremendous intelligence and loyalty.

Chapter 10

Collecting
Your Puppy

At long last, the big day dawns and it is time to collect your puppy. Hopefully, you have your home and your garden prepared, and you have got everything that was on your puppy's shopping list.

If possible, arrange to collect your puppy early in the day. This will mean that the pup has most of the day to settle into his new home before he has to be left alone at night. Although all the family will be keen to go and collect the puppy, it is better to go with just one other adult. This will mean that you can attend to instructions from the breeder without distractions, and one adult can drive home while the other looks after the puppy. You will need to bring:

- A towel or a blanket for the puppy to lie on (you will probably be holding him in your lap).
- Kitchen paper (in case of accidents).
- A bowl and some fresh drinking water (if you are travelling a long distance).
- The means to pay for your puppy (or the balance if you have paid a deposit).
- If you have to travel alone, you will need to bring a puppy carrier, lined with bedding.

THE PAPERWORK

When you arrive at the breeder, do not rush off in search of your puppy. It is more important to listen to instructions and to complete the formalities. The breeder will provide you with the following:

The pedigree: This will usually take the form of a five-generation pedigree tracing your puppy's relatives through parents, grandparents, great-grandparents etc. Often the dogs who have become Champions will have their names written or underlined in red. This is a fascinating document, and one you should treasure.

Registration documents: The puppies will be registered with the national Kennel Club, and you should receive the necessary documentation. You will then have to complete papers for transfer of ownership.

Details of worming treatment: The breeder will have already started a worming program for the puppies. You will need instructions as to when the next treatment is due, and what product has been used.

Details of vaccinations: If you are collecting your puppy at around eight weeks of age, he will probably be unvaccinated. If your puppy is a little older (some of the Toy breeds are sold a little later), he may have received his first vaccination (see page 202).

Eye testing/ear testing certificates: Depending on the breed, the puppies may be eye-tested to ensure they are clear of inherited eye disorders. The Collie breeds will often be tested for this. Some breeds, such as Dalmatians, are more prone to deafness, and so the puppies are generally tested before they are sold. For information on inherited disorders, see Chapter 27: A-Z of Canine Disorders and Diseases.

Diet sheet: A detailed breakdown of what the puppies are eating. Most breeders will suggest the numbers of meals per day (usually four), and when the meals should be given. Guidance will be given for the first few weeks, and then recommendations are generally given as to how to proceed as your puppy grows.

Sample of food: It is common practice for breeders to supply food for the first few days after your puppy has arrived in his new home. This is to ensure the puppy gets precisely the diet he has been accustomed to. A pup will very often suffer from an upset stomach if he has to cope with a sudden change of diet, as well as the trauma of moving home (see page 97).

Insurance: Some breeders provide health insurance to cover the first couple of weeks following change of ownership.

Receipt: A written acknowledgement of the fee you are paying for your puppy.

Contact details: You may well need to seek advice as your puppy grows up. The breeder will usually supply their own telephone number, and they will often provide an additional back-up number in case you need help in a hurry.

SAYING GOODBYE

Listen to all the last-minute instructions from the breeder, who will probably want you to telephone to report how the puppy is settling. A lot of owners keep in touch with the breeder, and this is much appreciated. Breeders love to know how the puppies they have reared have turned out, and the chance to see photos of a pup as he grows up is considered a great bonus. Not only is it fun to receive the photos, it can also be extremely helpful as breeders can assess appearance and conformation, which may influence their future breeding plans.

THE JOURNEY HOME

Although your puppy will be leaving his mother, his brothers and sisters, and the only home he has ever known, he is unlikely to show any signs of distress. A confident, healthy puppy will be happy to go off with his new friends, and will enjoy getting all the attention.

In most cases, the breeder will try to ensure that your puppy has not eaten prior to his journey home. For most pups, this will be their first experience of car travel, so it is better not to attempt it on a full stomach. If possible, the puppy should be held by an adult, and travel in the back seat. This means that if he does wriggle free, the driver will not be distracted. It is best to settle the puppy on a towel or a blanket, so there is some protection in case of accidents. The puppy may whimper a little to begin with, but most will be reassured by a warm, comfortable lap, and a few kind words.

If you are travelling alone, your puppy will need to go in a puppy carrier. This should be placed in a secure part of the car, such as the rear, and you must ensure that the carrier cannot tip up if the puppy scrabbles around, or if you are negotiating a sharp bend. You will almost certainly have a noisy journey home, but at least you will know your puppy is safe and cannot do himself any damage.

It is not unusual for puppies to be a little car-sick, so make sure you have your kitchen paper at the ready. If it is a long journey, you may need to stop. You can give your pup a little water to drink, but remember that an unvaccinated puppy must not be put on the ground. Generally, it is a good idea to complete the journey as quickly as possible. With any luck, your puppy will be exhausted by all the excitement and will settle down to sleep until you arrive home.

Chapter 11

Arriving Home

All the waiting is over, and now your puppy has arrived in his new home. There will be huge excitement from all members of the family, and everyone will want to hold the pup and cuddle him. Try to keep things as calm and as orderly as possible. Your puppy will be feeling confused by the strange surroundings, and by all the new people in his life. Give him a chance to find his feet rather than overwhelming him with too much attention.

EXPLORING THE GARDEN

After the journey, your pup will need to relieve himself, so start as you mean to go on, and take him out into the garden. You can take him to his toilet area (see page 69), and he will almost certainly oblige. Give him lots of praise, and then give him a chance to explore.

At this stage, your puppy will probably feel thoroughly bewildered, so reassure him in a warm, friendly tone of voice. There are some pups who are bold right from the start, but most will be quite tentative, sniffing around, and following you wherever you go. Use your puppy's name, and encourage him to come to you. Give lots of praise, so your pup starts to feel he is safe when he is with you.

MEETING THE FAMILY

Once your puppy has had a chance to go out in the garden, you can introduce the rest of the family. Obviously, the way you go about this will depend on your family set-up. Generally, give the pup a chance to go up and sniff each new person, and allow him to make the overtures rather than picking him up and passing him around like a parcel.

If you have small children, you will need to supervise introductions carefully. Try to curb overexcitement, as the puppy will get hyped-up if there is any yelling or screaming.

• Sit the children on the floor, and give each of them a food treat for the puppy.

- Let the pup go to each child in turn, and be rewarded with a treat.
- Allow the children to stroke the puppy, but do not let them pick him up. It is all too easy for the puppy to wriggle and fall.
- You can get out one of your puppy's new toys, and supervise a game. At this stage, a few minutes' gentle play will be sufficient for the children and the puppy.

LEARNING RESPECT

Children and puppies can develop great relationships, but it is essential to instill a sense of mutual respect. The puppy must learn how to behave with the smaller members of his human pack, and children must learn that a pup is not a plaything which they can swamp with attention one moment, and then discard the next.

Puppies and small children should never be left alone together. A game can get out of hand, and the pup, or the child, could inflict an unintentional injury. Make sure an adult is always available to supervise play sessions.

Here are a few guidelines which will ensure that both puppy and children respect each other.

- The pup must never bite or mouth when he is playing.
- He must not jump up at children, or chase after them.
- The puppy must have his own toys, so you have something to give him if he tries to play with the children's toys.
- He must learn to take treats and toys "Gently" when they are offered to him.
- Children must learn not to get over excited when they are playing with the puppy.
- The puppy must not be picked up. He should be played with at ground level only.
- The puppy must not be manhandled by children pulling his ears or his tail. It would be surprising if a pup did not object to this.
- Children must learn the 'house rules', such as not allowing the puppy on the furniture, or the pup will be quick to take advantage. If the children are too young to understand this, make sure the adult that is supervising is quick to step in and prevent any transgressions.
- Children must try to be tidy, keeping their own toys out of the puppy's reach. If the children are too young to do this, it is an extra job for the adults in the family.
- The pup should never be disturbed when he is sleeping. Puppies need their rest, and, if a pup is suddenly woken up, he may snap or growl.

MEETING THE RESIDENT DOG

It may be that you already have a dog at home. If this is the case, you will need to be tactful in the initial stages so that the adult dog learns to accept the newcomer.

It helps if you can introduce the dogs on neutral territory as the adult dog will not feel so threatened by the 'intruder'. However, this may not be possible if you have an unvaccinated puppy. In this situation, the garden is generally the best meeting place to choose.

Allow the two dogs to go up to each other and sniff each other. The puppy is likely to show submissive behavior to the adult, and may even roll on to his back. Some pups are more pushy, and may try to initiate a game, jumping up at the adult, trying to play chase. Leave the two dogs to sort themselves out. They are working out their own hierarchy, and this will be achieved far more effectively without human intervention. Do not introduce toys at this stage, as they can become a source of contention.

Make sure the adult dog is allowed to rest undisturbed when he wishes. Even the most mild-tempered dog can become intolerant of the antics of a playful puppy. You must also make sure you spend some quality time with your adult dog. As your puppy will not be ready to go out for walks, you can use this time to play with the older dog, and make him feel special.

In most cases, the relationship between puppy and adult soon becomes established. It may be that the older dog always remains the boss, but sometimes the puppy will take over this role. Do not worry if this happens. Dogs work out their own relationships, and, if the older dog is prepared to take a back seat, you must accept the status quo. As long as both dogs are receiving plenty of attention from their human family, they will be happy.

TOP TIP

If the adult dog gives a warning growl, do not rush to pick up the puppy and then reprimand the adult. This is a clearly understood signal that the puppy must respect an older dog, and if you become overprotective of the puppy, it will lead to trouble. The adult will feel his nose has been put out of joint, and the puppy will think that you will always come running to his rescue – so he will not learn to respect the older dog.

FELINE FRIENDS

Dogs and cats are classed as natural enemies, but this does not have to be the case. If relationships get off to a good start, the pup will quickly learn that the cat is not a furry plaything that he can chase whenever he feels like it.

If you have a cat, initial introductions must be carefully supervised. A cat is unlikely to be impressed by a bouncy, excitable puppy, and, if you let nature take its course, the fur will soon be flying. Try the following course of action.

- Put the puppy in his crate, and allow the cat to come up and investigate. Reassure the cat, talking in a low, soft voice.
- Before you let the puppy out of his crate, make sure your cat has an upward escape route. A cat will instinctively climb out of reach when threatened. This is much better than leaving a door open, which would encourage the cat to bolt and the puppy to chase after her.
- Let the puppy out of his crate, and hold him on your lap.
- Ask a friend or a family member to hold the cat.
- If the cat wants to go, this should be allowed. She should not be restrained against her will. However, it is important to hold on to the puppy so that he does not try to jump on her.
- Encourage the pup to look away from the cat by offering a treat. Every time he switches his attention away from the cat, reward him. If the pup has his eyes glued on the cat, withhold the treat.
- Once the puppy has shown that he will respond to you, he can meet the cat at closer quarters. She has her escape route if she feels threatened, and she is will make it clear if the puppy oversteps the mark. Obviously, you do not want your puppy to be on the receiving end of sharp claws, but if the cat hisses, and spits, the puppy will learn to mind his manners.

Do not worry if it takes a little while for this relationship to gel. Allow the cat to proceed at her own pace, and do not allow any unsupervised interaction until you are confident that your puppy has learned not to chase. In time, your puppy will learn to respect the cat, and, in fact, some dogs and cats become good friends.

SMALL ANIMALS

If you keep small animals as pets, such as rabbits, hamsters, or birds such as budgerigars, they should be off-limits as far as your puppy is concerned. All cages and hutches should be secure, and you should not use a garden run for rabbits, guinea pigs etc. until your puppy has learned not to disturb them. Again, it is important to supervise all interactions in the initial stages, so your puppy learns the correct behavior.

- The rabbit/guinea pig/budgie should be secure in their cage before you attempt an introduction.
- Allow your puppy to go up and sniff, but then attract his attention by offering a treat.
- Correct any signs of overexcitement, such as barking or jumping up at the cage with a firm "No".
- Every time your puppy responds to you rather than the animal, give a reward.

Eventually, your puppy will learn to live alongside small animals. He will understand that the cage is off-limits, and the occupants will quickly lose their novelty value. However, do not take unnecessary risks. Never leave your puppy unsupervised with small animals. Something unexpected could happen, such as the animal letting out an unexpected shrill cry, and your pup may decide to investigate. It is not fair on your small animals – or your puppy – to test this relationship too far.

EXPLORING YOUR HOME

Your puppy will want to explore his new home, so make sure you have shut off any rooms where he is not allowed.

At this stage, the stairs will be considered too big an obstacle to negotiate, but it is a good idea to have a stairgate in place (see page 68). An ambitious pup may try to follow you upstairs, and could easily fall and injure himself.

It is a good idea to show your puppy his bed or his crate, as exhaustion will soon take over. Puppies have periods of hectic activity contrasted with long periods when they need to sleep. When your pup looks like he is slowing up, try putting him in his bed or in his crate for a rest.

CRATE-TRAINING

Your puppy will probably be used to going in a pen with his brothers and sisters, but this is likely to be his first experience of going into a crate on his own. A puppy may show some initial hesitation, but most soon appreciate the crate as their own special den, where they can rest in peace and quiet.

Try the following routine to accustom your puppy to his crate.

- Make the crate as inviting as possible, with comfortable bedding, and some toys to play with.
- Encourage your puppy to go in the crate by offering a treat, and then stroke the puppy while he is in there. Do not attempt to shut the door at this stage.
- If your puppy is very tired, he may snuggle down to sleep, but he is more likely to want to get back to you. Stay sitting by the crate for a few minutes, talking quietly, and encouraging your puppy to settle.
- Then shut the door, but stay within sight so your puppy does not feel deserted.
- Try a few short sessions with your puppy in the crate, leaving him for short periods. Do not make a big fuss when you leave your puppy or when you return to let him out. Keep your manner calm and low-key and your puppy will soon learn that going to his crate is a simple matter of routine, and nothing to worry about.

In fact, you will probably find that your puppy appreciates a chance to rest undisturbed, and there is many a puppy (and adult dog) who will go into the crate of their own free will to find some peace.

MEALTIMES

Most puppies will be getting four meals a day at the time when they move homes. Often, the breeder provides food to last over the first few days, or you may have bought in a supply of the diet the breeder has recommended.

It is very important not to introduce any changes while your puppy is settling in. This is a traumatic period for the boldest, bravest puppy, and if he has a new diet to cope with, as well as the stress of trying to adapt to a new environment, it will inevitably lead to an upset stomach. Feed the diet your puppy is happy with, and, if possible, try to keep to a similar schedule so disturbance to the routine is kept at a minimum.

Do not worry if your puppy shows little interest in his food, or does not finish the whole meal. To begin with he will miss the rivalry of feeding with his littermates, and so he will not have the same incentive to get his share. He will also be feeling a little strange and bewildered, and food will not be a top priority.

Give your puppy the chance to eat as much as he wants, and then take the food away. Start again with a fresh bowl of food for the next mealtime.

If your puppy is not eating his food after a few days, or is experiencing any stomach upset, ask your vet for advice.

For further information, see Chapter 13: Diet and Feeding.

THE FIRST NIGHT

By the end of the day, your puppy will be beginning to find his feet and to feel reasonably confident in his new home. Now comes the hard bit – settling the pup for his first night.

There is no way of making this situation easy. Just as the pup is getting to know his new family – they all disappear and leave him on his own. Not only is the pup expected to settle in a new place on his own, he also has to cope without the warmth and comfort of brothers and sisters.

Some owners start with the best of intentions, settling the puppy in his bed, determined to leave him until the next morning. However, an hour of piteous crying can break the sternest resolve, and, hey presto, the puppy is nestled up in bed, sleeping comfortably alongside his new owner.

WHAT'S THE PROBLEM?

What's wrong with a puppy sharing your bed? Quite simply, nothing. However, you should consider the following points:

Do you really want the puppy to share your bed, or are you going to try and settle him in his own bed after a few days?
If you are planning to relocate your puppy, you may be making a rod for your own back? Once the pup has got the idea of sharing your company in a warm cozy bed, he will put up a fight if you try to move him

Do you want an adult dog to share your bed?
A puppy can be very sweet, and will not take up much space. But, depending on the breed you have chosen, you may find there is little room left for you.

Can you put up with the doggy odors that will pervade your bedroom?
It is very hard to keep a room clean and fresh if you have a big, hairy mutt on the bed!

What does your partner think about the new bedfellow?
You must both be happy with the situation, or, inevitably, problems will arise.

Are you confident that your dog will respect you if he gets his own way with the sleeping arrangements?
It is important to start right, and if one of the more dominant breeds, such as a Rottweiler or a Doberman Pinscher, thinks you are a pushover, you may find your authority is disputed in others areas (see Chapter 22: The Adolescent).

If you have thought about the above points, and you are still happy with the situation, that's OK. You are entitled to make your own rules. However, if you would prefer to have your dog sleeping in his own bed, you should adopt the following regime.

BEDTIME TIPS

Feed your puppy his last meal of the day at around 8-9pm. You do not want to feed the puppy too late in the evening, but, remember, he only has a small stomach, and it will seem like a long wait for breakfast. A hungry puppy will never settle.

Before going to bed, take your puppy out to relieve himself.

Line the front of the crate with newspaper, or place some newspaper outside the bed. A young puppy will need to relieve himself during the night, and he will use the newspaper rather than fouling his bed. If you do not provide this 'toilet area', the puppy will end up getting dirty and uncomfortable which will add to his distress.

Tempt your puppy into his bed/crate with a treat, and leave him with a toy that is completely safe, and will withstand chewing (a cotton tug-toy, or a hard, rubber toy would be suitable).

Check that the room is a suitable temperature – not too hot, nor too cold.

Shut the door, and go to bed – with ear-plugs if necessary!

It is important not to keep coming to check on your puppy, or he will feel that he is being rewarded for making a noise. As long as you are confident that your puppy cannot get up to any mischief, you should allow him to cry himself to sleep. For this reason, a crate is a great option because you know exactly where your puppy is, and you know he cannot harm himself – no matter how loud his cries!

TOP TIP

Try leaving a ticking clock in the room where your puppy is sleeping. Some puppies seem to find it very comforting!

If you are firm to begin with, your puppy will soon get used to the routine of being put to bed at night. He may protest for a few days – and he may be an early riser to begin with – but if you do not alter your behavior, he will soon realize that being alone at night is the norm, and he will learn to settle down peacefully.

House-Training

There is no doubt that house-training is a top priority when your new puppy arrives home. It is the part of puppy rearing that most people dread, but, in fact, it can be fairly painless if you are prepared to work hard for the first few weeks. Puppies are quick learners, and if you put the message over clearly and consistently, your pup will soon learn that he must only relieve himself when he is outside the house.

GETTING STARTED

House-training starts from the first moment your puppy arrives home (see page 92). Do not make the mistake of leaving it for a couple of days until your puppy has settled; start as you mean to go on.

Always use the toilet area you have allocated, and think up a command to use when you take your puppy out. To save embarrassment from neighbors, it is wise to use something straightforward like "Be clean" or "Busy".

When you get to the appointed area, your puppy will sniff around, or he may try to start a game. Be patient, and wait for him to perform. As soon as he does, give the command "Be clean", and give him lots of praise. In time, your pup will learn to associate the command with the action, so that you can ask him to "Be clean" when you take him out.

ESTABLISHING A ROUTINE

The key to house-training is to do the thinking for your puppy. At this stage, he is too young to ask if he can go out – you must work it out for him. Generally, you will need to take your puppy out at the following times:

• First thing in the morning.
• Every time he wakes up from a sleep during the day.
• After mealtimes.

- After a play session.
- Every time you see him sniffing or circling.
- Last thing at night.
- A minimum of every two hours.

Although this may seem like a punishing routine, it is well worth sticking to it. Your puppy will quickly understand why he is being taken out and will learn to respond to the "Be clean" command. The fewer the accidents he has in the house, the more likely he is to associate the garden with where he performs.

WHEN ACCIDENTS HAPPEN

Inevitably, your puppy will have the occasional accident in the house. Nine times out of ten, this will be because you have not been vigilant enough, or you have failed to read the warning signs.

There is, therefore, no point in getting angry with the pup – even though you are not best pleased about finding a mess on the carpet. Unless you catch your puppy in the act, he will have no idea why he is being told off. He will probably think he is being reprimanded for coming up to you, which will not help his future training. If you find a mess, simply clear it up and vow to supervise your puppy more closely.

If you catch your puppy 'red-handed', you can turn the mistake into a lesson. Quickly pick up the pup and take him out to his allocated toilet area in the garden. Give the command "Be clean", and hopefully your puppy will oblige. When he does, remember to give lots of praise – at least your puppy got it right in the end!

TOP TIP

Patience is a tremendous virtue when you are house-training. Even though you may get frustrated at times, you should bear in mind that a puppy will learn far more quickly if he is happy and relaxed, rather than becoming stressed by failing to understand what he is doing wrong.

NIGHT-TIMES

When your puppy first arrives home, he will be too young to go through the night without relieving himself. The best plan is to line the front of the crate, or the area alongside his bed, with newspaper. A puppy will instinctively try to keep his sleeping quarters clean, and he will soon get the idea of using the newspaper.

The process of becoming clean at night will almost certainly be quicker if you are using a crate. A puppy that has the freedom to roam is likely to be less fastidious. When your puppy cuts down to having three meals a day (see page 111), you can feed his evening meal a little earlier, and this will make it easier for him to be clean until he is let out in the morning.

HOW LONG DOES IT TAKE?

There is no set answer for calculating how long it will take for your puppy to be house-trained. To a large extent, it depends on the amount of effort you put in. If you work hard at establishing a routine, and supervising your puppy, he will get the general idea within a couple of weeks. However, you will need to continue with the routine of taking him out, and doing the thinking for him for at least a couple of months.

When a puppy reaches about six months of age, it is all too easy to become complacent, thinking that you have cracked house-training. You may not have had an accident for weeks – and then suddenly your puppy starts to make mistakes.

This is usually because you have moved on too quickly. Your puppy knows he has to "Be clean" outside, but you have become lax in taking him out, so it is hardly surprising that his house-training breaks down.

If this happens, go back to basics, and work really hard at taking your puppy out, giving his command, and then rewarding him with lots of praise. Soon, the pattern of being clean outside will be so firmly established that the dog will ask to be let out.

CLEAN UP!

It is important to keep your garden clean, particularly if you have children. Clean up every time your puppy performs, and find a convenient method of disposing of the waste.

When you get to the stage of taking your puppy into the outside world, you can take him to his toilet area first and ask him to "Be clean". Hopefully, this will mean that your pup will not need to go when he is on the streets or in the park.

However, it is much better to be safe than sorry, so make sure you always have the means to clean up after your dog. This is a vital part of responsible dog ownership, and it is your duty to the community to make sure your dog does not foul public places.

SOLVING PROBLEMS

Despite the best endeavors, sometimes house-training breaks down – or never seems to get properly established in the first place. There are a number of common problems which crop up, but, fortunately, most are quite easy to solve.

Problem: I take my puppy outside at regular intervals throughout the day. I leave him in the garden for at least 10 minutes, but, when he comes in, more often than not, he has an accident.

Solution: Cutting corners does not work with house-training. It is not good enough to let your puppy out at regular intervals – you have to stay with him. It is vital that you are there to give the command, and to reward with lots of praise. Although hanging around in the garden may seem tedious, it is time well spent. Your puppy needs to understand what is required, and be praised when he does the right thing.

Problem: My puppy was coming on very well with his house-training, and when he was nine months old I was confident that he could be trusted when he was away from home. Unfortunately, the house where we were staying had a concrete yard, and my pup refused to go on it. Needless to say, we had a very difficult week. What went wrong?

Solution: Most dogs are not fussy about what surface they use as a toilet area, but there are some who get really concerned about a change of surface. This characteristic has been reported more commonly among females, but males may also develop problems. It has been known for a dog to 'hang on' virtually all day, waiting to get to a grass surface rather than using concrete or gravel.

The best plan is to prevent the problem occurring by getting your puppy accustomed to using a variety of surfaces right from the beginning. The pup is then most unlikely to develop a phobia about a particular surface.

If your pup has got into the habit of only going on grass for example, you must work at weaning him on to a different surface. Select a concrete area in the garden and start to use this as the puppy's toilet area. Take your pup to the area and give the command "Be clean".

Reward with lots of praise and a game when your pup obliges. You will need to be patient as it may take a while for your pup to accept the change, but keep working at it. You want your dog to be a thoroughly adaptable creature who can cope with any change of circumstance.

Problem: I seem to spend hours hanging around in the garden, waiting for my pup to do his business, but he seems more interested in playing. What should I do?

Solution: Typically, this scenario occurs when the owner takes his puppy out, and then the second the pup has performed, they go back into the house. The puppy starts to associate relieving himself with rushing back into the house, leaving the garden where he would much rather be. The pup, therefore, decides to adopt some delaying tactics, so that he can stay in the garden for longer.

The solution is very simple. When the pup has performed, give him lots of praise and then have a game. Just a few minutes of play will suffice; the pup will give up his waiting game as he will start to look forward to the fun that follows.

Problem: My puppy had an accident in the house and I cleaned it up thoroughly. However, he seems to have developed a liking for this spot, and keeps returning to it to make a mess.

Solution: This is instinctive behavior, where the puppy returns to the same spot to mark his territory. You may think you have cleaned the spot thoroughly, but dogs have a very acute sense of smell, and your pup can still detect that this is the spot he used.

The answer is to buy a deodorisor (there are a number manufactured specifically for doggy odors), and use it liberally on the spot.

This will deter your pup from future use. At the same time, step up your vigilance and make sure you are taking your puppy out often enough. If a pup needs to go and is not taken outside, he may become quite sneaky, finding a discreet spot in the house to use instead.

Problem: My puppy is very good with his house-training, but when visitors come to the house, he gets really excited and then urinates.

Solution: This is the result of submissive behavior. The puppy is using doggy behavior to show that he is inferior in status and does not pose a threat.

Most puppies grow out of this as they mature, but some pups who lack confidence may continue to exhibit this type of behavior. Obviously, you want to try to put a stop to it, as not only is it antisocial, it also points to an underlying problem where the dog is over-anxious and easily stressed.

Try to build up the puppy's confidence at every available opportunity. Run through some simple training exercises (see Chapter 20: Basic Exercises), so you have good reason to reward your pup and tell him how clever he is. It is also important to allow your puppy to spend some time on his own (see page 186), so that he becomes more independent and less needy.

Most house-training problems are solved with hard work and patience. However, if you are experiencing on-going problems, seek the advice of a reputable dog behaviorist (see page 182) who should be able to find out what is going wrong.

Part 6

Caring For Your Puppy

Diet And Feeding

The pet food industry is a multi-million dollar business, and, if you go into any supermarket or pet store, you will be confronted by huge displays of dog food, backed up by advertisements claiming the merits of each brand on sale. How do you go about choosing the best diet for your dog? This is a very important decision as your dog's general health, development and wellbeing will all be affected by the food he is given.

EARLY DAYS

To begin with, do not attempt to make any changes in diet. Continue with the breeder's recommended feed while your puppy is settling into his new home (see page 62). This will also give you a chance to assess the following factors:

- Is your puppy enjoying his food and eating it with relish?
- Is the diet suiting his digestion? The best guide to this is to check your puppy's stools. If they are too loose, or he has trouble passing motions, the diet may be at fault.
- Is the diet within your financial budget?
- Is the food readily available?

If you are worried about the diet from your puppy's point of view, it is best to discuss the matter with your vet. If there are financial considerations, or problems with supply, you will need to examine some options.

COMPLETE

This has become an increasingly popular method of feeding dogs, and although the food does not look very palatable to our eyes, most dogs are quite happy with it. The advantages are:

Easy to feed: This is the quickest, simplest method of feeding, where very little or no preparation is needed.

Buying in bulk: This does not suit all owners, but many people find it easier to buy a big sack of food, rather than constantly needing to top up supplies.

A balanced diet: The diet is scientifically formulated to cater for all your dog's needs. Supplements are not required – in fact, they upset the balance of the diet.

Changing needs: Most manufacturers provide a diet to suit the changing needs of a dog. For example, you start with a diet geared for growth, and then move on to a maintenance diet when your dog is fully grown. You can also get a diet made for veterans, one for brood bitches while they are feeding a litter, a performance diet for racing dogs, and even a diet to cope with obesity.

Some breeds, regardless of their workload, have specific needs. For example, Boxers generally do better on a diet that is relatively low in protein. Your puppy's breeder will give you specific advice. If your puppy has special needs, check the food analysis on the packaging to ensure that the nutritional balance is correct for your breed. Guidance is also given as to what quantities to feed as your puppy matures.

TOP TIP

When you start feeding a complete diet, most puppies will prefer it if it is soaked in warm water. If your pup shows a reluctance to eat his food, add a gravy cube to the warm water. This invariably does the trick!

CANNED

Canned dog food, fed with biscuit, is still favored by many dog owners. Again, there is a vast difference, in terms of food value, between the brands, so you will need to check the label for details. This is a fairly quick and easy method of feeding, and most dogs seem to enjoy the food. Shopping for heavy cans, and then disposing of the waste is a minor disadvantage.

HOME-MADE

You may have ambitions to be creative with your puppy's cuisine, and have plans to feed a home-made diet of assorted fresh meat, vegetables, and biscuit or pasta. Think very carefully before going ahead with this idea. It is almost impossible to provide a diet that has the correct balance of minerals, vitamins, proteins and carbohydrates, and you could, unknowingly, be feeding a diet that is deficient in a vital element. Unless you are prepared to analyze the food you are feeding, and constantly check that the balance is correct, you are better off leaving it to the experts.

FEEDING FOR GROWTH

Whatever diet you choose, remember that good-quality, balanced nutrition is essential if a puppy is to achieve his full potential in terms of growth and development. During the growing period, bones, muscles and tissues are developing, in addition to the normal energy that the puppy is expending. That is why a puppy needs a much greater food intake for his size than an adult dog.

CHANGING DIET

If you decide that a change of diet is required, do not make the switch in one go. Your puppy needs time to adjust to the new food, so introduce a little of the new food at each meal. Gradually cut down on the original food and increase the new diet until the changeover is complete. This should be phased over a two-week period so that your puppy gets used to the new food without risking a stomach upset. If your puppy is not thriving on the diet, ask your vet for advice.

NUMBER OF MEALS

Most puppies of around eight weeks will be getting four meals a day. Some breeders suggest that these are divided between meat and cereal feed, but if you are feeding a complete diet, you will feed this for every meal.

The meals should be well spaced throughout the day to give your puppy the chance to digest each meal, and it also means that he will not have to wait too long between meals. A recommended mealtime plan is as follows:

8am Breakfast	12.30pm Lunch
5pm Teatime	8.30pm Supper

Each meal should be the same in terms of quantity. The manufacturer will provide feeding guidelines based on your dog's weight. By the time your puppy is 12 weeks of age, you can probably cut out the teatime meal, and by the time your pup is six months old, he should be fed twice a day. Obviously, you will need to adjust the quantity you are feeding to ensure your pup is getting sufficient nutrition to meet his needs.

A good indication that you are feeding the correct amount is if your puppy eats up all his rations, and then looks around for any spilt food. Obviously, he should not be looking desperate in his search for food, but he should look as though he has enjoyed his meal and is not too full.

If your puppy starts to leave food in his bowl, wait for 10 minutes, and then dispose of it. In most cases, your pup is telling you that he does not need so much food, so it is probably time to cut out one of his meals.

When your dog is 12 months old, you can feed just one meal a day. This was common practice among dog owners until fairly recently. Now, many people prefer to split the rations and feed two meals. This has the benefit of giving your dog two treats a day, but, more importantly, it is easier for a dog to digest smaller quantities. This is particularly important for the heavyweight breeds, such as Bullmastiffs and St Bernards, who can be prone to bloat. This is a condition where the gut twists on itself, and it is often fatal (see page 223).

DANGERS OF OBESITY

While it is essential to provide an adequate, balanced diet for a growing pup, it is equally important not to overfeed. This is particularly important from six months onwards, as overfeeding can lead to over-rapid bone growth. In the heavier breeds, this can lead to joint disorders such as osteochondrosis of the elbows or

A new-born puppy will increase his size forty-fold or more by the time he is an adult. The most rapid growth period for a puppy is from birth to six months. By the time a pup is six months of age, he will have attained half his final bodyweight.

shoulders, and hip dysplasia (see Chapter 27: A-Z of Canine Disorders and Diseases).

A greedy pup can easily become an overweight adult, and this brings a whole host of health problems, resulting from putting too much strain on the major organs.

Do not be fooled by those pleading eyes; harden your heart and put your dog's health first!

FADDY FEEDERS

Most dogs have a healthy appetite and see mealtimes as the highspot of their day. However, there are a few animals who pick at their food, never finishing a meal. There may be a number of reasons for this:

There may be a physical cause

If you are seriously concerned about your puppy's lack of appetite, get him checked over by the vet. It may be that your pup is teething and has a sore mouth, which is why he is less than enthusiastic about his food. There may be another underlying physical cause, so it is wise to get the vet's opinion.

You are feeding too much

This is the most likely reason, and the most simple to rectify. Cut out one of the meals, and you will soon see if there is an improvement in the situation

The feed may be too dry

Complete food can be fed dry, as long as fresh water is freely available. However, some puppies find this unappetizing, and prefer to have the food soaked in warm water.

The puppy may be too distracted

It is easy for a puppy to get distracted when he is eating his food, particularly if he is still in the process of settling into his new home. This is more likely to happen if a sensitive pup is being fed in the kitchen, for example, where there is a lot of coming and going. Try feeding your pup in a quieter spot, and stay with him to give added reassurance. You may well find that the pup just needs to feel a little more secure in order to concentrate on his food.

Your puppy does not like the food

If none of the above solutions have worked, it may be worth changing the diet. If you do this, you must check that the nutritional balance is correct for your breed. The transition to a new diet should be carried out gradually (see page 110).

Your pup may be playing you up in the hope of getting some finer food!

There are some puppies who like to play games with their owners. They pick at their food, and the caring owner drops in a piece of chicken to encourage their appetite. The pup realizes he is on to a good thing, and refuses to eat his standard diet.

Don't get caught in this trap. As long as there you are confident that there is no physical reason for your puppy's faddiness, there is no excuse for serving up tempting tidbits. Give your puppy his standard diet and remove the bowl, regardless of how much he has eaten within 10 minutes. Your pup may end up feeling a bit hungry, but that will encourage him to eat his next meal. It will not take long for your pup to realize that he must be content with the food he is given.

BONES AND CHEWS

Puppies and adult dogs love having a bone to gnaw on. It provides occupation, and it helps to keep teeth clean. However, they can cause problems, so check through the following Dos and Don'ts.

Do feed marrow bones, which are available from butchers and from some pet stores. You can also get sterilized bones, filled with a meaty substance, which many dogs enjoy.
Do not feed poultry bones, e.g. chicken. They splinter and can cause serious injury.

Do supervise your puppy when he has a bone, in case he has a problem.

Do not allow your puppy to go off with his bone, and then refuse to give it up.

Do teach your puppy to give up his bone when you ask. If your puppy is reluctant, try swapping it with a treat or a toy

Do not allow your puppy to show any guarding or possessive behavior when he has a bone. You can prevent this by taking the bone from him at intervals, and then giving it back. This shows the dog that you are in control, and he can only have the bone when you allow it.

Do choose chews with care. They must be tough so that your pup can only gnaw off fragments at a time. If your pup tears off a piece of chew and swallows it, it may prove to be very indigestible.

INVALID DIET

Hopefully, you will experience few health problems with your puppy, but there may be times when he seems a little off-color, or he may get an attack of diarrhea. Seek veterinary advice to find out the cause. If your pup is suffering from diarrhea, you may have to withhold food for a short period (see page 220), but make sure that fresh drinking water is available.

When your puppy is ready to eat again, he should be fed simple food that is very easy to digest. Fish or chicken with rice or pasta is an ideal invalid diet, and can be fed to puppies who are recovering from illness, or following an anesthetic.

SUMMING UP

The science of nutrition is highly complex, but, if you follow the guidelines in this chapter, your puppy will thrive. Remember the following points:

• Fresh drinking water must be available at all times. If you are feeding a complete diet, this is particularly important.
• Milk can be offered in moderation, but as the puppy matures he loses the ability to digest lactose, and so too much milk can lead to diarrhea.
• If you are buying a complete feed, store it in a dry place, and check that you do not go past the 'best before' date.
• Do not feed your puppy from the table. This will encourage him to beg and to become a nuisance at family mealtimes.
• If you are feeding treats (during training sessions, for example), deduct the food from your puppy's overall ration, or he will become obese.
• Do not feed your puppy and then go out for an energetic spell of exercise. This can lead to problems with digestion, and, in the heavier breeds, it could result in bloat (see page 223).
• If you are worried about your puppy's diet, or his eating habits, consult your vet.

Chapter 14

Regular Checks

Most puppies are easy to look after, and, once you are happy with their diet, there will be few areas of major concern. The most important aspect of caring for a puppy is observation. If you know what is normal for your puppy, you will be quick to spot any changes, whether they be physical or behavioral. Keep a check on the following:

Appetite: Is your puppy eating his standard rations?
Energy levels: Is your puppy as energetic as usual?
Stools: Keep a check to ensure there are no problems with diarrhea (see page 220) or constipation (see page 217).
Coat: Is the coat shiny and healthy-looking?

In addition, you will need to give your puppy a regular, routine examination, so you can check on more specific areas. The ideal time to do this is during a grooming session (see page 120). As you work through the puppy's coat, you will be able to detect if there are any bald or sore patches, or any lumps or bumps that are not usually there. Early detection is the key to preventing major problems from arising, so make sure you include this general check-up in your care regime.

HANDLE WITH CARE
It is important to train your puppy to accept all-over handling from an early age. Some puppies are more sensitive than others, and may object to this familiarity. Choose a quiet room that is free of distractions. It is best to start handling your puppy while he is on the floor, or when he is sitting in your lap.

• Start by stroking your puppy all over, talking to him in a soft, soothing voice.
• Move your hand to the puppy's head, and stroke his ears. Then lift the ear flap so that you can see inside each ear.

- Your puppy may resist an attempt to check his teeth, so be prepared with a treat. Gently open the mouth, using a command such as "Open". Hold the mouth open for just a few seconds, and then reward with a treat.
- Move on to your puppy's feet. Each foot should be picked up in turn, so that you can check both the nails and the pads.
- Some puppies will roll on to their backs when you are playing with them, and this gives you the opportunity to tickle your pup's tummy, so that he is used to being touched on the more sensitive skin.
- Finally, run your hand down your puppy's tail, and then lift the tail up. The vet may have to take your dog's temperature, or the genitalia may need to be examined, so your puppy must learn to accept being handled in this area.
- When you have finished, have a game with your pup, so that he thinks the whole session has been fun.

If you meet any opposition, do not fight shy of touching that area in future. There must be no such thing as a no-go area, because you never know what treatment your dog may need to receive in later life.

Be firm with your puppy, saying "No" if he growls or attempts to struggle free. Start again, and reward your puppy if he allows a fleeting touch of the sensitive area. Build this up over subsequent sessions, touching the area for a longer period, until your puppy is completely relaxed. Make sure you always reward your puppy with a treat or a game.

DENTAL CARE

The wild ancestors of the dog would have killed their prey with their teeth, and then they would bite and tear at the carcass until they had eaten their fill. The domesticated dog takes life easy, enjoying the food he is provided with. However, this can lead to problems as dogs must adapt to a completely different diet. The food is often soft and mushy, and there is no need to bite, chew and gnaw. As a result, human intervention is often required to keep the teeth and gums healthy.

MILK TEETH

Puppies cut their milk teeth about 14 days after birth; there are no molars (teeth located at the back of the mouth for grinding) in this set. When you first get your puppy, you will soon become aware of his needle-sharp milk teeth, and it is a good idea to introduce some bite inhibition training at this stage (see page 134).

TRIALS OF TEETHING

The milk teeth are shed and replaced by adult teeth between four and six months. This can be a very trying period for some puppies. Their gums may become sore, and they will have a strong desire to chew as the adult teeth are coming through. In some breeds,

An adult dog has 42 permanent teeth. These are made up of 12 incisors (6 on the upper jaw, 6 on the lower jaw), 4 canines (2 on the upper jaw, 2 on the lower jaw), 16 premolars (8 on the upper jaw, 8 on the lower jaw), and 10 molars (4 on the upper jaw, six on the lower jaw).

particularly those with erect ears such as German Shepherd Dogs, ear carriage may be affected during teething. Be careful when you inspect your puppy's mouth at this stage as it may be extra-sensitive.

To help your puppy through this stage – and to save your house from destruction – provide lots of different items for your puppy to chew. He may enjoy chewing on a marrow-bone or a sterilized bone (see page 113), or he may prefer the soft texture of a cotton tug-toy. Give lots of variety so that your puppy can please himself.

TEETH CLEANING

With the soft food that most dogs are fed these days, there is a tendency for tartar (a hard deposit) to develop on the tooth surface. Food particles can get trapped between the teeth and the gum margins, and this can lead to inflammation of the gums and foul breath. Infection can also enter at this point. It is therefore vital to keep your dog's teeth clean and avoid the build-up of tartar.

Chewing bones (see page 113) is an excellent way of keeping the teeth clean and healthy, but this is not always practical on a regular basis. So teeth-cleaning is often chosen as a preferred method of maintaining dental health. This should present no problems, particularly if your pup is accustomed to having his mouth examined (see page 116). Dog toothbrushes, which may be long-handled or a small finger brush, are available from pet stores. You may wish to try both types and find out which you find easiest to use. More importantly, you can buy meat-flavored toothpaste, so most dogs are quite happy to have their teeth cleaned.

If a lot of tartar accumulates on the teeth, you may need a tooth-scaler to remove it. This is a relatively simple task, but if you are unsure about it, you can ask your vet to do the job for you.

NAILS AND FEET

Puppies' nails grow at a rapid rate, and the sharp claws can scratch and be very uncomfortable for the mother while the pups are still feeding. For this reason, the breeder will usually trim the nails, so your pup will be used to the procedure. You may find that once your pup is running around, particularly if he is being exercised on a hard surface, his nails will wear down naturally.

However, if the nails do not wear down, they will need to be trimmed. Nails that are too long can cause permanent damage to a dog's feet, as well as being very painful. If you have never trimmed nails before, you can ask your puppy's breeder or your vet to show you what to do. The task is made simpler with guillotine nail-clippers, although some people prefer to use a nail file. It is important to trim the tip of the nail only. The quick of the nail extends downwards, and it is easy to cut into it. This will cause bleeding, and may well put your dog off having his nails trimmed in future.

In pink nails, you can see the quick, but this is not possible with black nails. It is best to proceed with caution, and trim just a little at a time. Most dogs learn to accept this procedure without undue concern. However, if your pup appears worried, progress in gradual stages.

- First pick up each foot, and examine each toe individually.
- Get out the nail-clippers, but do not make any attempt to trim the nails. Allow your puppy to sniff them, and hold them close to his feet.
- At each stage, reward your puppy, so that he is not worried or frightened.
- Only advance to trimming the nails when you are confident that your puppy is relaxed about the procedure.

You will almost certainly find that the task is made easier if you have someone to hold your pup, while you concentrate on trimming the nails.

You will also need to check the pads on a regular basis. It is a good idea if you get into the habit of doing this when your dog returns from a walk. Examine the pads to make sure there are no cuts, and feel between each of the toes in case a sticky substance, such as chewing gum or tar, has adhered to the hair, which will cause soreness and discomfort. If your dog has run across a muddy field, balls of mud can also build up in this area.

In the winter, if salt and sand has been used on the roads, make sure you wash your dog's feet thoroughly to prevent possible skin irritation.

EYES

The eyes tend to mirror a dog's overall health and condition. They should be bright and sparkling, with a keen, alert expression. There should be no evidence of redness in the white of the eye. If you see any discharge, consult your vet.

Sometimes, debris collects in the corner of the eye, and this will need to be cleaned away. If you need to clean the eyes, use a piece of cotton wool (cotton) that has been moistened in warm water. Always use a fresh piece of cotton wool for each eye to prevent the possible spread of infection.

EARS

Examine the ears to check they are clean and fresh-smelling. Wax can build up in the ears. This can be softened with an ear-cleaning fluid, and then removed using cotton wool. The use of cotton buds is not recommended, as there is a danger that you could probe too deeply and cause damage. If the ear appears inflamed, dirty, or foul-smelling, consult your vet (see Otitis Externa, page 232). You can often detect an ear problem if the dog tilts his head at an unusual angle, or if he scratches his ear excessively.

NOSE

Contrary to popular belief, a cold, wet nose is not necessarily an indicator of health. However, the nose should be examined, and if there is any crustiness or discharge, consult your vet. The color of the nose may be pale in some months, particularly during the winter months when there is reduced sunlight.

CONDITION AND WEIGHT

Like people, some dogs will put on weight more easily than others, and some are naturally lean.

It is therefore a good idea to keep a note of your dog's weight once he is full-grown, and to weigh him on a regular basis. You can then detect any changes in weight at an early stage, and this will be of great assistance if you need to consult your vet.

Chapter 15

Coat Care

Dogs come in a wonderful variety of shapes, sizes and colors – and there is also spectacular variation between the coat types, ranging from the luxuriant, longcoated Afghan Hound to the Chinese Crested which has virtually no coat at all! When it comes to choosing a breed, coat type is a very important consideration (see page 23), as you must ensure that you have the time (and patience) to give your dog the care he needs.

Regular grooming is essential for all breeds for the following reasons:

- It gives you the opportunity to check your dog thoroughly, thus spotting any signs of trouble at an early stage (see page 115).
- It is a means of removing mud, dirt, and debris from the coat.
- It removes dead hair from the coat, which is particularly important when a dog is shedding his coat.
- In longer-coated breeds, you will prevent the formation of mats and tangles, which can become very uncomfortable for the dog.
- You will be able to spot any signs of flea infestation (see page 201).
- You will spend time interacting with your dog, which will improve your relationship with him.
- Grooming can be very therapeutic.

PUPPY GROOMING

Even if you have chosen a low-maintenance breed, such as a shortcoated Beagle, your puppy must learn to accept being groomed. This process should start within the first week of your pup arriving home so that it becomes a simple matter of routine.

If you have a longcoated breed, the puppy coat will not need a great deal of attention to begin with. But do not make the mistake of delaying grooming sessions until the coat becomes longer, or you will be storing up trouble for yourself. You want your pup to enjoy being groomed, so his first experiences must be entirely pleasurable. If you wait until the coat is matted or tangled, your pup will resent the attention.

To begin with, accustom your puppy to general handling (see page 115). When he has got used to being touched all over, you can introduce a soft, bristle brush. This will feel light to the touch, and will be sufficient for a soft, puppy coat.

- Start by laying the brush on the coat, and give a couple of gentle strokes with the brush.
- Praise your puppy, and then repeat the exercise.
- If your pup twists round to bite the brush, say "No", and then gently hold him in position while you try a couple more brush strokes.
- This will do for the first session. Give your pup lots of praise, and then have a game with him so that he connects the grooming session with having fun.
- Build up the grooming routine in easy stages, gradually increasing the amount of time your puppy needs to stay still.
- Remember to talk to your puppy as you groom, telling him how good he is, and always have a game or reward him with a treat at the end of the session.

COAT TYPES

Your grooming routine (and equipment) will depend on coat type. These can be divided into broad categories e.g. shortcoated and longcoated, but many breeds have individual coat characteristics. For example, a Labrador Retriever and a Greyhound are both shortcoated, but a Labrador has a double coat (a dense, undercoat with a hard, straight topcoat to protect him from the cold), whereas a Greyhound has a short, fine, close-fitting coat, and rarely has an undercoat. It is therefore important to talk to your puppy's breeder and find out specific grooming requirements.

TOP TIP

If you have chosen a breed that needs a lot of attention, train your pup to be groomed on a table. This makes the task a great deal less back-breaking, and therefore more pleasurable. Buy a rubber mat for your pup to stand on as the table may be slippery, which will make him feel insecure. Groom for a few minutes at a time, until your pup learns to settle on the table. In the early stages, always supervise your pup when he is on the grooming table to avoid the risk of accidents.

SHORTCOATED

These are the low-maintenance dogs that require the least amount of work. The following routine is a general-purpose guide for all shortcoated breeds.

- Use your fingertips to massage the coat against the natural lay of the hairs. This helps to loosen dead hair, and encourages the skin to secrete sebum which gives the coat its healthy sheen.
- Use a bristle brush, and work against the lie of the coat to pick up the loosened hairs. Then brush with the lie of the coat.
- If your dog is shedding his coat, a rubber handmitt can be used.
- Comb through the coat with a metal-toothed comb, working over your dog's body in a methodical order.
- If you want the coat to get a really good shine, give a rub over with a piece of velvet or chamois leather.

THICKCOATED

There are a number of breeds, such as the Akita, the Chow Chow and the Alaskan Malamute, which have a dense woolly undercoat, and a thick, straight topcoat. Breeds with this coat type often originate in countries with harsh climates, and so they have a coat to withstand all weathers.

Generally, this coat should be treated in the same way as a short coat. A slicker brush (a fine, wire pin-brush) is a useful addition to the grooming kit, and a wide-toothed comb will be easier to work through the coat.

LONGCOATED

The true longcoated breeds include breeds such as Afghan Hounds, Lhasa Apsos and Yorkshire Terriers, who have a spectacular coat which needs intensive, daily grooming.

- Plan your grooming session, so that you work over the dog systematically, covering all areas of the body.
- A pin brush, which has fine metal pins with rounded ends, should be used to work through the coat. Your pup will need to be trained to stand, and lie on his side, so that you can reach all areas easily.
- Lift up the coat, so that it can be brushed through, layer by layer.
- Repeat the exercise, using a wide-toothed comb.
- Use a fine-toothed comb if you need to tease out any mats or tangles.
- The face hair of some longcoated breeds, such as Shih Tzu and Yorkshire Terriers, are combed upwards, and then tied with a band into a top-knot. It is important to accustom your pup to this as soon as the hair is long enough to tie back.
- You may need to cut excessive hair growth that will be uncomfortable for your dog. In

The Yorkshire Terrier grows such a long, silky coat that show dogs are often kept in crackers, which are special wrappers to protect the hair from breaking.

longcoated breeds, hair often grows between the pads, and inside the ears, and this will need to be trimmed back. For the purposes of hygiene, hair should be trimmed around the anus.

- If you are showing your dog, there will be specific requirements for trimming, so you will need to seek expert advice.
- Some of the longcoated breeds, such as the Shih Tzu and the Lhasa Apso, can be clipped into a puppy trim if they are not being shown. This looks smart, and certainly cuts down on the workload. Many owners of pet Yorkshire Terriers also opt to have the coat cut short.

The longcoated sheepdog breeds, which include the Old English Sheepdog (Bobtail), the Bearded Collie, the Rough Collie and the Shetland Sheepdog, are also highly labor-intensive in terms of grooming. Talk to your puppy's breeder to find out what grooming equipment to buy. In some cases, this will change as the coat grows, so, for example, a bristle brush will be needed for a Bobtail during puppyhood, but then he will need a pin brush or a slicker brush.

If you are not planning to show your Bobtail, you may consider having the coat clipped, which is a popular option among pet owners.

MEDIUM-COATED WITH FEATHERING

There are a number of breeds that do not have the luxuriant coat of those mentioned above, but they have a medium-length body coat with profuse feathering on the neck, chest, legs, underbelly and tail. The coat varies in texture depending on the breed, but the Setter and Spaniel breeds, plus the Golden Retriever, all fall into this broad category. Ask your puppy's breeder to recommend the grooming equipment that best suits your dog.

- The body coat can be brushed with a slicker brush, although a bristle brush is preferred for some breeds.
- The feathering needs careful attention as it mats and tangles very easily. Tease out tangles with a fine-toothed comb.
- A pin brush can be used to brush through the feathering once it is tangle-free.
- Most of the breeds in this category will need routine trimming, as outlined for longcoated breeds. There are specific requirements for show dogs, so seek expert advice.

NON-SHEDDING COATS

There are a few breeds that have non-shedding coats, which is a great bonus for people who have an allergy to dog hair.

The Poodle is the most popular breed in this category, but he needs to have his coat bathed and clipped every six to eight weeks (see page 78). There are a number of different poodle clips, which all look highly glamorous, but the Lamb or Sporting trim is the most popular among pet owners.

The Poodle still needs to be groomed between his trips to the grooming parlor. Regular brushing with a slicker brush is required, plus a comb-through using a wide-toothed comb.

The Hungarian Puli and the Komondor have a similar coat to the Poodle, but, instead of being clipped, it is allowed to grow into long dreadlocks. These are formed by using oil or Vaseline and twisting the hair between the fingers.

WIRECOATED

Some of the terrier breeds (Jack Russell, Airedale, Cairn, and the West Highland White, for example) have a harsh coat that is easy to keep smart with regular brushing with a slicker brush.

However, they need to be hand-stripped at least twice a year. This can be done with clippers and stripping knives, or it can be more of an on-going process where the hair is plucked out using finger and thumb. Hand-stripping is always used for show dogs, but pet owners generally prefer to rely on a trip to a professional groomer (see page 78). The Schnauzer breeds (Miniature, Standard and Giant) also need the same attention.

BATHING

Dogs should not be bathed frequently, as they will lose the natural oil in their coats. However, there are times when your dog has rolled in something unpleasant, or when the coat is shedding, when you really feel that a bath is a good idea.

There is no need to bath a young puppy. If your pup gets muddy, wait for the mud to dry and then brush it off. Some puppies are messy feeders, but you can solve this by using a damp cloth and wiping off the food before it has a chance to dry. If you have a white dog, such as a Samoyed or a Bull Terrier, do not make the mistake of thinking that frequent bathing will keep the coat clean. It is regular grooming that cleans the coat.

As your puppy gets older and more adventurous, he is more likely to discover the delights of rolling – and then a bath will be necessary. By this age, your puppy will be thoroughly accustomed to grooming and handling, so a bath should not be too much of a trauma. The best place to use is a shower cubicle, with a hand-held shower head. You can also use a bath; again, it helps if you can use a shower appliance. Place a rubber mat on the base of the shower cubicle or bath before you attempt to bath your dog. This will prevent your dog from slipping, and he will be far more co-operative if he feels secure.

BATHING ROUTINE

Start by assembling everything you need before you get your puppy involved. There are lots of brands of dog shampoo and conditioner available, including insecticidal treatments (see page 201). It is important to buy shampoo and conditioner that is made specially for dogs, as human shampoo or other types of detergent could have an adverse effect on your dog's skin. You will need a jug for mixing the conditioner (if you plan to use it), and plenty of dry towels.

If this is your puppy's first bath, recruit an assistant so that you can concentrate on the bathing while they hold on to the pup. On this occasion, you may find it easier if your pup is wearing a collar so that you have more control.

- Give your puppy a thorough grooming, making sure you have teased out any mats or tangles. If you wait until after bathing, you will find the job much harder.
- Lift the puppy into the bath, or call him into the shower cubicle, and give him lots of praise. Make sure he is happy and settled before you apply the water.
- Check the water to ensure it is lukewarm, and then wet the coat thoroughly. Start at the neck and work down the body. Make sure you get the underside wet as well. Do not get water into your pup's eyes or ears.
- Talk to your puppy reassuringly as you work. Most puppies will not get upset, but there are a few that may make a bid to escape. This is where a collar comes in handy, as your assistant can hold on to your pup, and you can give a command to "Stay' or "Stand".
- Once the coat is wet, you can apply the shampoo. This can be poured straight from

the bottle, or you may find it easier to dilute it in warm water in a jug.

- Work the shampoo into a rich lather, making sure you keep well away from the pup's eyes, ears and mouth. Most puppies enjoy this part of the process, and the more you tell your pup what a "Good boy" he is, the happier he will be.
- Make sure you have worked the shampoo into the entire coat, and then rinse if off. Work methodically from the neck down through the body, making sure the soapy water drains away from your pup.
- Conditioner should be added at this stage. It is matter of preference whether you use conditioner, but it is useful in longcoated breeds as it makes the coat easier to brush through after bathing. Conditioner is easier to apply when it is diluted and then poured from a jug. Again, work the conditioner into the coat and rinse thoroughly.
- Make absolutely certain that there is no trace of shampoo or conditioner left in the coat before turning off the water.

DRYING YOUR PUP

- Do not make the mistake of releasing your pup the moment you have finished rinsing. His coat will be saturated with water, and he will be only too keen to get rid of it with a good shake!
- Keep your pup in the bath or shower cubicle, and use the towels to soak up the excess moisture from his coat. Your pup will still be wet – but you will not be in danger of getting soaked.
- If you have a longcoated breed, take care not to rub the coat or it will tangle.
- Lift your pup out of the bath, or release him from the shower cubicle. His instinct will be to shake. If your pup is small enough to carry, you will be able to get as far as the garden before this happens – otherwise it is a matter of luck!
- Once your pup has had a good shake, you can continue drying with towels. If you have a shortcoated breed, you can finish with a good brush all over.
- Some owners use a hair-dryer, and this is essential if you have a longcoated breed. The dryer must be put on a medium/low setting, and you must be careful not to direct the dryer into your dog's face.
- Initially, a pup may be frightened of the hair-dryer, so proceed in easy stages. When you turn the dryer on, praise your pup and give him a treat. Do not direct the dryer too close to the coat until your puppy appears calm and relaxed.
- As you dry, brush through the coat, working through it layer by layer.
- When you have finished, give your pup a treat or have a game with him so that he understands that bathtimes are fun.

Chapter 16

Exercise

There is no doubt that some breeds are more energetic than others, and the amount of exercise a dog needs varies tremendously. The Border Collie, for example, is seemingly tireless, and requires an owner with energy to match. The Mastiff, the heavyweight of the canine world, is quite happy to take life easy in the slow lane, and does not appreciate a strenuous regime.

The key to finding out the energy levels of different breeds is to find out what they were originally bred to do. A Jack Russell Terrier may seem small and undemanding, but, in fact, he was bred to follow horses, and then go to earth after fox. Stamina was the name of the game, and this characteristic is still very much part of the Jack Russell make-up. No self-respecting Jack Russell would be happy to spend his life lounging on a sofa; he wants to go out and about, investigating new sights and smells.

In contrast, the Pug was bred to be a companion dog. A royal favorite originating from China, the Pug likes nothing better than to sleep in comfort on the lap of his owner. This was the job he was bred to do.

Obviously, it is very important to find out the exercise requirements of the breeds you are attracted to, and make sure you can fulfil them, before making your final choice of breed. It is all about matching the lifestyle you can offer to the specific needs of a breed. If you get that right, you and your dog can look forward to a happy and rewarding life together.

GARDEN EXERCISE

The average eight-week-old puppy will run and play with great bursts of energy, swiftly followed by long periods of rest. As he gets bigger, the periods of activity will lengthen, and the pup will need less sleep. However, the importance of rest for the young puppy should never be underestimated. Not only is he using up energy through play, he is also growing at a very rapid rate. When a puppy flops down to sleep, he should never be disturbed; sleep is vital to his wellbeing.

To begin with, your puppy will get all the exercise he needs playing in the garden or yard. He will be developing his muscles and his co-ordination as he explores his surroundings and plays with his toys. While you are waiting for your puppy's vaccination course to be completed (see page 202), you can do some lead-training in the garden, so that he will be ready to go out when he is fully protected (see page 168).

LEAD-WALKING

When your puppy is fully vaccinated and is walking on a lead, you can venture into the outside world. Your pup will find this an exhausting experience. He will be encountering new sights, sounds and smells, and he will feel very small and vulnerable. It is not so much the physical effort of walking on the lead, but more the mental strain of taking on board a whole new world.

Keep your outings very short to begin with – just long enough for your pup to start getting used to his new surroundings.

As your pup gets bigger, you can increase the amount of time you spend going out and about, as this is an important part of his socialization (see Chapter 18: A Program of Socialization). However, you must still limit the amount of time you spend walking with your puppy on-lead. A ten-minute session is ample for puppies under the age of six months. This will provide good exercise, but will not overtire your pup. It is much better to return home after a positive experience, rather than exhausting your pup who may start to resent lead-walking sessions.

When your pup is over six months of age, you can increase lead-walking sessions gradually, but they should not exceed 30 minutes in length. If you have a large breed, lead walking should be kept at 15-20 minutes until the dog is fully grown.

FREE-RUNNING

All dogs relish the opportunity to run free, but this is not always possible or desirable. Before you allow your puppy off the lead, you must ensure the following:

- Your pup must be trained to return to you when he is called – no matter the distractions (see page 164).
- You must choose a safe place, well away from passing traffic.
- You must check local legislation to ensure that your dog is allowed off the lead.
- You must be confident that your pup is well socialized with other dogs so that he will not get involved in fights.
- Your pup must be used to children, so that he does not jump up or get overexcited if he sees them playing.
- If you have a breed with strong hunting instincts, such as a Siberian Husky, or a breed that may chase, such as a Greyhound, it is advisable to allow free-running only in enclosed areas where there is no prospect of meeting other animals.

If you are happy to let your puppy off the lead, you must keep a close check on the amount of time he is allowed to run free. During the growing period, the bones and joints are very vulnerable, and serious, long-term problems will result if a dog is over-exercised. See Hip Dysplasia page 225, Osteochondritis Dissecans (OCD) page 231.

This applies to dogs of all breeds, but most particularly to the larger, heavier breeds. A free run of ten minutes will be sufficient until your dog is full-grown. It is far better to give him a couple of short free-running sessions, e.g. morning and evening, rather than overdoing it in one lengthier session.

RESTRICTED FREEDOM

If you do not have a suitable place to free-run your pup, this does not mean that he should be limited to lead-walking where he is restricted to being close by your side. The extending lead is a wonderful invention, which gives your pup the opportunity to roam further afield, investigating exciting sights and smells, while remaining under your control.

It is a good idea to practice using the extending lead in your garden before venturing into the park, so that you are competent at operating the mechanism, and your pup realizes that he cannot dive off at full tilt.

SWIMMING

Swimming is a great form of exercise, and the majority of dogs take to it with little persuasion. This is particularly true of the retriever breeds (e.g. Labradors and Goldens), where it is a hard job to keep them out of water.

TOP TIP

If you have a dog that loves to swim, you must train him only to go into water when he is given permission. If he is allowed to plunge in every time he sees water, he could end up in a dangerous situation. To start with, keep your dog on the lead when you are near water, and if he tries to pull towards it, command "Leave", and distract him with a game. Work at this over a period of time until you are confident that your dog is responding to the command. Then, you can let him run free, and you can choose whether he is allowed to swim or not.

It is better to wait until your dog is full-grown before he starts swimming, but you can introduce your pup to water, making sure he is well within his depth. Give your pup lots of encouragement to enter the water. If he likes retrieving, throw his retrieve toy into a shallow stretch of water. Give your pup lots of praise as he goes in, and then call him back to you. Do not overtire your pup; a couple of retrieves will be sufficient at this stage.

Before your puppy (or adult dog) is allowed in the water, check the following:

- There are no strong currents in the water.
- There is an easy place for your pup to get out.
- You can see clearly below the surface of the water.
- Your pup is trained to "Wait" until you allow him to go into the water.
- Your pup will respond when you call him out of the water.

FUN AND GAMES

Exercising your pup does not simply mean rushing about until you are both tired out. A pup thrives on a mixture of mental and physical exercise, stretching his mind as well as his limbs.

This type of exercise can be provided in a number of ways that will help to enrich your relationship with your dog.

RETRIEVE GAMES

If your pup likes playing with toys, it is relatively simple to teach him to retrieve (see page 171). Keep a special toy for your retrieve games, and your pup will get really excited when you bring it out. Running out to retrieve provides excellent exercise, as well as being a good training exercise.

HIDE AND SEEK

You can take the retrieve game a step further by hiding the toy, and teaching your pup to seek it. Dogs have an amazing sense of smell, and most will quickly get the idea of scenting out their favorite toy. You can turn this into a family game by getting children to hide in the garden, then each child calls the pup in turn. To begin with, your pup will be confused, wondering where the sound is coming from, but he will soon work it out. Make sure the pup is given a treat when he 'finds' a child.

ON THE RIGHT SCENT

Let your pup use his nose to follow a trail of treats laid out in the garden. As he gets more proficient, you can increase the distance between treats, and then end up with a special treat or a toy at the end of the trail.

ANYONE FOR TENNIS?

If you do not have the opportunity to give your pup free-running exercise, he can still enjoy strenuous exercise in the garden. Equip yourself with a tennis ball and a racquet and fire off some shots for your pup to retrieve. This demands very little effort from you, but your pup will benefit enormously. If your pup is still growing, limit the number of retrieves so he is not put under too much strain.

These are just a few ideas to show how much fun you can have exercising your pup. You can probably think of lots more ideas – it doesn't matter what you do, the important point is that you are giving up time to be with your dog and to interact with him. A dog that has the attention of his owner, the mental stimulation of playing a game he enjoys, plus the freedom to run about, will be 100 per cent contented.

Part 7

The Well-Adjusted Pup

Chapter 17

The Importance Of Socialization

All too often, we take it for granted that a dog should adapt and conform to our human world. We forget that each dog has his own set of instincts and desires, and these may have very little to do with what we deem acceptable behavior. For example:

- A dog may have a strong instinct to chase, but he is not allowed to chase livestock.
- A pup may have strong guarding instincts, but we condemn any display of aggressive or possessive behavior.
- A pup instinctively uses his mouth to explore, but we forbid mouthing and biting.
- A pup will always be on the lookout for food, but he is not allowed to steal or to scavenge.
- A pup may prefer to keep away from loud, frightening noises, but we expect him to cope in a stressful, urban environment.

How do we overcome this conflict of interests? We cannot expect a puppy to conform to our way of life just because we have taken him into our home. He has to learn what we consider 'correct' behavior, and he must accept that he must adhere to this code of conduct in order to be a member of the human pack. It is our duty to make this learning process as easy as possible, and we can do this by constructing a comprehensive program of socialization.

STAGES OF DEVELOPMENT

In order to socialize a puppy, it is helpful if we understand how his mind and body are developing. We can then provide learning experiences which he is able to cope with, and we will be able to have some understanding of problems that may arise.

Scientists have studied dog behavior, and they have worked out the following stages of mental development.

CANINE SOCIALIZATION (24-49 days)

This lasts from day 29-49, and is primarily concerned with a puppy's interaction with his mother and his littermates. This is a pup's first set of learning experiences, which will give him an understanding of canine manners.

A pup will be cared for by his mother, but, just as importantly, he will also be disciplined. If he nips her as he suckles, she will turn on him with a warning growl. If the pup gets too boisterous, he will be reprimanded.

In the same way, the puppies in the litter will learn from interacting with each other. The more assertive pups will push their littermates out of the way when a food bowl is put down.

Games of chase will often end up in a tussle, and the more docile pup will whimper, showing he is ready to 'give in'.

By watching their mother, and interacting with each other, the puppies learn how to communicate through body language and through vocalization.

HUMAN SOCIALIZATION (50-84 days)

This covers the period when a puppy first arrives in his new home. He will be highly impressionable to all learning experiences, and will be ready to 'bond' with his human family.

During this period, spend as much time as you can with your puppy. This will help the bonding process, and the pup will start to look on you as his leader. At this stage, your puppy must learn that he cannot behave with people in the same way that he did in the litter. Biting and mouthing is not acceptable, and so the pup must be taught bite inhibition. This is particularly important if you have children in the family, as a game can quickly end in tears.

- Hold a treat in your hand and offer it to your puppy. As he takes it, use the word "Gently", and praise your pup.
- If the pup tries to snatch at the treat, or uses his teeth, withdraw your hand, crying out "Ouch" in a sharp tone of voice.
- Offer the treat to your puppy again, repeating the word "Gently". Do not give the treat to your pup until he is ready to take it without biting or mouthing. Praise him when he gives the correct response.
- Repeat this exercise several times a day until you are confident that your puppy has got the message.

At this stage, you can allow children to offer a treat to the puppy. Make sure you are on hand to supervise, and be quick to intervene if your pup forgets his manners. You can also teach the same exercise using a toy. Your pup will learn he cannot snatch or grab his toy, a lesson which is, again, invaluable when he is playing with children.

FEAR IMPACT (56-77 days)

This is when a fright or harsh handling can have a permanent effect. It is therefore important to take care with all encounters during this period. You will probably be taking your pup to the vet for his first inoculation during this period, so work at making the experience as untraumatic as possible.

Do not be overprotective, but be ready with a treat as soon as your pup has been injected so that your pup has good associations with the vet. In fact, many vets will be aware of how important it is to make the pup's visit a positive experience, and you may well find that the vet or the veterinary nurse has some treats to offer.

TOP TIP

If your pup shows fear during this phase, do not make too much of a fuss in your efforts to reassure him. Stroke him, or maybe have a game with him, and encourage him to ignore the problem. If you take his fear seriously, your pup will think that there really is something to be frightened of.

SENIORITY CLASSIFICATION (12-16 weeks)

Your pup is now finding his feet, and may show a desire to become more independent. Some pups attempt to become more dominant and try to force their desires on you. Be firm and consistent during this stage. Do not allow your pup to mouth or bite, and do not get involved in serious games of tug or the pup will take it as a battle of wills and a test of his developing strength.

At this stage, it is helpful if your pup learns the "Leave" command so that your puppy learns to give up his toy on request. When you are ready to finish a game, offer your pup a treat in exchange for giving up his toy. As he lets go of his toy, say "Leave" and then praise him.

Give the puppy his toy again, and repeat the exercise a couple of times. Most pups catch on pretty quickly, and will be ready to make a fair exchange.

In time, your pup will associate the word "Leave" with giving up his toy, and you will not have to reward him on every occasion. However, it is a good idea to reward on a random basis, so that your pup knows there is an incentive to give up his toy.

Never allow your pup to go off with his toy at the end of a game. You may be quite happy for him to continue playing with his toy, but the more assertive puppy will think he has won the 'trophy' and is therefore superior to you.

FLIGHT INSTINCT (4-8 months)

This is a variable period, depending on the individual. It tends to coincide with the onset of physical adolescence, which may be later in some breeds than in others. Generally, the bigger breeds mature later. It is worth talking to your puppy's breeder who will be able to tell you when your pup is likely to hit adolescence so that you can be prepared for any changes in behavior.

When a youngster is approaching the onset of sexual maturity, he will often start to question the established status quo and may challenge your authority. This is a time when established training, such as the recall, tends to break down. Careful handling is needed during this phase (see Chapter 22: The Adolescent).

FEAR OF NEW SITUATIONS (6-14 months)

The type of behavior associated with this stage often coincides with growth spurts. You may find there are times when your pup suddenly appears to have 'forgotten' his lessons in socialization, and he may develop an irrational fear of something, even though he has seen it many times before. For example, he may see a man in the park carrying a large, plastic bag. All of a sudden, the pup becomes tense and his hackles rise. He may give a low, rumbling growl, or he may bark.

This often occurs when the pup is hitting adolescence and is feeling insecure about his personal status. He is no longer a carefree, fun-loving puppy; he is attempting to appraise the world through adult eyes. If you do not overreact, you will find that this behavior has no long-term significance. Adopt a calm, confident manner, and your pup will soon realize that his fears are groundless, and he will continue on his way as if nothing out of the ordinary had occurred.

TOP TIP

Do not make your pup confront his fear, or it may become deep-seated. Distract his attention, and show there is nothing to fear. Continue with your socialisation and training programme, and you will generally find that your youngster will outgrow this behaviour as he reaches young adulthood.

YOUNG ADULTHOOD AND MATURITY (12 months-4 years)

This is the final stage of development when your dog attains his full mental and physical powers. This phase covers a wide margin of age, as it can vary enormously from breed to breed. Small Toy dogs will be fully mature at 12 months, whereas the canine heavyweights will take considerably longer to realize their full mental and physical potential. With these breeds in particular, it is essential to continue training and socialization, as the dog's mind is still malleable, and, if you suspend his education, he may see it as a reason to assert his own authority.

When a dog reaches full maturity, he is still capable of learning, but for the most part his behavior has become established.

A SENSE OF TIMING

We can see that making the most of opportunities and getting the timing right is crucial in shaping a dog's present and future behavior. Do not be in too much of a hurry to rush your dog through his puppyhood, looking froward to the time when he becomes a settled individual.

Spend as much time as you can with your puppy, training him and socializing him as he moves from phase to phase. Be patient if he takes a step backward, and be firm if he attempts to become too assertive. Your hard work will pay off, for you will be repaid with a well-balanced, well-behaved, contented adult dog.

Chapter 18

A Program
Of Socialization

If you have purchased your puppy from a responsible breeder, some preliminary work will have already gone into socializing the litter. The breeder should spend as much time as possible with the litter, talking to the pups and handling them so that they are familiar with humans. Some litters are reared in the house, and these puppies will have an advantage as they will be exposed to all the sights and sounds of a busy household.

If the weather is fine, the breeder may be able to put the pups out in the garden, or in a run, so they will have seen a little of the outside world. However, the major responsibility of socializing your puppy rests with his new owner. When you take your puppy home, a new chapter in his life is beginning.

THE RIGHT START

A young puppy is highly impressionable, and he will take in every new experience that comes his way. When your puppy comes into his new home he will have plenty to absorb.

- He will be meeting his new family.
- He has to become familiar with his new home and garden.
- He will be meeting other pets in the family.
- He has to adapt to a new routine.
- He will be learning to become more independent, living without the companionship of his littermates.

Try to make all these experiences as easy for your puppy as possible. Be calm and confident in your manner, and your pup will take the lead from you. If your pup shows a particular anxiety, for example if he is worried by the noise of the Hoover, you can help him to overcome his fears.

- Turn off the Hoover, and sit down next to it. Make sure you have a treat to offer, and encourage your puppy to come towards you.
- If he comes up to you, praise him and reward him.
- Next, move the Hoover a few inches and, again, call your puppy to you. Praise him and give him a treat.
- Repeat this a couple of times until your puppy appears completely unconcerned.
- The next stage is to switch on the Hoover. Do not make a big fuss, but gently encourage your pup to come up to you for his treat. Talk to your pup, reassuring him, and give him another treat for staying with you.
- If your pup enjoys a game, you can distract his attention by playing with a toy.

In most cases, a pup will soon become indifferent to a new experience. That is why it is important not to make too much of it. The puppy is learning by being a little suspicious and then finding out there is nothing to worry about. Your job is to encourage him and reassure him, but not to mollycoddle him.

If you plan to use a clicker for training your puppy (see page 151), this is an ideal situation to use it in. Once you have introduced your pup to the clicker (see page 162), use it to encourage your pup to move towards the Hoover (or whatever he is frightened of). He will quickly learn that boldness pays off!

Once your puppy has had a chance to settle into his new home you can increase his learning experiences.

- Invite friends to the house so he has the opportunity to meet people outside the family.
- If you do not have children, make arrangements for some youngsters to come and visit. Few children can resist the chance to meet a puppy, and it will be a valuable experience for your pup.
- Ask a friend to arrive wearing a hat or dark glasses.
- Open up an umbrella and give your puppy a chance to explore.
- If you know anyone who plays an instrument, ask them round so that your pup can share in an impromptu concert.

TOP TIP

Use your imagination to invent as many different scenarios as possible. They will all be of benefit to your puppy, and will stand him in good stead when he is ready to venture into the outside world.

THE OUTSIDE WORLD

Although your puppy will not be fully vaccinated until he is 14-16 weeks old, you can still give him plenty of socialization. In fact, it is an ideal time to choose, as your pup will soak up all new experiences like a sponge.

Find out if your vet runs puppy parties, which are specially designed group socialization classes for pups of this age (see page 174). You can also take your pup out for small excursions if you are prepared to carry him. The best plan is to find a bench, and sit with your pup on your lap. This will give your pup the chance to have a look at everything that is going on, but he is not being exposed to the dangers of picking up an infectious disease.

CAR TRAVEL

Your pup needs to get used to travelling by car, and you can work on this while you are waiting to complete the vaccination course.

Ideally, your pup will travel in a crate in the rear of the car. This is the safest way to travel, as your pup is securely contained, and quickly learns that he must settle when he is in the car.

To start with, attempt a few short outings, so that your pup gets used to the motion of the car. Some puppies are a little car-sick to begin with, but this is seldom an ongoing problem. If your pup suffers from car-sickness, try to limit his access to food and water before going in the car. If the problem persists, consult your vet, who may prescribe some medication.

Some puppies bark or whine when they are in the car. It is important to stop this before it becomes a bad habit. In most cases, the puppy is attention seeking, so it is best to simply ignore his cries, and he will learn that there is no point in making a fuss. Some owners find that it helps to play the radio as it seems to soothe the pup.

When you reach your destination, observe the following car drill. (For information on teaching the following commands, see Chapter 20: Basic Exercises.)

- Open the car door, and tell your puppy to "Sit". Do not open his crate if he is scrabbling to get out. He must learn that the only way he gets out is when he is sitting.
- Open the crate door, and tell your puppy to "Sit" or "Wait". When your pup is sitting quietly, fasten his lead.
- Tell your puppy to "Wait" again, and check the traffic before allowing him out of the car.

This may seem like a long-winded procedure – but it is better to be safe than sorry. Accidents happen at lightning speed, and it only takes a split second for a puppy to jump out of the car and into the path of an approaching car.

GOING OUT AND ABOUT

When your puppy is ready to have his first outing walking on the lead, do not be too ambitious. Hopefully, your pup is already walking confidently on the lead (see page 168), but he will feel quite daunted when he has had to stand on his four feet.

Limit the outing to just five or ten minutes, and make the experience as positive as possible. Start off in a quiet area before attempting a more built-up location, and encourage your pup to keep walking by your side. If he is worried by a loud noise, or by a strange object, you can distract his attention by giving him a treat, and then encouraging him to keep moving. Do not be tempted to pick up your puppy and cuddle him every time he shows any sign of fear; you will only make him worse.

If your pup does seem particularly sensitive, confine yourself to quiet suburban streets, and give him a chance to build up his confidence before attempting a more challenging environment.

When your pup is walking happily on the lead in a built-up area, you can introduce some new experiences.

TOP TIP

Your pup is able to learn at such a fast rate that you can literally saturate him with new experiences. Take him with you whenever possible – even if it is just down the street to buy a newspaper. Your puppy will enjoy the outing, and, inevitably, there is always something new to learn.

- Go to a railway station and give your pup a chance to see and hear the trains.
- Take a ride on a bus, so that your pup gets used to getting on and off a big vehicle, and learns to settle under your seat.
- Go into a bank or a post office (first check that dogs are allowed) so that your pup learns to sit quietly while you are being served. You may well find that the bank has a revolving door, or a slippery floor, and this will give your pup something else to get used to.
- Go past some roadworks so that your pup sees and hears the men and machinery at work.
- Go to a park and sit on a bench close to where children are playing. Some puppies can be worried by the high-pitched cries of the children as they play.
- Find a game of football, and spend a few minutes watching the game. This is a particularly useful exercise if you have one of the Collie breeds who can become obsessed with 'rounding up' or chasing every ball they see.

• Go to a street market so that your pup gets used to walking in a crowd. There are usually lots of enticing smells, so this is also a good exercise in stopping your pup from sniffing every time he discovers something of interest.

STRANGE ENCOUNTERS

It is important that your pup learns to respect livestock, and so, if you live in an urban area, you may need to take a trip out to the country so your pup has a chance to meet cattle, sheep, chickens and horses.

Your pup is certain to be fascinated by the strange animals, and he has every right to be curious. However, you must prevent him from lunging at the animals, or showing an obsessive interest.

- Give your pup a chance to look, and then walk away a few paces. Call your pup and reward him for coming to you.
- Repeat this a few times, so that your pup is responding positively to you every time you call his name.
- Walk alongside the animals, keeping your pup on a loose lead. If he attempts to pull towards the animals, say "No" in a firm voice, stand still, and call the pup back to your side. Be ready with a reward.

The aim is to make yourself more interesting than the animals he finds so fascinating. If you work at this on a number of occasions, your pup will learn that animals are not there to be chased or harassed.

TOP TIP

No matter how good your puppy appears to be with livestock, never be tempted to take a chance. Your pup should always be on the lead and under close supervision when you are anywhere near field-kept animals.

CARRY ON THE GOOD WORK

Some owners make the mistake of working hard at training and socialization during the first 12-18 months of their dog's life, and then giving up, believing the job is done.

In fact, dogs benefit from training sessions all through their lives. It keeps them mentally active, and, if you have a dog with dominant tendencies, training will strengthen your status as leader.

As your puppy matures, he may not need an intensive program of socialization, but do not suddenly leave him high and dry and only take him out for his exercise. Dogs love being a part of everything that is going on, and a short trip in the car is infinitely preferable to being left at home. Get into the habit of taking your dog out with you whenever you can. You will enjoy his companionship, and your dog will thrive on the variety in his life.

Part 8

Principles Of Learning

Chapter 19

Understanding The Dog's Mind

In our relationships with fellow human beings, we use a number of tools so that we can communicate successfully.

First and foremost we use speech, which enables us to exchange thoughts, ideas and emotions in a complex and sophisticated manner. This is a conscious form of communication where we can plan what we are going to say, and we can decide what we wish to reveal or conceal.

On a more unconscious level, we use body language, facial expression and tone of voice, which give clues as to how we feel. These forms of expression are often involuntary, and can sometimes give a much more accurate picture of a person's feelings than a verbal exchange.

The problem is that we have come to rely so heavily on speech that we are gradually losing the skills needed to communicate in other ways.

In the animal world, communication may not reach the dizzy heights of verbal debate, but it is just as important.

- It is the means of forming individual relationships that are essential for breeding, and therefore for the survival of the species.
- It is used for establishing a hierarchy within a group so animals can live in harmony, strengthened as a group against common dangers.
- It is a method of passing on essential knowledge, such as the whereabouts of food or water, or the presence of an enemy.

How do animals communicate, without the power of speech? The answer is very simple, they rely almost totally on body language; facial expression plays a smaller part, and there is limited vocal exchange.

Obviously, this may vary from species to species, but it gives an accurate picture of how the wild ancestors of our domesticated dogs would have behaved.

CROSSING THE DIVIDE

If we take a dog into our human family, we are presented with the problem of trying to communicate with a creature that does not share a verbal language or a common body language. This may seem like an impossible state of affairs, but, in fact, the barrier between man and dog is far from insurmountable. As intelligent human beings, we can learn to understand a dog's body language so that we know how he is feeling.

- A confident, happy dog will wave his tail, and behave in a positive, extrovert manner.
- A submissive dog will slink down, lowering his height, flattening his ears and putting his tail between his legs. If he is trying to appear very submissive, he will curl back his lips.
- A dog who wants to appear dominant will stand tall, raise his head and hold his tail upright. He will meet a challenge with a hard stare.
- If a dog raises his hackles (lifting the hair) along his back, he may feel frightened or threatened.
- An aggressive dog may adopt a dominant stance, flatten his ears, curl back his lips, and show his teeth.
- A nervous or frightened dog may react aggressively, raising his hackles and showing his teeth, through fear. Alternatively, he may adopt a submissive attitude (see above).

A dog has a limited vocal vocabulary, but it is helpful to understand what he is conveying.

- A bark is an expression of warning, usually marking the approach of strangers. It is also a way of expressing exuberance and excitement, but this type of bark will be more repetitive and higher in pitch than the warning bark.
- A growl is a warning signal, meaning "keep off". It is usually low and continuous, sometimes broken by a snarl.
- A dog who is distressed or in pain may whine or whimper. A submissive dog may also use this form of expression.
- Some dogs may howl in unison, particularly if they are in a kennel environment. This could be a throwback to their hunting heritage when wolves would howl to get the pack together before setting out on a hunt. Some dogs with sensitive hearing will howl if they hear a noise that distresses them, such as a high-pitched musical instrument.

As we get to know an individual dog, we can become expert at reading his body language and interpreting his vocal vocabulary. It is a skill that is well worth acquiring, as it can help us to detect changes in mood and we can even become aware of barely discernible changes in a dog's physical health.

CANINE PERSPECTIVE

The adaptable dog learns to read our body language, and quickly picks up on the tiniest clues that we may not even be aware of ourselves. The dog who is attuned to his family will know how a person feels just through a small facial expression, or a slight body movement. That is why many people believe their dogs have extrasensory powers. This may or may not be the case, but there is no doubting the dog's almost uncanny ability to pick up on the clues that we fail to see.

Not only can a dog read our body language, he can also understand our spoken language – up to a point! A well-trained dog will learn to respond to verbal commands, offering the appropriate reaction to a given command. This does not mean that the dog understands the meaning of the words you are using. It makes no difference whether you say "Sit" or "Bananas", as long as you use the same word every time you ask for a particular behavior. The dog is responding to the sound of the word, and the tone of voice. He is equally happy to respond to hand signals, as is shown by dogs who compete in Obedience Trials, or to the sound of a whistle, which is used by many people who work their dogs with livestock.

UNDERSTANDING AND INTELLIGENCE

Now we have established the means of communicating with our dog, how much can we expect from him? It is almost impossible to quantify how intelligent a dog is, despite numerous studies to try to evaluate the canine IQ.

- Is a dog intelligent because he responds to a series of commands, or does the dog who runs off to pursue his own interests have superior intelligence?
- Is a Border Collie intelligent because he responds quickly and accurately to the shepherd's commands, or is he driven purely by instinct?
- Are some breeds more intelligent than others? Working sheepdogs and Border Collies carry off all the prizes in Obedience competitions, but this merely proves that this type of dog is easier to train than a slow-moving, powerful St Bernard, for example, or a skittish and slightly wilful Shih Tzu.

It is fair to assume that all dogs have a good level of intelligence, but how this is used depends on their training, their relationship with their owner, and the motivation that is on offer.

THE POWER TO REASON

Many owners believe that their dogs 'work things out', rather than relying on commands or using instinctive behavior. You can sometimes see a dog's reasoning powers in action. For example, if you are on a country walk, and you come across a stile that is difficult to climb, your dog must work out how to find a way through. He may try climbing the stile, but back off when he finds it too precarious. He may attempt to duck under the adjoining fence, or he may move further along the path and find an easier way through. The dog has a problem to solve, and, using his intelligence, he will try out the available options until he finds a solution.

LIVING FOR THE MOMENT

The one big difference between the human and canine brain is the human's ability to reflect on their actions. A person will worry about problems that lie ahead, such as unpaid bills, and dwell on the row at work they had the day before. In contrast, a dog lives for the moment. He does not plan ahead, nor regret the past. He never thinks about the consequence of his actions, and he does not act out of spite.

That is why there is absolutely no point in returning home to punish your dog for a misdeed that could have happened hours before. He will have absolutely no idea what you are angry about. He is incapable of connecting your present anger with his earlier crime.

ESTABLISHING LEADERSHIP

The dog is a pack animal, and, despite thousands of years of domestication, he retains the instincts of a pack animal. This is very useful when it comes to training your puppy, as he is ready to accept authority. This starts in the nest when the mother disciplines her puppies, and, in the wild, the youngsters would be disciplined by their elders so that they learnt their place in the pack hierarchy.

In a domestic situation, the puppy must learn his place in his human family. This does not mean that you have to assume the role of a dictator, forcing your puppy into a subservient role. But you must establish a relationship where the puppy respects your authority and does not question your commands. If you have children in the family, he must also learn to respect them.

If you are fair and consistent in your training, your puppy will be happy to accept his place in the pecking order, without ever feeling the need to question it. If leadership is poorly defined, dogs – particularly adolescent males – will have a go at taking over, which leads to major behavioral problems (see Chapter 22: The Adolescent). However, there is absolutely no reason for matters to reach this stage. Give your puppy a clear picture of where his boundaries lie, and he will be content to accept your authority.

BEING CONSISTENT

Bringing up puppies and children has great similarities, and a good parent, will often prove to be a good dog trainer. Children need to know what is allowed, and what is not allowed, and puppies are exactly the same.

A child who is allowed sweets one day and refused them the next day, without explanation, will become cross and fractious. The child will nag or make a fuss in the

HOUSE RULES
THOU SHALT NOT...
STEAL FOOD
DIG THE GARDEN
PEE ON THE RUG
SLEEP ON THE BEDS
CHEW SLIPPERS

hope of changing your mind. That child would be far happier – and far better behaved – if he or she knew that sweets were always bought on Saturdays, and not on any other day of the week.

Now picture a scenario from a puppy's perspective. You have told your pup not to jump up because you do not want to encourage a bad habit – particularly if your puppy is going to grow into a fair-sized adult. But then you come home and your puppy is so pleased to see you that you let him jump up to say a special hello. The next time he greets you like this, he has muddy paws and you are furious with him.

What is the result? A confused puppy who does not know what is expected of him. As far as he is concerned, the same action has provoked two entirely different responses. He has been praised for jumping up, and he has been thoroughly told off for doing exactly the same thing. It is not surprising if the puppy starts to question your authority.

Before your puppy even arrives home, you and your family should decide what is acceptable behavior, and then all members of the family can adhere to the 'house' rules. If your pup is getting a clear, consistent message from everyone, he will quickly learn what is expected of him.

There are other areas where being consistent will help your puppy's training.

- When you call your puppy, make sure all members of the family use the same name. For example, you may have decided to call your pup Ben, but if he is also called Benny, Benjamin and Benno, you will end up with a muddled pup, who is slow to respond to the recall (see page 164).
- When you start training, use the same word or words every time you give a command. For example, the command is "Down", not Lie down, or Lie, or Stay down. Remember, your pup does not understand the meaning of the words you are using, he is going on sound alone. You know that you are asking for the same response when you use a variety of different words, but your pup will not know what you want.
- Decide what areas of the house your pup is allowed in, and whether he is allowed to lie on the furniture. The rules you make are entirely a matter of personal preference, but you must stick to them. You cannot ban your puppy from the sofa one day, and then let him stay there the next because he looks so sweet and peaceful. If you are indecisive in your leadership, your puppy will quickly realize that he does not need to do what you ask.

PROVIDING REWARDS

There is a big difference in doing something because you *want* to do it rather than because you *have* to do it. A dog's mind works in exactly the same way. Your pup will learn to obey commands because he accepts your authority, but he may not show much enthusiasm. He will put in minimal effort, and his responses will be slow and lethargic. Compare this with the dog who is working for something he wants – a treat or a game with a toy – and you will be amazed at the change. Suddenly the dog is trying his hardest to do as you ask, responding quickly and enthusiastically to instructions. He is happy to be working because he is anticipating his reward.

It is your job to find out what type of reward provides the greatest motivation for your puppy. Most breeds cannot resist a food treat, and will work tirelessly for tiny rewards, other breeds are not so food-orientated. There are some dogs who will get more excited at the prospect of being given their favorite toy to play with, or maybe having a game of tug with the lead. If you find out what turns your pup on, you will have found the key to training him.

CLICKER TRAINING

This is a relatively new method of training, which is proving to be very effective with dogs of all breeds. It was first introduced by Karen Pryor when she was training dolphins, and she has adapted her training program to suit many different animals.

The clicker is a small box with a clicking mechanism that is activated when it is pressed. The trainer 'clicks' the dog when he performs a correct behavior, and then

TOP TIP

There are some dogs who are indifferent to toys, and also show a lack of interest in food treats. If this is the case, try finding something that is really tasty to use as your reward. A pup may not be impressed by being offered a few biscuits, but if he is given a piece of cheese, he may be transformed.

Try out a selection of mouth-watering treats on your pup, such as cheese, sausage or cooked liver, and find out what is his heart's desire. When you have found his favorite, make sure he is only given it during training sessions. Never use chocolate, or any other sweet food as a treat, as it will be very bad for your puppy's teeth.

follows it up with a food reward. The dog learns that he if gets clicked, he will get a reward, so he will work hard to produce the behavior that is required. The trainer uses the clicker as a means of saying "yes, that is what I want you to do", giving positive reinforcement to the dog's actions.

One of the big advantages of clicker training is that the dog can be 'clicked' at the exact moment he offers the correct behavior, so he is in no doubt that he has done the right thing. When the dog has learnt the behavior, cues or commands can be introduced.

Puppies love this method of training as it is varied and interesting, and they seem to thrive on the very positive system of learning.

Chapter 20

Basic Exercises

Training a puppy is fun – and it should always be treated as such. Training sessions mean quality time with your puppy, which you should both enjoy. If you are short of time, or you are feeling stressed after a hard day at work, it is better to skip training, and just have a game with your pup or take him for a walk instead. Inevitably, we show our feelings when we are training, and the perceptive puppy will soon pick up on 'bad vibes'. He will be less responsive, and tempers will quickly become frayed.

Training should be an entirely positive experience, so even though you want to plan a regular training program, make sure you choose times when you are most likely to be successful. It is not just your own mood you have to assess before starting a training session; it is equally important that your pup is feeling receptive. Here are some guidelines to get you off to a flying start.

DO'S

Do train when your pup is feeling fresh and lively.

Do choose some tasty treats to reward your pup. If he prefers toys, make sure you keep a favorite toy especially for training sessions.

Do choose a place to train that is as free from distractions as possible.

Do train little and often, rather than trying to cram too much into one session.

Do sound enthusiastic when you are training your pup. Tone of voice is an important means of communicating, so you must sound encouraging.

Do praise your puppy when he has done well. You can do this verbally, or by stroking him, and also by giving him a treat, or his toy.

Do be conscious of your body language. Your pup will pick up on positive vibes, and will work more enthusiastically for you.

Do end training sessions on a good note. If your pup is struggling with an exercise, go back to something that you know he can do well. This will give you the opportunity to praise him and reward him for his efforts.

TRAINING AND SOCIALISATION

The aim of every responsible owner is to have a well-behaved, well-adjusted dog who will go any-where, taking every situation in his stride. However, achieving this is not a matter of luck. You must work hard at providing a programme of training and socialisation as your puppy grows up so that he matures into the perfect canine companion.

Your puppy will learn to accept the resident cat – they may even become friends.

Supervise play sessions, so that both child and puppy learn a sense of mutual respect.

An adult dog and a pup will work out their own relationship.

Your pup will enjoy exploring the garden, and this will be sufficient exercise for him until he is ready to go into the outside world.

▲ To begin with, your pup will miss the company of his littermates.

▶ Training can start as soon as your puppy arrives home.

▲ A puppy has a limited concentration span, so keep training sessions short.

▶ Make sure your pup enjoys his outings, and is rewarded when he behaves well.

157

▲ Many breeds love to retrieve, and this game gives the opportunity for mental stimulation as well as physical exercise.

▶ Remember, owning a dog is fun – so spend time enjoying the wonderful relationship you can share with your canine companion.

◀ Swimming is an excellent way of providing exercise, as long as you choose a safe area (top photo opposite).

◀ As your pup gets bigger and stronger, you will be able to step up the amount of exercise he is allowed (bottom photo opposite).

159

◀ *Some pups may challenge your authority as they hit adolescence, but problems can be overcome with firm, fair and consistent handling.*

▼ *Reaping the reward of early socialisation, these giant-sized Mastiffs know how to behave around children.*

DON'TS

Do not train if you feel tired, irritable, or preoccupied. You must be prepared to give the job your full concentration.

Do not train when your puppy has just had a meal. He will not be interested in working for food treats, and he will prefer to rest.

Do not train your puppy when he is tired – for example, when he has just had a hectic game in the garden.

Do not use treats that are too big or too chewy. You will find that training will become a stop-start affair if you have to keep waiting for your pup to finish his mouthful!

Do not attempt lengthy sessions of training with a young puppy. A pup has a very limited concentration span, and he will quickly become distracted. Start off with five-minute sessions, and build up the time gradually as your pup matures.

Do not wait until your pup is six months old before you start training. A pup can start training from the moment he arrives home, as long as you keep training sessions short (see above).

TOP TIP

Food is a great way of motivating your puppy – but you do not want him to become overweight because he is getting through so many treats. The best plan is to work out how many treats you are likely to use in a training session, and subtract this amount of food from his regular mealtime rations.

LESSONS TO LEARN

You may have ambitions to train your puppy to a high standard so that he can go on to compete in one of the many canine sports, such as Obedience, Agility, Canine Freestyle or Working Trials. Alternatively, you may be content to simply teach the basics so that your pup matures into a well-behaved adult.

In fact, in the early stages, the approach, and most of the lessons you need to teach, are identical. If you are planning to compete, your training regime obviously becomes more intensive once your dog is fully grown, and is mentally and physically capable of working at a more advanced level. However, for the first 12 months of a dog's life, training should be relatively relaxed and informal.

Clicker training (see page 151) is an excellent method of teaching dogs of all ages and breeds, regardless of the standard you are aspiring to. The following exercises are outlined using clicker training, but can easily be adapted if you prefer to use reward-based training, without incorporating the clicker. In these exercises, food is used as a reward, but a toy will work equally well. When your pup has offered the correct behavior, click, and reward by throwing him his favorite toy, or having a game of tug.

INTRODUCING THE CLICKER

It takes most puppies a matter of minutes to understand how the clicker works.

- Get a bowl of treats at the ready, and take your pup and your clicker into a distraction-free training area.
- When you have your puppy's attention, click and give a reward.
- Repeat this four or five times, going to different parts of your training area (so that your pup does not think the clicker only works in one place).
- Next, click and delay giving the treat for a couple of seconds.
- Repeat this until you can see that your pup is actively looking for the treat as soon as he hears the click. At this point he has learnt that a click means a treat is coming.

SIT

This is the simplest exercise to teach, and it is rewarding because, almost immediately, you and your puppy can be successful.

- Get a treat and hold it above your puppy's head, so that he has to look up for it.
- As he tries to reach for the treat, your pup will naturally go into the Sit position.
- The moment he sits, click and reward.
- Practice the exercise a number of times so that your pup learns that if he goes into a Sit, he will be clicked and then rewarded.

This will be fine for your first training session. Do not attempt to teach too much at a time, or your pup will get distracted or confused.

- Next time you are training for the Sit, wait a few seconds after your pup has gone into the Sit before clicking. In this way the pup will learn to sustain the behavior until you are ready to click and reward him.
- You can now work at withdrawing your hand so that you are not luring your pup into position. First of all, lure your dog into the Sit, and then withdraw your hand. If your pup stays in the Sit, click and reward.
- Now you can try keeping your hands in your lap, or behind your back. Your pup knows he must earn a click, so he will probably offer a Sit. Then you can click and reward.
- If your pup tries to nose at your hands in the hope of finding a treat, just ignore him.

He will soon give up and will be ready to offer a Sit to get his click and reward.

- When you are confident that your pup has understood the exercise, you can introduce a verbal command or cue to give a name to the behavior he has learnt. This means that you will be able to ask for this specific behavior when you want it. As your pup goes into the Sit, give the command "Sit". Repeat the exercise a few times, and your pup will quickly associate the command with the action.

DOWN

This is an extension of the Sit exercise. Do not start teaching it until your pup has mastered the Sit, or he will confuse the two.

- Start with your pup in the Sit, and, holding a treat in your hand, lower it towards the ground.
- Your hand is acting as a lure, which your pup will follow. To begin with, he may only half lower himself, but you should click and reward to encourage this behavior.
- Keep practicing until your pup is following the lure and going into the Down position when you can click and reward.

Take a break here, and save the next stages for another training session.

- Start by luring your pup into the Down, click and reward.
- Next time, wait a little longer so your pup has to stay in the Down position before you click and reward.
- Gradually withdraw your hand as a lure. Your pup knows you have a treat, but he must earn it by lying down. The moment he goes Down, click and reward.
- When your pup is confidently going into the Down, introduce the verbal command. Practice a few times, saying "Down" as your pup goes into position.

You can encourage your pup to be steady in the Down by gradually introducing a few distractions.

TOP TIP

Once your puppy has learnt an exercise, you do not need to click him every time he does it. There is no need; he has learnt what you want him to do. Click and reward on a random basis to keep his mind fresh, but, increasingly, you can use the clicker when you are teaching new exercises, or when you are trying to string a number of exercises together (see page 168).

- Command your pup to go into the Down, and then walk around him. If he stays in position, click and reward.
- When your pup is in the Down, step over him, and stand with your legs either side of him. Return to his side, click and reward.
- Next, put your pup in the Down, and ask someone to walk past. If he stays in position, click and reward.
- If your puppy breaks position, do not make a big fuss. Quietly put him back in position and repeat the exercise. Your pup will soon realize that if he breaks position he will not get clicked, and so he will not get his reward.

This exercise can be built up slowly over a series of training sessions. Do not attempt to introduce distractions too soon or you will invite failure. You want your puppy to learn by offering the correct behavior; he will not learn if he keeps making mistakes.

COME

Puppies have an instinct to follow, and so you will probably find yourself tripping up over your pup as he constantly gets under your feet! You can make use of this right from the start, and it will prove to be the foundation of a good recall.

- Use every opportunity to train your puppy to come to you. When you see your pup running up towards you, call his name, click and reward.
- At mealtimes, click as your pup comes towards you.
- Make a game out of the exercise, using members of the family to call the pup to them, one at a time.
- Your pup will soon learn that if he comes when he is called, he will be clicked and rewarded. When you are confident that he understands the exercise, you can add a verbal command "Flash, come".
- As your pup becomes proficient, call him from one room to another. You can make this easier by rattling a few treats in a bowl as an added incentive.

You may be deceived into thinking you have cracked this exercise when your puppy is responding quickly and consistently in the house. But you will probably find that your puppy is unreliable when you try to call him outside. He will be distracted by enticing scents, and by the interesting sights and sounds of the outside world.

- Start by practicing in the garden before you attempt the exercise in the park.
- Make sure you sound really enthusiastic when you call your puppy so that he thinks coming to you is the most fun thing to do.
- You can use body language to encourage your pup, holding your arms out, and then welcoming him in as he comes towards you. Don't forget to click as your pup comes

to you, and then give his reward.
- It is a good idea to have a game with your pup, as well as rewarding him with food. Throw a retrieve toy, or have a game of tug, so that your pup associates coming to you with having fun.

Your puppy will not be ready to go to the park until he has completed his vaccination course (see page 202), so you will be able to practice at home before attempting a more difficult test.

For your first recall exercise in the park, use a training line. This is a length of cord running to 9-12 ft. It is fastened to the pup's collar, but it does not need to be held. It is there as an insurance so that you do not have to worry about your puppy running away.

- Ask a friend or a member of the family to hold on to the pup as you walk approximately 12 ft away.
- As you call the pup, your assistant releases him. Click and reward as your pup comes to you.
- This exercise can then be reversed, so that your pup is called the opposite way.
- Repeat this a couple of times, and then stop and have a game with your pup.
- Use the training line for the first few outings to the park so that you can concentrate on building up a strong response in the new environment, without the risk of your puppy running away.
- When you are confident that your pup is focusing on you, try introducing some distractions while you call your pup. Ask a friend to walk past, or try the exercise close to where some children are kicking a ball.
- When your pup is coping with people distractions, try a few dog distractions. Ask a friend to walk past with a dog on the lead. This will be very tempting for your puppy, but use lots of encouragement, and be ready to click and reward a positive response.

Before you move on to a recall off-lead, check that the park allows dogs to run free, and make sure that the area you choose is completely safe, well away from passing traffic. Do not delay too long before you try your puppy off the lead as he is far more likely to keep close to you when he feels slightly vulnerable in a new place, rather than waiting until he is six months old and raring to go!

- Let your pup off the lead, and allow him to have a sniff around. Call your pup, sounding bright and enthusiastic, and, hopefully, he will respond. Be ready to click and reward.
- If your pup is a bit reluctant to stop what he is doing and come to you, turn your back on him and walk for a few paces. Call him again. You will usually find that the

pup is more eager to come if he thinks he is being left behind.

• When your pup responds to your call, reward him and have a game. Do not make the mistake of putting him straight back on the lead, or he will associate coming to you with the end of his walk. Let him wander off again, and call him back. Repeat this a number of times, and when you are ready to put him back on the lead, have a game first.

When your puppy is responding consistently well to the "Come" command, you may wish to build the exercise into a more formal recall (see Putting It All Together, page 168). Do not attempt this too early as, in the early stages, you want your pup to respond enthusiastically, rather than being concerned about a more formal, disciplined approach.

TOP TIP

Some dogs need additional motivation so that they become enthusiastic about coming to you. Call your pup in a variety of different situations – when his meal is ready, as you open the car door, when you are holding his favorite toy. This will help to reinforce the message that "Come" means the start of fun, rather a command which marks the end of free time.

WAIT/STAY

Before you work on a formal recall, your pup needs to learn to "Wait" on command. Some trainers use the command "Wait" when they want a dog to maintain his position before moving on to the next command. If they want the dog to stay for an extended period of time, they say "Stay". This is a matter of personal choice, and probably has greater significance for those who want to get involved in advanced training. Whatever you decide, be consistent so that your puppy understands what is expected of him.

When you teach the Sit and the Down exercises, your puppy is learning to stay in position (see above). Your aim is to teach your pup to maintain his position until you give the next command or release him.

At first glance, this may seem an unimportant exercise unless you want to get involved in more formal training. However, it has a wide variety of applications.

• You can command your pup to "Wait" as you open a door so that he does not go rushing out.
• You can tell him to stay in position if you are grooming him.
• You can tell him to "Wait" when you open the car door. This can be a lifesaver, preventing your pup from diving out into oncoming traffic.

The Wait exercise is easy to teach:

- Start by asking your puppy to "Sit". Step a couple of paces to one side, and then return to where you were standing. Click and reward.
- Repeat the exercise, taking a couple of paces in front of your puppy and behind him. Click and reward when you return to your puppy's side. If he tries to get up to follow you, just say "No" in a quiet tone of voice, and put him back in position. Repeat the exercise, and click and reward a correct response.
- You can then try dropping the lead, and repeating the exercise. If he is staying in position, you can try walking a small circle around your pup.
- Gradually build up the distance you can leave your puppy, and the amount of time he has to stay in position. Always return to his side before you click and reward.
- It may help if you use a hand signal (hand held up, palm facing towards your pup) to reinforce the message that he must stay in position.
- When your pup has understood the exercise, you can introduce a verbal command "Wait" or "Stay".

You may find that your puppy tries to follow if you turn your back on him to walk away.

- Start by walking backwards and wait a few paces away, still facing him. Return to his side, click and reward.
- Next, walk backwards, and then make a half-turn, so you are standing side on. Pause for a few moments before returning to your pup. Click and reward.
- If your pup is maintaining his position, you can try walking backwards, and then turning so that you are facing away from him. Repeat the command "Wait" so that your pup knows he must stay in position even though you are looking away from him. Return to his side, click and reward.
- Build up the exercise in easy stages, walking away from your pup for just a short distance, and waiting just a few moments before returning to his side. You are building up his confidence so that he is happy to be left for a limited period of time.

You can train your puppy to stay in the Down in exactly the same way as outlined above. In fact, you will find that your puppy is less likely to break the Down position, so you may prefer to ask him to go into the Down when you are extending the duration of the exercise.

If your puppy breaks position, do not get cross and shout at him. It is not wrong that he wants to be with you, he must simply learn that he has to wait a few minutes before you rejoin him. Simply put your pup back in position, and repeat the exercise. If necessary, go back a few stages and make it easy for him. You want the opportunity to click and reward a correct behavior. Once the Down is firmly established, you can go on to increase the complexity.

PUTTING IT ALL TOGETHER

Once your puppy has fully understood the Sit, Wait and Come exercises, you can put it all together and train a formal recall. This is not essential for basic training, but is a way of practicing the three different elements. It also adds variety to your training sessions which will be more stimulating for your puppy.

To begin with, the clicker is used to positively reinforce a single, correct behavior. In fact, it is used to reinforce the stages that go towards making up a correct response. So, as we have seen, a pup is clicked the first time he lowers himself towards the ground when we are looking for a Down. Then, in stages, he is clicked for getting into the right position and then staying there.

In the same way, an exercise that includes a number of elements, like the recall, can be trained stage by stage before putting it all together. The puppy is clicked for each element, then for getting two elements right, and finally for completing the exercise.

The puppy knows he is working for a reward, and, as he matures, he is able to cope with working a little harder, and waiting a little longer before he gets the 'yes' reinforcement of the clicker and the reward that follows.

Do not attempt a formal recall until you are confident that your pup has mastered each of the three elements: Sit, Wait, and Come, as separate entities. It is particularly important not to confuse a young puppy, or you will end up ruining his correct response to the simple "Come" exercise. When you are ready, put the routine together as follows.

- Start with your pup at your side, and ask him to "Sit".
- Ask your pup to "Wait". You can use a hand signal to reinforce the verbal cue.
- Walk away from your pup, about-turn and face him. Some trainers suggest setting off on the foot furthest from the puppy's side, so that he is not tempted to follow.
- Repeat "Wait" and pause for a few moments. It is important that your pup learns he must wait until he is called, rather than anticipating what you want him to do.
- Call your puppy to you, sounding bright and enthusiastic. In the initial stages, you may wish to click your puppy as he comes in, and reward him straightaway.
- If you wish, you can move on to the next stage, and ask your puppy to "Sit" as he reaches you.
- He is then clicked when he is in the correct position, and the exercise is finished with a reward and a game.

LEAD-TRAINING

The aim of every owner is to have a dog who walks happily on a loose lead. This makes walking your dog a pleasure, rather than putting up with a dog who strains and pulls to get ahead, or one that lags behind, stopping for a good sniff at every scent he comes across.

The first stage is to get your puppy used to wearing a collar. Choose a soft, lightweight collar (see page 62) to minimize the feeling of restraint.

- Put the collar round your puppy's neck. Click and reward.
- Slip the strap through the fastening. Click and reward.
- Fasten the collar, making sure it is not too tight. Test by slipping two fingers under the collar. If you can do this with ease, the collar will be both comfortable and secure. Click and reward.
- Let your pup scratch the collar if he wants to, but, better still, distract his attention away from the collar with a toy. If he starts playing a game, he will soon forget he is wearing a collar.

You can finish the session at this point and take off the collar. Repeat the exercise a couple of times a day, and each time leave the collar on for a little longer. You can try leaving it on while your pup is eating a meal, or practicing his Sit exercise. Most puppies soon get used to wearing a collar, and within a few days you will be ready to move on to the next stage.

- Put on your puppy's collar and then attach his lead.
- To begin with, allow the lead to trail. If you are in the house, make sure it does not get snarled up.
- Then pick up the lead and hold it loosely. Call your pup to you, and if he takes just a step towards you, click and reward.
- Try again, calling your puppy, and maybe patting your thigh to encourage your pup to follow. Click and reward for any movement towards you.
- Finish the session when your pup has managed to follow you for a couple of paces. Break off and have a game.
- Over a number of sessions, gradually build up the paces you can take with your pup following you on a loose lead. Click and reward at every opportunity so that he realizes that walking by your side is the behavior you want.
- You are now ready to move out into the garden, and try the exercise with added distractions. Keep training sessions very short – just a few minutes at a time – and encourage with lots of vocal praise, as well as using your clicker.
- If your pup tries to pull ahead, or lags behind, *do not* yank him back into position. Stop walking and call your pup to you. Click and reward any movement back to your side. In this way the pup learns that he is only rewarded when he is in the correct position – and he also learns that pulling or lagging behind is counterproductive.

You can work on your early lead-training sessions so that your puppy has got the idea of walking by your side before you venture into the outside world.

TOP TIP

It can be very hard not to put tension on the lead, but the handler who does this can, unwittingly, encourage the puppy to pull against the tension. If your pup is showing a strong desire to pull, try walking your pup with the lead tied around your waist rather than in your hand.

If your pup tries to pull, halt. Your pup will soon find that he cannot get you to move. As soon as he allows the lead to go slack, click and reward. When the pup has moved back to your side, you are ready to move off again. The pup has nothing to pull against, and he is not being manhandled into the correct position. He only makes progress when he is at your side. Create opportunities to click and reward correct behavior.

- For the first couple of outings, go to the park and work at establishing lead walking in this new environment. Your pup will probably feel vulnerable, so give lots of encouragement. Create the opportunity to click and reward by stopping and starting a few times, so that your puppy has to make the effort to keep pace with you. The more often he is rewarded, the quicker he will learn to walk by your side.
- As your puppy becomes more confident, introduce a few turns and changes of direction. You can also try changing your pace. The puppy will have to concentrate to keep at your side, and this gives lots of opportunities to click and reward.
- When you are happy with your puppy's progress, try introducing distractions, such as people or dogs walking past. Inevitably, your pup will pull to get where he wants to go. Be ready for him. Stop, call him, and click for any movement back to you. Hopefully, the treats will help to regain his attention, and he will return to your side. Do not move off again until your puppy is in the correct position.
- Wait until your puppy is walking confidently on the lead before taking him to a built-up area. This is an important stage in his socialization program (see page 141), but you do not want to combine a lead-training session with a lesson in getting used to the noise of traffic.
- When he is ready to try a more challenging environment, limit outings to 5-10 minutes. This is ample for a young puppy.

RETRIEVE

This exercise is by no means essential, but it gives you something new to teach, and is the basis of playing games and exercising your pup. Some breeds are natural retrievers; many of the sporting/gundog breeds have a very strong instinct to go out and fetch and to carry. They were bred to retrieve game and to carry it back without harming it, and so most dogs of this type will relish a chance to show off their skills.

For other breeds, including most of the terriers and hounds, retrieving is a completely alien exercise, but, with patience, many can be taught what is required, and they thoroughly enjoy the new game. A number of the smaller breeds, bred principally as companion dogs, show a surprising aptitude for retrieving, and they love the opportunity to show off to an admiring audience.

- Choose a toy that your pup seems to show a particular liking for. It should be light in weight, and easy to pick up. Some dogs prefer to hold an article that is soft in texture.
- Get your pup interested in his toy. Some pups will want to play with it, others tend to be a little more suspicious. Throw the toy a couple of feet away, and be ready to click if your pup moves towards it.
- If your pup has been clicked and rewarded for moving towards the toy, wait until he goes up and sniffs the toy before clicking again.
- Your pup is starting to learn that the toy holds the secret to being clicked. He may try

nosing it, or, better still, picking it up. Be ready to click and reward any progress.

That will do for the first session. If you are training a retrieving breed, he will probably be running up to the toy and bringing it back in a few sessions. Another breed, such as a Whippet, may take a few sessions to get as far as going up and sniffing the toy. Be patient, and make sure your training sessions are fun, even if progress is slow.

- As your puppy starts to show more interest in the toy, delay clicking until he has picked it up. He may take a little while to get the idea, but if he knows that he has got to 'earn' a click, he will try out a number of behaviors until he gets the "yes" click.
- If your puppy is showing no interest in picking up his toy, try a different approach. Encourage your puppy to take the toy from your hand, and as soon as it is in his mouth, click and reward.
- Work at getting your pup really excited about his toy. Pick it up, hide it behind your back, throw it – anything that will motivate your pup to run out and get it. Be accurate with your timing, so your pup understands the behavior you are reinforcing.
- When your pup has run out and picked up his toy, call him back to you. To begin with, make it easy for him and position yourself just a few feet away. Do not click until your pup has picked up his toy and is moving back towards you.
- Work on this stage by stage until your pup comes up to you and waits for you to take the toy. Then it's time for a big reward!

TOP TIP

If your pup decides the best game is to pick up his toy and run away with it, you can take preventative action. He may come back to you if you withhold the click, and therefore he will realize he is not getting a treat. But if he is very determined, tie the toy to a length of cord. Your pup will run out to pick it up, but if he tries to run away with it, you can give a gentle tug, and direct him back to you. You then have the opportunity to reinforce the correct behavior. Try this for a couple of sessions, and then you should be able to dispense with the cord.

Dogs love to retrieve, and once your pup has understood what is required, he will become a great enthusiast. This is a wonderful exercise which combines mental stimulation and physical exertion, as well as the sheer enjoyment of playing a game.

PARTY TRICKS

The value of teaching your puppy to perform a trick should not be underestimated. You may think that it serves no useful purpose if your pup shakes hands, sits up and begs, or rolls over on to his back to 'play dead', but that misses the point.

If you spend time teaching your pup a trick, you are stimulating his mental powers and you are spending time interacting with him. This will improve your relationship, and you will also find that your pup loves the opportunity to show off, and then to get lots of praise for his efforts.

As with the other training exercises, build up the trick stage by stage, rewarding each correct response, until you are ready to put the whole trick together.

ENDING ON A GOOD NOTE

Remember, whatever you are attempting to teach, always end a session on a good note. Puppies have long memories, and if training ends in a cross, unsatisfactory manner, your pup will quickly start to lose his enthusiasm. Training must always be light-hearted and positive, based on a system of praise and reward. If you always bear this is mind, your pup will be a willing pupil and will always try his hardest for you.

Chapter 21

Branching Out

Training does not have to be a solitary occupation. In fact, there are many benefits for both puppy and owner in going to a group training session.

PUPPY PARTIES

Generally, a puppy will not have completed his vaccination course until he is around 14-16 weeks of age. This is a long time to be confined to the home base, particularly because a puppy is at his most impressionable at this time, and is ripe for learning experiences.

There are a number of ways to get round this problem (see Chapter 18: A Program of Socialization), but the invention of puppy parties has made the single biggest difference to the early socialization of puppies.

These are usually organized in a veterinary practice, and it gives the opportunity for young puppies to meet together under supervision. Procedures vary from practice to practice, but in many cases puppies are allowed to attend after they have had their first inoculation.

The advantage is that not only are puppies being socialized in a relatively protected environment, they are also meeting pups of a similar age. This means that class members are at roughly the same stage in terms of learning and experience. They can interact with each other, but they do not run the risk of being frightened by bigger, stronger animals. Meetings are fairly informal, but the pups develop their canine skills, learning to communicate with other pups, and they also have the chance to meet lots of different people.

TRAINING CLASSES

When your pup is fully vaccinated, you will be ready to join a training class. You may feel that you are better off working with your pup at home, but, in fact, both you and your pup will get a lot from attending a well-run club.

- Your puppy will meet other dogs, and their handlers.
- You will be given guidance on how to teach basic obedience exercises.
- If you encounter behavioral problems, or get into difficulties when you are training at home, you can ask your training instructor for advice.
- Your pup will learn to respond to you, even though there are the distractions of other dogs and people.
- You have the opportunity to develop your training skills, which is important if you want to get involved in advanced training.
- You will enjoy a social night out, with the opportunity to talk to lots of other doggy people.

Before you go rushing off to join a training class, do some research into clubs in your area so that you find the one that will be most suitable for your needs. It is a good idea to go along to a training session without your puppy so that you can have a look at how the classes are run. Check out the following points.

- What method of training is used? It should always be reward-based, with no attempt to force or punish puppies to get results. A number of training classes specialize in clicker training (see page 151), and you may consider this a plus point.

- Does the instructor(s) seem knowledgeable? Is the teaching well structured, and are the instructions given clearly?
- Are the dogs kept under proper control at all times? This is particularly important as your puppy will be meeting adult dogs, and a bad experience could have a very damaging effect.
- Are the classes divided so that dogs of similar ages or abilities are working together? This may depend on the size of the club, but you will make far better progress if instruction is geared to the stage you have reached.
- Does the club prepare dogs for the Canine Good Citizen scheme (see below)? This is an excellent program for all dog owners, and it is well worth taking part in.
- Does the club specialize in ring training? This will only be relevant if you plan to show your puppy. But, if this is the case, he should be learning his show ring manners from puppyhood.
- Does the club specialize in any of the competitive canine sports? Some clubs have advanced classes for those who want to compete in Obedience. The clubs that teach Agility, Flyball, Working Trials etc, are usually confined to their specialist area, and, if you want to get involved, it will be a matter of finding a specialist club when your puppy has mastered basic obedience.

CANINE GOOD CITIZEN

It is entirely a matter of personal preference as to how far you wish to progress with your puppy's training, but every responsible owner should aim for a reasonable standard of obedience. Unfortunately, there are those in the community who are 'anti-dog', and it is vital that we give them no ammunition in their attempts to restrict the rights of dog owners. If all our dogs are model citizens, there is nothing to object to.

The English Kennel Club and the American Kennel Club have devised a scheme specifically to help owners produce canine good citizens. Your dog must pass a series of tests, which include:

- Accepting grooming and handling
- Responding to basic obedience commands
- Meeting another dog
- Walking on a loose lead in a controlled manner
- Walking confidently through a crowd of people
- Being approached and petted by a stranger.

If you have been working hard at your training, these tests should not pose a major problem, but you may need to polish up your pup's skills before having a go. There are many participating training clubs in the United Kingdom and in the United States where you can enroll to prepare your dog for the tests. To find out more information, contact your national Kennel Club (see Appendix I: Useful Addresses).

SPECIALIST ACTIVITIES

As your puppy grows up, you may decide you want to broaden your horizons and have a go at one of the many canine sports. Find out as much as you can about the sport you are most interested in (there are books, videos and websites that give information on most subjects), and then decide if it is suitable for you and your dog. There are specialist training clubs for all the disciplines, and you will certainly need to seek expert help if you want to compete.

If you need further information about the rules and regulations of each discipline, contact your national Kennel Club.

COMPETITIVE OBEDIENCE

Rules and regulations vary depending on your national Kennel Club, but basically this discipline involves the following exercises, which get increasingly difficult as your dog becomes more proficient.

- Precision heelwork at varying paces, on and off the lead.
- Recall – either to the handler who is standing still or when the handler is on the move.
- Stay – the dog must stay in the Sit or the Down for an extended length of time.
- Retrieve – the dog must go out and fetch an article and return it cleanly to the handler.
- Sendaway – the dog must be sent from the handler and lie down within an allocated area.
- Scent discrimination – the dog must pick out a specific scent cloth.
- Distant Control – the dog must stand at a distance from the handler and respond to a series of commands (Sit, Stand, Down).
- In the United States, dogs must also compete in an Agility section, which includes retrieving a dumb-bell over a solid jump, a broad jump, etc.

Generally, Competitive Obedience is dominated by Border Collies, Working Sheepdogs, German Shepherds and Golden Retrievers. However, there is absolutely no reason why other breeds cannot be successful. In the US, a wide variety of breeds compete, from the tiny Toys to the canine giants, and the standard remains remarkably high.

AGILITY

This is a tremendously popular, fast-moving sport, so both dog and owner need to be fit. However, the strain of running and jumping could be harmful to a growing puppy, so training should not be attempted until your dog is fully grown.

In Agility competitions, dogs must tackle a series of obstacles, competing against the clock. Marks are deducted if the dog takes the wrong course, knocks down a jump, or misses the contact point (a marked area indicating where the dog must get on or get off a particular piece of equipment). The obstacles include

- Hurdles
- Seesaw/teeter
- Tunnel (this may be rigid or collapsible)
- A-frame: a steep, A-shaped frame which the dog must scale and then descend
- Dog walk : a narrow walkway raised off the ground, sloping at both ends
- Tire: this can be set on a post like a lollipop, or supported within a frame
- Weaving poles: a series of poles set close together which the dog has to weave through
- Pause table: the dog must jump on the table and stay in the Down for a timed period
- Long jump/Broad jump.

Agility is open to all breeds. If you have a small dog, the heights of the obstacles, such as the hurdles and the tire, are lowered. Speed is all-important, and so, again, Border Collies and Working Sheepdogs excel, and Australian Shepherds. But many other dogs of all shapes and sizes get involved, and it is a sport that is clearly enjoyed by all who take part.

FLYBALL

This is rather like a canine relay race where teams of dogs compete against each other. The aim is for each dog to clear a series of hurdles to reach the Flyball box. The dog must then operate the pedal so that a ball is sprung from the box. The dog must catch the ball, and return over the hurdles to his handler before the next team member sets off. A dog is faulted if he drops the ball or knocks over a hurdle, and he will have to run the course again after the last team member has finished.

This is a highly competitive sport, and the standard is very high. The top teams have all recorded times of under 17 seconds. The sport is open to all breeds, but it is the quick, agile dogs that tend to do best.

CANINE FREESTYLE/HEELWORK TO MUSIC

This is the most recent innovation in the dog world, and the sport is catching on fast. It has its roots in Obedience, with the dog performing a series of exercises with his handler. But, in this sport, the exercises are performed to music and dog and handler 'dance' together.

This is a great crowd-pleaser, and, as long as your dog is well trained, all breeds can do equally well.

WORKING TRIALS/TRACKING

In the UK, Working Trials involves Tracking, Agility and Obedience. In the US, many of the Working Trials skills are tested in Competitive Obedience (e.g. heeling on- and-off-lead, stays, retrieving a dumb-bell over a solid jump), and so the titles of Companion Dog and Utility Dog are used in Obedience (with the addition of Obedience Trials Champion). In the US, the tracking element of Working Trials is treated as a separate sport.

Despite these differences, the basic principles of testing the handler's control, and the dog's obedience, agility, and nosework are the same. This sport demands a great deal of dedication, as the dog must reach a high standard in a number of different disciplines.

German Shepherds and Rottweilers have traditionally excelled in this area, but many of the gundog/sporting breeds, as well as Border Collies and Working Sheepdogs, are also successful.

WORKING TESTS

Many breeds were developed to perform a specific job, and Working Tests give the opportunity to test these various abilities. They range from earthdog tests for terrier breeds, to herding tests for the pastoral breeds, and field trials for the sporting/gundog breeds. For more information, contact your national Kennel Club.

Part 9
Growing Pains

Chapter 22

The Adolescent

Puppies do not stay as sweet little bundles of fur for long, and that is why you should consider the full implications of owning a dog for 12 years or more before being seduced by an appealing pup.

One of the most difficult phases of human development is the teenage years, when childhood is left behind, and the youngster hits adolescence. This marks a time of great physical development, which brings with it a fair degree of mental turmoil as the individual adjusts to their new status in an adult world.

In fact, you can draw a strong parallel between human and canine behavior at this time. As a dog approaches sexual maturity, his body is developing and becoming increasingly influenced by hormonal changes. Like a human teenager, he needs to re-evaluate the world and his place in it. This applies equally to male and female dogs, although changes in behavior may be more apparent in the male.

BEHAVIORAL CHANGES

The age at which a dog hits adolescence varies from breed to breed (see Chapter 23: The Question of Neutering), and also from individual to individual. Some dogs become quite problematical during this time, while others sail through to adulthood, and see little reason to question the status quo. These are some of the changes you may detect in your adolescent youngster:

- Your pup may sometimes seem moody, and a little off-color. Bitches, in particular, may be a little subdued as they approach their first season.
- Established training routines, such as the recall, may break down.
- Some pups may get boisterous, almost as if they are showing off their new-found physical strength.
- You may find that your pup thwarts the house rules, and tries his luck at lying on the sofa or stealing from the bin.

- Your pup may be alarmed or frightened by new situations (advice on dealing with this type of behavior is given on page 136).
- You may detect a tendency to be more possessive over food or toys.

This may sound as though your adolescent dog is undergoing a total change in personality – but do not panic. Generally, the problems you encounter at this time are easily resolved if you are tactful in your handling. Some changes you may notice, such as the moodiness, are transitory and will disappear as your dog's hormones stabilize behavior.

Neutering your dog or bitch may have beneficial effects, and the pros and cons of taking this step are discussed fully in the following chapter. This chapter focuses on the more common behavioral problems that may come to the fore during the adolescent period.

SEEKING PROFESSIONAL HELP

If you find that behavioral changes are on-going, and do not respond to the training methods outlined below, you may need to seek advice from an experienced dog trainer or behaviorist. It is far better to tackle a problem in the early stages than allow it to become part of a dog's established behavior.

There are many professional dog trainers and behaviorists, and you will see their services advertised in specialist dog papers. However, the best route is probably to inquire at your veterinary practice. In many cases, the practice will have contact details of reputable trainers and behaviorists working in the area, and you will have the confidence of knowing that they are specifically recommended.

FAILURE TO RESPOND TO THE RECALL

There is nothing more frustrating than having a dog who fails to respond to the recall. It is even worse when you know you spent time training the exercise and your pup formerly responded correctly.

It will not help if you lose your temper when your pup turns a 'deaf ear'; you must try to understand what is happening. The pup was taught to come when he was called and was rewarded with treats or by having a game. As he got older, the treats may have been given on a more random basis, or you may have got out of the habit of playing a game. Now your pup is an adolescent, he is ready to question everything. He is saying: "Why should I come when you call when I have interesting scents to follow, or when I can go off and play with another dog?"

If your pup is asking questions, you must answer them. "You come when I call because I am more interesting and more important than anything else on offer. You come when I call because I am your leader, and you want to be with me."

Obviously, you are not going to get anywhere by telling your puppy this; you must prove it by your actions and behavior.

- Go back to basics, and give your pup the opportunity to respond correctly. Call him when you have his meal ready, or when you are going out in the car, or when you are leaving the house for a walk. In this way, you are emphasizing that coming to you means having fun.
- When you call your puppy, make yourself appear really exciting, jumping up and down, or throwing a toy in the air, so that he *wants* to come to you.
- Every time your pup responds by coming to you, give him a reward and make a really big fuss of him. Until the recall behavior is re-established, reward at every single opportunity so that your pup knows a treat is coming.
- Work at all your training exercises at home, making the session as positive and enjoyable as possible. This will remind your dog that you are his leader, and, in fact, he will be happy to obey you.
- Invent some new exercises to teach your pup. This will add variety to your training sessions, and will also exercise your pup's mind.

You may have made the mistake of only calling your pup at the end of the walk, and so he has worked out that it is not worth his while to return to you. If this is the case, remember to vary your routine, calling your pup on a number of occasions throughout the walk, and then allowing him to go off again after you have rewarded him. It may also help if you go for some different walks; taking routes that your pup is not familiar with. If he is unsure of his surroundings, he will be more likely to look to you for leadership, and to respond to your commands.

This problem is not hard to solve, but do not allow matters to drift until your pup has got into the habit of ignoring you.

BOISTEROUS BEHAVIOR

Some of the bigger, extrovert breeds can become a little too boisterous as they enter the adolescent period. This applies particularly to male dogs who seem to take a delight in their new physical strength and maturity.

You will have discouraged your puppy from jumping up to get attention, anticipating the time when this type of behavior would be positively dangerous in a big dog, but now your exuberant youngster has decided to ignore this rule. You may be able to cope with a powerful Labrador hurling himself at you, but, if your dog is likely to meet children or elderly people, the results could be disastrous.

- Your pup has to learn that he only gets attention when all four feet are on the ground; if he tries to jump up he will be ignored.
- Every time you call your dog to you, stroke him and give him a treat – as long as he

has four feet on the ground.
- If he tries to jump up, turn away from him. Dogs hate to be ignored, and so your pup will wonder what he has done to earn this rebuff.
- Call your pup to you again, and reward him if he stays on the ground. If he attempts to jump up, turn away and ignore him – your pup will soon get the message.

If you are expecting visitors, make sure you are controlling your pup rather than allowing him free rein.

- When the visitors arrive, your pup must be on the lead.
- Give the visitors a treat, and tell them that this can only be given to your pup if he stays on the ground.
- Take your pup to each visitor in turn, and tell him to "Sit".
- Once your pup has been stroked and rewarded for staying at ground level, move on to the next visitor.

It may take a few weeks to retrain your pup, but if you use every opportunity to reinforce the fact that he only gets attention when he is on the ground, he will catch on. Remember to limit his chances to misbehave by keeping him on the lead until his initial enthusiasm for greeting visitors has worn off.

BREAKING THE HOUSE RULES

If you have been consistent in your training, your pup will know exactly what is, and is not, allowed in the house. If he attempts to thwart the rules by lying on the bed, or jumping up to steal food that has been left on a kitchen counter, he is, quite simply, trying it on. He knows the rules, but he also fancies lying somewhere more comfortable than the floor, or sees no reason why he should not take the food that he can easily reach.

In the wild, an adolescent may decide to challenge the established authority of the senior members of the pack. He is fed up with being told what to do, and having to wait for the top dogs to eat before he has a turn. In a domestic situation, your adolescent pup is challenging you in the same way. He is questioning your authority and your superior status.

Some breeds have a tendency to be dominant, and if you have a Rottweiler or an Akita, for example, a challenge of this sort is inevitable, particularly if you have a male dog. However, this type of behavior can be seen in varying degrees in dogs of all shapes and sizes, and it is important to nip it in the bud. A dog who thinks he can disregard human authority is not to be underestimated. You may think that a warning growl if you try to move your pup off the bed is nothing to worry about, but if this is allowed to escalate, the dog will be beyond your control.

If you are seriously concerned about your dog, and he is failing to respond to the guidelines suggested, do not delay in seeking advice from a reputable dog trainer or behaviorist.

If your adolescent pup is attempting to usurp your authority, you need to lower his status so that he is ready to accept his inferior position in the human pack. You can do this in the following ways:

- Feed your pup after the family has eaten.
- Command your pup to "Wait" in doorways, so that you always go through the door first.
- If you play with your pup, make sure you always 'win' the toy at the end of the game.
- Do not allow your pup to sleep on the bed, or lie on the sofa. You may have allowed this previously, but, if your dog is showing dominant tendencies, you need to establish a clearer demarcation line between what you can do and what your dog is allowed to do.
- Spend time training your pup to re-establish your authority. Try not to become too draconian in your manner. Make the sessions fun, so that your pup enjoys being with you, and likes doing what you ask.

In most cases, you will find your pup responds to these measures. If you are not making any progress, seek help.

GUARDING/POSSESSIVENESS

You may find that your pup does not like to be approached when he is eating, even letting out a warning growl. You may find that the pup resents anyone coming too close to his bed, or he may start being possessive over a particular toy. This type of behavior is symptomatic of the adolescent pup who no longer accepts his position in the human pack. He is guarding what he sees as his own property, and he is building up his own sphere of influence. Attempts to challenge his new-found authority are met with a warning to keep away.

Although the behavior is being expressed in a slightly different way, it is, again, an indication of the dog who is trying to become dominant. Use the same technique outlined above to lower his status, and work at his training to improve your relationship with him.

In addition, you will need to focus on the areas where your pup has attempted to assume control.

- When your pup is eating, drop some treats into his bowl. In this way, he will not resent interference with his food bowl.
- When your pup becomes more relaxed by accepting the treats, take the bowl away for

a moment. Give him a treat, and then give him the bowl again. Your pup must understand that you are in charge of his food. You are a fair leader, but he must accept your authority.

• Confiscate all your pup's toys, and only get them out when you are training, or specifically to have a game. When the game or the training session is over, take charge of the toy. Your pup needs to see that the toys are not his possessions; they can only be played with when you give the go-ahead.

• If your pup goes to his bed, stroke him and give him a treat while he is there. He will see that, although you have invaded his personal space, he has benefited from it.

COPING WITH SEPARATION

It is not necessarily the adolescent dog who becomes over-anxious when separated from his owner, but it is a relatively common behavioral problem that may well get worse at this time. Separation anxiety may be expressed in different ways.

• A pup may become destructive when he is left on his own.
• You may come home to find your pup has urinated or defecated in the house.
• The neighbors may alert you to the fact that your pup has been continuously barking while you have been away.

All forms of behavior are equally antisocial, and you can be certain that they will only become worse if you do not try to find a solution.

The pup who becomes distressed when he is left has the opposite problem to the dominant dog. Instead of trying to empower himself and challenge your authority, he is saying, "Help! I am not confident enough to be left on my own without the protection of my leader". This may seem very touching, but, as we have seen, the consequences of this insecurity are far from appealing.

If you have followed the advice given in earlier chapters, your pup should never experience separation anxiety. He is used to being left alone for short periods, and he is confident that you will return. If, for whatever reason, your pup has failed to accept periods of solitude, you can tackle the problem in the following ways.

• Invest in an indoor crate. If your pup is confined, he cannot be destructive and he is a lot less likely to soil his own bed.
• Train your pup to go into his crate (see page 97), and gradually increase the amount of time he is left. It may help if you feed your pup in his crate so that he starts to see it as a special safe place.
• Buy some boredom-busting toys (see page 65). These are an excellent way of keeping your pup occupied while you are away. If he is busy trying to get treats out of his toy, he will have no time to bark or to be destructive.

- It may help if you leave a radio playing. The sound of human voices may act as reassurance.
- When you go out, make as little fuss as possible so that your pup does not become tense.
- Try a few mock departures, going out for a few minutes, and then returning so your pup is kept guessing.
- When you return, do not rush up to the crate and make a huge fuss of your pup. Be quiet and calm, and maybe wait a few moments before releasing him. This will help to take all the tension out of comings and goings.
- Work at your training, giving exercises in which you know your pup will be successful. This will help to build up his confidence.

When you are at home, make sure your pup spends some time away from you. A stairgate is a useful way of shutting your pup in one room, but allowing him to see you in an adjoining room. Your pup will learn to settle without needing to be in close proximity to you.

If you have an anxious pup, do not give in to him because you feel sorry for him. Separation anxiety not only results in antisocial behavior, it means your pup is unhappy and insecure – a far cry from the outgoing, confident dog that you wish to share your life with.

TROUBLESHOOTING

Hopefully, your pup will soon outgrow the agonies of adolescence, and will mature into a calm and settled adult. However, if your pup or adult dog shows any changes in behavior that you cannot cope with, do not delay in seeking advice from the professionals.

Chapter 23

The Question
Of Neutering

By the time your puppy reaches adolescence, you will need to decide whether altering (neutering) is a sensible option. This is a big decision, so you will need to weigh up the pros and cons, and evaluate the implications for both health and behavior.

THE FEMALE CYCLE

Female dogs, or bitches, become sexually mature soon after six months of age. Smaller breeds, especially the Toy breeds, are often later, but most bitches should have their first season by the time they are one year old. Thereafter they will have a season approximately every four to twelve months, averaging every six months.

The season is characterized by a swollen vulva, with a small bloody discharge, although in some cases this can be quite copious. There may also be an increase in frequency of urination. The day that the bloody discharge is first seen should be counted as day '1' of the season.

Ovulation normally occurs between the 11th and 13th day of the season, and this is the time when the bitch is receptive to a mate. However, ovulation can be early or even markedly delayed. I knew of a Greyhound who got pregnant on the 26th day of her season. The variation in the exact timing of fertility can make mating a 'hit or miss' affair – particularly if you are planning to travel a long distance to find a suitable stud dog.

To determine more accurately the exact day on which mating should occur, blood samples can be taken on alternate days, looking at levels of progesterone. Around the time of ovulation, progesterone drops markedly.

The bitch, although only fertile for a few days, will be 'attractive' to males for the duration of her season. This can lead to some tricky social problems, particularly if there are both male and female dogs in the same household.

A bitch will continue to have seasons throughout her life; female dogs do not go through a menopausal phase.

SPAYING

Neutering a female dog (spaying) has a number of pros and cons, but on balance the benefits outweigh the problems. The main reasons for spaying are to:

1. Prevent seasons
2. Prevent accidental mating (misalliance)
3. Eliminate false pregnancies
4. Prevent pyometra and endometritis
5. Decrease the chances of mammary tumors
6. Tackle other medical conditions, e.g. diabetes and vaginal hyperplasia.

The surgery involves removing both the ovaries and the uterus, i.e. it is an ovario-hysterectomy. This is different to humans, as in dogs the ovaries are removed to prevent future potential seasons.

Spaying can be carried out at a young age (in the USA from 3-4 months) or after the bitch has had a season. There is an argument that if a female is spayed before she has had a first season, then she is more likely to become incontinent. If she has had a season, then it is best to wait three to four months before having her spayed. There are two reasons for this:

• To ensure that her uterus and the associated blood vessels, etc. are at their most inactive.
• To ensure that she is not spayed whilst being pregnant, or even having a false pregnancy.

The operation is almost always only a 'one day at the surgery' affair. The incision is made in the middle of the abdomen at the bottom, or higher up on the flank. The flank approach is more common in America. The wound will normally be stitched, and stitches will need to be removed about ten days post-operatively.

HEALTH BENEFITS

Apart from the obvious advantages of eliminating seasons, and potential accidental mating resulting in unwanted puppies, the main reason for neutering is to diminish the likelihood of mammary tumors (or breast cancer) and prevent uterine infections.

Mammary tumors: These are extremely common in entire (un-neutered) females. In fact, a study has shown that 90 per cent of entire bitches develop mammary tumors by the time they are ten years old – a frightening statistic.

However, if a bitch is neutered before she has a single season, she is unlikely to ever develop mammary tumors.

Pyometra: The other main medical reason for spaying is to eliminate the possibility of pyometra. Pyometra means 'pus in the uterus', and it is literally that. It is an infection of the uterus that occurs more commonly in older dogs, usually appearing four to six weeks after they have been in season. It can take two forms – an open pyometra or a closed pyometra.

In an open pyometra, the cervix reopens, allowing the pus formed in the uterus to discharge from the vagina. A creamy-white vaginal discharge is seen. Treatment may involve antibiotics, and possibly surgery. However, in a closed pyometra, the cervix remains closed and so the pus builds up in the uterus. This quickly becomes an urgent surgical condition – involving surgical removal of the uterus in an anesthetised sick dog. It is obviously a risky operation. The largest uterus full of pus I have ever removed weighed just over 9 kilograms.

False pregnancies: These can occur four to nine weeks after a previous season. The bitch will show signs associated with pregnancy, even though she has not conceived. The signs range from mammary development, with or without milk production, to nest-making, and even straining. Unfortunately some of the behavioral changes can be antisocial, such as possessiveness. A false pregnancy can be easily treated with a range of different drugs, but the preferred treatment is spaying. It is important not to spay the bitch while she is having a false pregnancy, as it may lead to recurrent false pregnancies.

Other medical conditions prevented or cured by spaying include cystic ovaries, vulval abnormalities and vaginal prolapse (particularly in giant dogs). Bitches that develop diabetes should always be spayed, as this may effect a cure. The high levels of circulating hormone that occur after a season can be one of the hormonal triggers of diabetes.

REASONS AGAINST SPAYING

There are some downsides to having your bitch neutered. These include:

She has to have an operation

As spaying involves opening up the abdomen, whatever way the surgery is done, there is always the possibility of some operative and post-operative complications. It is important to discuss these with your veterinarian to allay any fears you might have.

In bitches that are spayed young, there is the potential for incomplete development of the vagina to occur – leaving the dog with a small, almost involuted, vulva. This can act as a source of local infection, and it is sensible in dogs that have very small vulvas to allow them to have a single season prior to neutering.

She will have an increased predisposition to putting on weight

All bitches are prone to putting on weight after they have been neutered. However, careful dietary management can prevent obesity problems developing. As a rough guide, it is sensible to decrease a bitch's food by approximately one-third after she has been spayed. Where possible, an increase in exercise will also help.

She may develop some coat changes

There is a link between estrogen and the coat quality – and in removing the ovaries you are removing a large amount of the natural circulating estrogens. However, the adrenal glands normally take over producing some estrogens. In some breeds, for example Cocker Spaniels and Irish Setters, they may develop a thinner, wispy coat after spaying. This can be corrected by supplementing the diet with essential fatty acids, e.g. Evening Primrose Oil.

There is some link to urinary incontinence

Urinary incontinence has two factors that are important in its development. One is a lack of circulating estrogens, and the other is a bladder that is positioned too far back in the abdomen. The naturally occurring estrogens in the body are related to the sphincter muscle mechanism at the exit of the bladder – i.e. the hormone helps maintain a watertight seal. After spaying, a decrease in the levels of this hormone, combined with an abnormal positioning of the bladder, can lead to incontinence. Another possible consequence is that spaying may disrupt the anatomical position of the bladder, perhaps due to adhesions, thus leading to incontinence. This type of incontinence can easily be treated.

THE MALE DOG

Male dogs become sexually mature soon after six months. Most dogs are born with their testicles partially descended. They soon descend into the scrotum, and are normally present by twelve weeks of age. However, a 'retained' testicle can still descend at any time up to six months of age.

The testicles act as the source of the hormone testosterone. This is the hormone that produces many of the male characteristics. These include:

- Territorial aggression
- Aggression
- Wandering
- Hypersexuality
- Dominance.

Males can be castrated from six months of age. The surgical procedure includes complete removal of both testicles, from a single incision just in front of the scrotum. The scrotum is left behind, and so an 'empty' sac remains. It is normally a 'day-patient' operation, and the dog is ready to go home in the evening. The wound will be stitched, and the stitches will need to be removed after about ten days.

MALE BEHAVIOR

The main reasons for castrating a dog are to prevent or diminish aggression, and to decrease sexually related antisocial behavior. The aggression may be in the form of aggression to other dogs, or people, or just excessive territorial defending.

Castration as a method of treatment for these problems is contentious, with many people having very strong opinions. Other methods of treatment which should also be considered include chemical castration using progestogens. Firm discipline, improved training, and increased exercise can all play a part in altering antisocial behavior. So it also worth consulting a behaviorist before deciding on surgery.

Castration will diminish wandering, the situation where an entire male, who can smell a bitch in season, may go off in search of her. A dog can smell a bitch in season up to three miles (5 kms) away – that's the power of lust!

Neutering a male also helps diminish domination problems. A dog in a family situation will see the family as part of his pack – i.e. he sees us as all dogs. There will be a pecking order within that pack, and an entire male dog will feel he should have a top-ranking place – in fact, he would like to be at the top. It is important that the dog should accept his inferior status at the bottom of the pack in order to avoid problems of aggression.

HEALTH BENEFITS

There are also some medical reasons for neutering male dogs. These include:

- Testicular cancers
- Hypersexuality
- Anal adenomas
- Prostatic problems.

TESTICULAR CANCERS

This cancer is more common in older dogs. Depending on exactly where the cancer is positioned in the testicle, the tumor can lead to either feminization of the dog (because female hormones begin to be produced), or to excessive production of testosterone.

There are three types of testicular cancer:
1. Interstitial cell tumors, the most common kind. It frequently causes no change in the size of the testicle and so is often not diagnosed. It is not malignant, but may cause prostatic problems.
2. Seminoma, which occurs most commonly in middle-aged and old dogs. It causes a marked enlargement of one of the testes. It can spread elsewhere.

3. Sertoli cell tumor, again more common in middle-aged and older dogs. There is no change in the size of the testicle, but the tumor can produce female hormones, thus leading to feminization. It is the most common tumor found in retained testes.

Fortunately, the predisposition to malignancy is far less than in humans. In fact, most canine testicular cancers are benign.

In dogs that have an undescended testicle, the retained testicle is far more likely to become cancerous, particularly if the missing testicle is still within the abdomen. If this missing testicle has not descended by the time the dog is six months old, it should definitely be removed. However, in these cases, there is no reason to remove the other testicle. The 'retained testicle' is an inherited condition – and dogs with this condition should not be used at stud.

REASONS AGAINST CASTRATING

There are some downsides to neutering a male dog. A neutered male is more prone to putting on weight. The hormone testosterone acts as a metabolic hormone, and so helps to keep the dog lean. However, reducing food by one-third after castrating the dog should help maintain fitness.

The most common reason for not wishing to castrate a male dog is anthropomorphic – it is often the men in the family who feel sorry for the dog and sympathize with him! This type of sentiment should be ignored, and the decision to neuter should be taken after evaluating health and behavioral benefits for the dog.

Part 10
Health Care

Canine Anatomy

The dog is a mammal. He is a hunter, descended from wild dogs and wolves. Man first started to domesticate dogs in the Stone Age, and it was soon found that the dog's sense of social hierarchy could be exploited so that they would accept man as their pack leader.

Anatomically, dogs are designed as fast runners and hunters, although specialized breeding has meant that some breeds of dogs (e.g. the Dachshund) may not be too successful at running, while others may not be all that successful at hunting (e.g. the Bulldog).

THE HEAD

The skull is elongated with a small brain set well back in the cranium. The size of the brain varies, but a Greyhound's brain is approximately 10cm long. The length of the nose depends upon the breed. Long-nosed breeds are called **dolichocephalic**, while short-nosed breeds are called **brachycephalic**.

Dogs have an acute sense of smell, as well as good hearing. Short-nosed dogs tend to have more problems with breathing, due to the cluttered anatomical structuring in their nose and the large soft palate at the back of their throat. Their nose often occluded, making it difficult for them to get air into the lungs. This occlusion becomes even more marked in warm weather when the lining of the nose expands, making breathing even harder.

Long-nosed dogs, however, also suffer problems – the long nose often acts as a trap for foreign bodies.

THE EYES

The eyes of herbivores (e.g. rabbits) are always positioned at the side of the skull so that they can watch for predators, while the eyes of the hunters are always positioned 'forwards' so that they can see their prey, and determine how far away they are. In all dogs, the eyes are situated so that they point forwards. Eyesight depends upon the breed of dog, tending to be less acute in the small, short-nosed breeds.

At the middle corner of the eye (the **medial canthus**) is the entrance to the **tear duct**. There are two holes in each eye that lead to a pipe (the tear duct) that drains the tears away from the eye. The duct leads to the end of the dog's nose. This is one of the reasons for dogs having a wet nose. This is very commonly blocked in the short-nosed breeds, where the duct may have a 'kink' in it. Blockage of the duct means that tears, having nowhere else to go, can spill over and down the skin below the eye.

THE EARS

The ears are made up of outer, middle and inner parts. The **outer ears** vary depending on the breed. In some, such as the German Shepherd Dog, the ears are erect, sticking upwards like an inverted funnel. In other breeds, the ears face downwards, e.g. Spaniels. If the ear falls down, it can block the circulation of air in the outer ear, causing a build-up of 'stagnant' earwax. This leads to the typical, chronic problems of the Spaniel ear. The outer ear carries sound waves to the middle ear.

The **middle ear** contains three small bones (the malleus, incus and stapes) that transmit these sound waves to the inner ear.

The **inner ear** contains the hearing nerves, the cochlear apparatus, as well as the organs of balance, the vestibular apparatus.

THE TEETH

The teeth have been designed to assist the dog in catching prey and then eating meat and bones. The long, large **canine** teeth straddle the small incisors. Their purpose is to assist the dog in clinging on to any prey that he might have caught. The **incisors** are designed for gnawing flesh from bones. Further back, behind the **premolars** and **first molars**, are the large **carnassial**, or bone-crunching, teeth.

Of course, a puppy is not born with these large teeth. Most puppies are born without any teeth at all. Milk teeth, 28 in total, erupt soon after birth. At four to six months, they are replaced by 42 permanent teeth. In dogs with long muzzles, there may be a considerable gap between the teeth; in short-nosed dogs, there is often overcrowding of teeth which may also have shallow roots. In addition, some of the teeth may be set at an angle. As a result, dental problems are more common in the shorter-nosed breeds.

THE SKIN AND COAT

The coat of the dog is covered in fur. There are two types of hair: a thick, longer, guard hair, and a finer more 'downy' undercoat. The relative presence of these two types of fur varies depending upon the breed of dog. The larger hairs act as a waterproof barrier, as well as a protective layer, while the finer hairs act as a warm jumper.

Theoretically, dogs should shed their coat twice a year, However, with central heating, most house dogs often lose their coat all year round. Some breeds need to have their coat clipped, others stripped – and some do not shed hairs at all.

There are no sweat glands in the canine skin. This means that a dog must lose heat in another way, and this is usually achieved by panting.

THE LIMBS

The legs of a dog were originally designed for fast running. However, selective breeding has created an enormous variation in size and shape of limbs. As a general rule, dogs with very large, long limbs tend to suffer more problems. They are particularly vulnerable during the growing period. Some of the giant breeds grow at such a fast rate – from 28 ins (70 cms) to 59 ins (1.5 m) in height in just a few months – that developmental abnormalities can easily occur. Such abnormalities include problems such as Osteochondrosis Dessicans (OCD), hip dysplasia, and panosteitis (see Chapter 27: A–Z of Canine Disorders and Diseases). In small Toy breeds, these developmental conditions are not common.

Every dog has five toes on the front feet, four main toes and a dewclaw. However, the hind feet may only have four (with no dewclaws present), five toes (dewclaws present), or even six toes (two dewclaws, e.g. the Pyrenean Mountain Dog). In many cases, particularly in working breeds, the dewclaws are removed in the first three days of life, as they can 'catch' and cause problems.

THE ABDOMEN (TUMMY)

The abdomen contains the intestines, reproductive organs, liver, kidneys and spleen.

The liver is tucked up under the ribs, resting behind the diaphragm. It is normally difficult to feel the liver; often it can only be felt when it is enlarged or has been displaced backwards. The liver has multiple functions, and so is often one of the organs most commonly disrupted during a disease process.

Immediately behind the liver is **the stomach**, lying slightly to the right of the midline. Its exit (the pylorus) lies in the middle. The position of the stomach is important because in large breeds, e.g. the Irish Wolfhound, the stomach can have sufficient room to twist on its own axis. The effect of this twist is to block both the entrance and the exit of the stomach. The food contents in the stomach then begin to ferment, causing a dilated and balloon-like stomach. As it is rotated, this is most commonly noticed on the left-hand side. This is an urgent condition, often requiring surgery.

The stomach empties into the small intestine, the duodenum. Here the **pancreas** and the **gall bladder** empty their secretions into the gut. The pancreas produces the enzymes necessary for digesting food and the gall bladder produces bile.

The **small intestine** empties into the **large intestine**, and at this junction there is a small vestigial caecum or **appendix**. The appendix does not tend to cause any problems.

There are two **kidneys** and the right kidney is placed slightly further forwards than the left. They are tucked up under the muscles of the back, with the right one partially hidden by the ribs. Their main function is elimination of waste products. Each kidney produces urine, which is then carried to the bladder by **ureters**. The two ureters lie just beneath the lumbar muscles. Insertion of one or both ureters into the bladder at the wrong place can be revealed as incontinence.

The **bladder** lies at the back end of the abdomen, just in front of the pelvis. In a bitch, it empties via the urethra into the **vagina**. In the male, it empties via the urethra, passing through the middle of the prostate and out through the **penis**. The **prostate** is located in the pelvic region and has the rectum passing over it. In consequence, any prostatic problems rapidly lead to pain on passing motions or urine. Pain is felt in the upper caudal end of the abdomen.

The **spleen** lies low down in the middle of the abdomen. It acts as a reservoir of blood that can empty large amounts of red blood cells into the bloodstream when there is a sudden need.

THE THORAX (CHEST)

The thorax contains the **lungs** and the **heart**. It is a bony box designed to protect these vitals organs, bounded by the spine on top, ribs either side and the sternum below. These bones act as a protective coat, as well as a supportive structure for the movement required in breathing.

Separating the chest from the tummy is a muscular wall called the diaphragm. It is the forward and backward movement of the diaphragm that acts as the driving force for breathing. However, there is some assistance from the inward and outward movement of the ribs; the whole process is complicated by being linked to a dog's movement, especially when running.

The heart lies in the middle of the chest, with one lung either side. It is easiest to hear the heart sounds with a stethoscope placed just behind each elbow. The average heart rate of a dog depends upon his size, larger dogs having a slower heart rate than smaller ones. The normal heart rate is approximately one hundred beats per minute.

Chapter 25

Health Care Programs

The health of your dog is in your hands – you provide his home and you are responsible for all his needs. To ensure that you have a healthy and happy dog, it is important to prevent as many problems and diseases as possible.

There are a number of areas in which good dog management can prevent problems, namely:

- Diet
- Control of internal parasites
- Control of external parasites
- Vaccinations
- Neutering
- Dental care
- Foot care
- Training.

DIET

The old saying 'We are what we eat' has a great deal of truth in it, and it can certainly be applied to dogs. Diet in dogs of all ages is critically important. In one piece of research, it was shown that over 30 per cent of dogs presented at veterinary surgeries are overweight with all the concurrent problems that follow. Even more problems are dietary-related, such as kidney failure, diabetes or heart disease.

Good dietary management needs to start from the first day your new puppy walks through the door. It is vitally important that you start as you mean to go on. There are many different ways to feed your dog and it is important to find one that suits both your lifestyle and the type of dog you have.

However, as a basic rule, never forget that a dog is a dog – definitely not a cat (so do not feed on cat food!).

Different breeds also have different dietary requirements. This is particularly true of the large/giant breeds, where a lower level of calcium and phosphorus is required in the food. Don't forget that these giant breeds grow from just a few hundred grams in weight to over sixty kilograms within eight months.

All puppies require higher levels of protein, carbohydrate, vitamins and minerals than adult dogs, so, once your dog has reached maturity, his diet needs to be altered to a maintenance version. Again, his dietary requirements change as he gets older, and dogs are generally classified as being senior when they get to seven years old (slightly earlier in large breeds).

At this older age, a dog is in a state of catabolism (breaking down), rather than anabolism (building up), and so requires lower levels of protein and carbohydrate but higher levels of fibre in the diet. By balancing intake with age and lifestyle, common problems such as obesity can be avoided. Finally, as a dog gets older, his year-on-year requirements get less (a 90-year-old human eats a lot less than a 30-year-old).

It is sensible to get good professional advice on diet as soon as you get your new puppy so that you start as you mean to go on.

CONTROL OF INTERNAL PARASITES

Routine worming is a critical part of the preventative measures that can be carried out at home. Puppies pick up worms from their mother, in the uterus, before they are even born. They then pick up more in the mother's milk. The worm burden is reduced by good worming of the mother during pregnancy. Ideally, she should be wormed from day 40 of the pregnancy until two days after the puppies are born.

However, it is safe to assume that your puppy has worms. At this stage, we are particularly concerned with the large, fleshy **roundworms** – *Toxocara* and *Toxacaris*. These worms take three weeks to develop from eggs into adults capable of laying more eggs. Therefore, the aim is to kill the worms before they are able to lay any more eggs, i.e. to worm every two to three weeks. This should continue until the pup is twelve weeks old as, each time you worm him, you will not succeed in killing all the worms.

After twelve weeks of age, a fecal sample can be checked for worm eggs, and, if necessary, worming can be repeated.

Once your puppy starts to go out and about, different types of worms become a problem, including **tapeworms**, **pinworms** and **threadworms**. As a routine, it is sensible to worm him every three to four months with a 'multi' wormer – i.e. a wormer that will kill all the different types of worms. If you do not wish to worm him, then get a fecal sample checked routinely for any parasite eggs.

In the USA, there is one other parasite that needs to be controlled – the canine **heartworm** *Dirofilaria immitis*. Heartworm is one of the more important conditions seen in dogs in the USA, but rarely seen in the UK. Having said that, it is seen in quarantine kennels, and, with the advent of the Pet Passport Scheme, may well be seen more frequently in the UK.

The heartworm parasite has an unusual life cycle. The adult worm, growing up to 6-10 ins (15-25 cms) long, lives in the heart. The female produces live young called micro filariae. These circulate in the bloodstream, especially in the peripheral circulation. When a mosquito bites the dog, it ingests the larvae with the blood. When it bites another dog, it spreads the parasite to the new dog.

Once a dog has been infected with adult worms, treatment is difficult, and so prevention is all-important. Control includes using a drug that will kill the migrating larvae before they reach the heart. Usually, this is in the form of a tablet given monthly.

EXTERNAL PARASITES

CONTROL OF FLEAS
Flea control is a top priority. Once your puppy goes out into the world, flea infestation is virtually inevitable. A pup can pick them up from other dogs, from cats, and from hedgehogs and other wildlife. In fact, it is only the dog and cat flea that will actively reproduce, but the other types of flea can give a nasty bite to both you and your dog.

The Life Cycle
The flea life cycle is fairly straightforward, but it is important to understand it, so that you take effective preventative measures. The adult flea must have a blood meal before laying eggs, i.e. it must bite the dog. It will then lay its eggs – up to 50 eggs a day in total. These may stick on to the dog's coat, but they often fall off into his bedding or on to the carpet. The egg hatches and, after going through several larval phases, pupates.

Finally, the pupa hatches into a new adult flea. The timescale for this development depends upon the ambient temperature in the home, but is normally between 12 and 174 days. This newly emerged flea then looks for a new host to bite!

Prevention And Treatment
The important fact to remember is that most of the flea's life cycle takes place off your dog – but in your home. In fact, for every flea on the dog there are 100 in the home! This is why prevention is so important. If you can stop the fleas before they get into your home, it makes life much more comfortable all round.

There are a large number of products on the market at present, and it is worth discussing the options with your veterinarian.

Treatment can be in the form of oral medication, which prevents the flea from completing its life cycle, along with a spray or powder which will kill any adult fleas that are present. Insecticidal baths can be used, but this is not a lasting treatment. A spot-on treatment disperses a chemical through the fat layer of the skin, and will give protection for around two months.

If your puppy does pick up some fleas, it is important to treat both him and the home. If you only treat the pup, you will leave generations of fleas in the home, waiting to re-infect him.

TICKS

A dog living in the country may pick up ticks from sheep or deer. In urban areas, the hedgehog is the primary host. In the USA, ticks are the carriers of Lyme disease, so preventative measures are very important. There is a wide variety of products available, so ask your vet for advice.

LICE

This is not a widespread problem, but where lice do occur, the dog will suffer intense itching. Insecticidal baths are recommended, although insecticidal sprays also work.

HARVEST MITES

It is generally the dog's head and feet that are affected by these tiny, red mites. Infestation usually occurs if a dog has been walking in fields and woods. Ask your vet to recommend a spray or an insecticidal shampoo.

VACCINATIONS

In general, most puppies are vaccinated against the following five diseases.

- Canine Parvovirus
- Canine Adenovirus I, (Canine Hepatitis)
- Leptospirosis
- Canine Distemper
- Parainfluenza.

In many countries, it is also mandatoty to vaccinate against rabies, and if your dog is going into boarding kennels he may have to be vaccinated against kennel cough.

Vaccinations for the five main diseases tend to be given together, in a single injection.

The timing of your puppy's first injections varies, depending on the incidence of disease in your area, and the policy of the veterinary practice. The aim is to achieve full vaccination as early as possible so that your puppy can start socializing. However, every puppy acquires maternally derived antibodies (MDA) in the first milk (colostrum), which provide a level of cover against disease for the first few weeks of life. It is important not to vaccinate while these are still active.

Normally, vaccinations are started between eight and nine weeks of age, and then a second vaccination is given at between eleven and twelve weeks. There is great variation between the claims of the different vaccinations as to when a puppy is fully protected against the diseases they cover, so it is important to check with your veterinarian how soon your puppy can go out. To maintain the required level of immunity, your dog will need to have an annual vaccination, to top up the levels of antibodies. This is known as a 'booster'.

There is currently much discussion regarding the need for vaccinations, and the possible side effects. Every dog owner must make their own mind up, preferably after discussions with the veterinarian. My feelings on the subject are simple: if you vaccinate 100,000 dogs and have problems with 100, that is a great pity. But, if you do not vaccinate those 100,000 dogs, many may well die from diseases that are preventable.

If you decide not to continue with annual booster vaccinations, it is important to take your dog in for an annual check-up – this provides the opportunity to pick up problems and prevent them becoming more serious.

Kennel cough is one of the vaccinations that is often not given routinely. This disease is caused by a bacteria (Bordetella bronchiseptica) and a virus (Canine Adenovirus 2). They gain entry via the nose, multiply there and then spread down into the throat to cause laryngitis and tracheitis (a sore throat). This vaccination is unusual in that it is delivered via the nose – to provide a local immunity to stop the bugs multiplying to begin with.

Dogs contract this disease from close contact with other dogs, especially in a 'strained' environment, e.g. kennels. However, a dog can contract the disease anywhere, for example at a dog show or when out walking. This vaccine only lasts for six months and so needs to be repeated twice yearly.

Rabies is commonly vaccinated against in the USA, but not in the UK, which is still a rabies-free country. However, now that the UK has introduced the Pet Passport Scheme, rabies vaccination is becoming more common and usually requires one or two injections, then an annual booster.

NEUTERING
See Chapter 23 for information on the health benefits associated with neutering.

DENTAL CARE
Caring for your dog's teeth is critical. Dogs will not brush their teeth on their own, and so you must do it for him. The earlier you start the better, so that both he and you get into the habit. Always use a proper dog toothpaste and brush. Your veterinarian should give you some tips on how to make it fun and easy (see page 117).

FOOT CARE
As your puppy gets older, the nails may not wear down properly, especially if he never

exercises on hard ground/roads. Nails that are too long cause great discomfort, and may even result in lameness.

People are often daunted about clipping their dog's toenails. However, provided you are always careful and do not take off too much in one go, then it is simple enough (see page 118). Ask an experienced dog owner or your vet to show you what to do the first time. The important thing is to look for the quick, and then to allow a couple of millimeters beyond that. This can be quite tricky in black dogs, where the nails will also be black and the quick, which carries the blood supply, is hard to see.

TRAINING

Training is one of the most important aspects of preventative health care. It is important for your quality of life, as well as your dog's, that he is as well adjusted socially as possible, and that he is a good, responsible member of society. This does not necessarily mean that he can perform a series of obedience exercises; it is more important that he is able to cope with any situation.

Socialization should start as early as possible. From the first day you get your puppy, teach him how to be examined by you, paying particular attention to his feet, ears, eyes and mouth. This will make life easier on occasions when you need to give medication, or when you try to remove a thorn from his foot.

Take your dog to a club for training, and ask your veterinarian whether he holds puppy socialization parties. The most important thing – and I cannot stress it enough – is that the more your puppy experiences, the more well balanced and adaptable he will be.

Chapter 26

First Aid And The Medicine Chest

Most dogs are athletic, though of course this depends on their shape, size and weight. As a general rule, the larger dogs are more athletic, and so are more prone to athletic injuries.

These particularly include musculoskeletal injuries, i.e. damage to the muscles or bones. When emergencies do occur, they often happen at a most inconvenient place and time – so it is well worth always being prepared.

First-aid Measures

There is a vast range of injuries that can befall a dog, and it is important to become conversant with basic first aid to avoid panic. However, your first priority should always be to try and contact professional help. So always carry the telephone number of your veterinarian with you.

Having contacted help, there are some basic first-aid measures that can be carried out while either waiting for help to arrive, or while travelling to the surgery. These include:

- Controlling bleeding
- Prevention of infection
- Basic stabilization of fractures
- Minimizing swelling
- Providing relief of pain
- Maintaining fluid intake (where appropriate)
- Controlling body temperature
- Maintaining an open airway.

The order of this list is not significant, and the order in which you should assess the priorities of treatment varies from case to case. However, as a rule of thumb, your priority in acutely traumatic cases should be to assess:

> A – for AIRWAY, has the dog got an open viable airway (see later)?
> B – for BREATHING, is the dog breathing?
> C – for CARDIAC, is the heart still working?

These are known as the ABC of emergencies, and are the first three things you should always check in acute emergencies, such as a road traffic accident. After checking for these, you can then assess the other areas.

CONTROLLING BLEEDING

Bleeding can be controlled by simply putting a finger on a single source of bleeding, and holding it there. It can also be controlled using a pressure bandage that is wrapped over the source of blood. Ideally, a double thickness of cotton wool (cotton) can be held in place over the site by a bandage. The bandaging does not need to look like a work of art – it just needs to hold the 'finger' in place.

If there is severe bleeding from a limb, particularly if it is near the foot, then a temporary tourniquet can be applied above the injury. Any tourniquet should only be left in place for a maximum of 15 minutes. If it has stayed in place for longer, loosen it for a few minutes every 15 minutes.

Once the dressing has been applied, do not be tempted to remove it or change it for at least an hour. You may dislodge the blood clot and start the bleeding again.

If the limb is raised, so that it is higher than the body, this will also help to stop the bleeding. Veterinary help should be sought as soon as possible.

PREVENTION OF INFECTION

Prevention of infection is desirable where practical. Obviously, you will not have access to antibiotics, but basic cleaning of a wound with lots of clean, fresh water will help remove contaminants such as dirt, etc.

If a wound needs stitching, the sooner veterinary attention is sought the better. While waiting for help, cover the wound with an appropriate dressing (e.g. Melolin) to prevent further contamination.

If a wound does not need stitching, e.g. a graze or scratch, then clean with a safe and reliable antiseptic. Use Hibitane solution diluted 1:1000 in water, or Betadine diluted 1:10 in water, or, if neither is available, use very dilute salty water. Soak a piece of clean cotton wool (cotton), clean the site with the disinfectant and then, where possible, cover with either a plaster or a bandage.

THE FIRST-AID KIT

This should contain the following items:

• Disinfectant, e.g. Hibitane

- Cotton wool (cotton)
- Melolin wound dressing (non-adherent)
- Bandages
- Blunt-ended scissors.

It is important to always seek professional help if you have any concerns about the injury.

BASIC STABILIZATION OF FRACTURES

Only lower limb and tail fractures lend themselves to emergency support. Even if you are unsure as to the presence of a fracture, it is better to err on the side of caution and support the injured area.

Good support can be easily achieved by wrapping the limb or tail in one or two towels and then binding these in place with bandages. Alternatively, cotton wool (cotton), two or three layers thick, can be used. However, in the case of a compound fracture, i.e. where bits of bone are sticking through the skin, the affected area should be covered in a sterile dressing first. Do not attempt to push the pieces of bone back under the skin, as this may increase contamination. Cover them with wet, sterile Melolin or a similar dressing, and then apply your stabilization bandage.

Makeshift splints can be constructed by using rulers, packing-case slats, or even blunt pencils in the case of small dogs. However, it is important not to bandage the hard splint in immediate contact with the skin, otherwise it may lead to increased discomfort.

In all cases of suspected fractures, it is important to seek immediate veterinary help. Delay in seeking help will cause unnecessary suffering, as well as decreasing the chances of a successful repair to the injury. The veterinary surgeon will determine the exact extent of the injury by palpation and probably by radiography (X-ray).

MINIMIZING SWELLING

Swelling around an injury is usually due to bleeding, or the accumulation of inflammatory fluids. The problem with swelling is that it increases pain, decreases movement, and can interfere with the healing process.

Swelling can be decreased by the application of ice-packs, or by cold water hosing. In large dogs, you can put the whole foot/leg into a bucket of cold water. The effect of this cold compress is to constrict the smaller blood vessels, assist blood clotting, and help remove the fluid from the area.

Ideally, the cooling treatment should be carried out for 10-15 minutes, and then repeated every hour until veterinary help arrives. If it is possible to bandage the area, apply the bandage after the first cold treatment, ensuring that the limb is dry first. However, be careful that your cooling treatment does not affect the dog's core temperature (see Controlling Body Temperature, page 208). If in any doubt, seek advice first.

PROVIDING PAIN RELIEF

There is more than just medical treatment involved in the relief of pain. Petting, stroking and talking to your dog will help relieve his anxiety and panic. It will also help to reduce the tension and fear associated with the injury. Don't forget that dogs have a strong bond with humans – they trust us. It is, however, important to remember that, when a dog is in great pain, he may not recognize you as his friend and may lash out and bite.

Do not give any medication until you have consulted with your veterinarian. He may advise that you can give some aspirin or paracetamol, but check first.

Where possible, place the dog in a quiet comfortable place while administering first aid. Avoid heat stress in hot weather, and keep the patient warm in cold weather.

MAINTAINING FLUID INTAKE

The first five steps outlined above apply to cases of trauma, such as a road traffic accident (RTA). However, sometimes first-aid measures are required in cases of disease.

In the disease process, a dog may become dehydrated, either as a result of decreased drinking or due to increased loss of fluids (e.g. diarrhea). The dehydration can be as debilitating as, or even more so than, the condition itself.

You can help by ensuring that the dog always takes in an adequate level of fluids. However, dogs will often be thirsty and may drink large quantities of water, and then bring it all back up. It is thus important to ensure that the dog drinks only small amounts, little and often.

If the dog will not drink on his own, then try syringing some fluids into his mouth. The fluid replacement can be improved by mixing one teaspoonful of salt and one tablespoonful of sugar with one pint of water. It is important to offer very small amounts of fluid at a time, and, if the dog is struggling, you should stop. This is not a treatment; it is purely a way of helping the dog's level of hydration while you await professional help

CONTROLLING BODY TEMPERATURE

In all cases of trauma or disease, it is essential to attempt to keep the body temperature stable. This may mean keeping the dog cool in the case of heat stroke (hyperthermia) by using fans, ice-packs, etc. But it is more likely to involve keeping the dog warm, and preventing shock and hypothermia. You can use hot-water bottles, wrapped in a towel to avoid burning, and blankets. Lots of tender loving care (TLC) will also help.

MAINTAINING AN OPEN AIRWAY

If a dog is having difficulty breathing, then every little thing that you can do may help. Remove his collar or harness, and talk to him quietly. If you comfort him, this will help to relax him, which will assist his breathing.

A road traffic accident is probably the most common emergency encountered. It is a highly stressful and emotional event, but your dog needs you to keep your wits about you. Time is often of great importance, and the sooner you get veterinary help the better.

Although we are trained not to move human road traffic accident patients, unless to safety, it is often advisable to move your dog as fast as possible to the veterinary surgery. I am often telephoned by people asking me to go to the site of a road traffic accident – but, in fact, you lose time by doing this.

In most cases, the vet will need to return to his surgery to initiate treatment. Few surgeries have fully-fitted veterinary ambulances, and so, as a general rule, it is better to get your dog to the vet as quickly as possible.

However, you must weigh up each individual case on its own merits – and it is worth discussing with your veterinarian what he, as an individual, would recommend.

The specific roadside treatment follows the guidelines discussed earlier – but speed is the all-important element.

A-Z Of Canine
Disorders And Diseases

Chapter 27

ABORTION OR MISCARRIAGE

This can occur as a result of trauma or minor developmental abnormalities; infections like a Herpes virus or a Streptococcus (a bacteria), or trauma from a man-made accident, such as a road traffic accident, are often also responsible.

The signs are easy to spot. The bitch may appear off-color, often with a temperature. There may be uterine contractions, a discharge from the vagina or the puppies may be expelled. If you see any of these signs, you should contact your vet as soon as possible.

ABSCESS

An abscess can result from trauma such as a bite or a claw wound, or be due to a foreign body, such as a grass seed, entering the body. The signs are localized pain, swelling, heat, with perhaps some discharge or pus. Often the dog will have a slight fever. If the abscess has burst, then treating with salty water and flushing it out may be sufficient.

However, if the abscess has not burst, it might need lancing, in which case you will need veterinary intervention. This may be followed up with some antibiotics and painkillers.

AGING OR SENILITY

Unfortunately this happens to all of us, and dogs are no exception. You will see a gradual slowing-down of activity, with decreased stamina – your dog may not be able to manage those long walks any more.

However, aging is really a combination of lots of little problems, which may include arthritis, dental disease, liver or kidney failure, cataracts in the eyes, or even heart disease.

There are lots of different types of medication that may help, and different combinations of them are used depending on the specific problem. Routine check-ups will often lead to early detection.

AGGRESSION

Aggression occurs most commonly in male dogs. It can be due to hormonal problems, nervous problems or even psychological problems.

The signs may be fighting other dogs, showing aggression towards people, or being over-zealous defending territory. One of the differential diagnoses, of course, is rabies.

There are many control methods for aggression, and improved training will certainly help. It is a good idea to seek the help of a reputable dog behaviorist. Castration may prove beneficial in male dogs (see Chapter 23: The Question of Neutering).

ALLERGY

An allergy is a hypersensitivity, and may be a reaction to a wide variety of things. The most common is an allergy to flea bites. However, allergies to food and furnishings appear to be becoming more common.

ALOPECIA (HAIR LOSS)

There are numerous causes of hair loss in dogs. These may be hormonal, such as hypothyroidism or growth hormone deficiency, or nutritional. External parasites, particularly fleas, are often to blame, but ringworm, burns, chemical irritants, infections and allergies can also produce the condition.

Depending on the cause of the hair loss, the treatment is variable. Treating the underlying cause, such as removing the fleas, is the most important element.

ANEMIA

There are two types of anemia: regenerative anemia where more red blood cells are being made. Non-regenerative anemia, where no replacement cells are made by the body. Regenerative anemia can occur when the dog is losing blood, such as in an accident. Other causes include poisoning, particularly with a Warfarin-type poison, or excessive parasitic infestation, such as with hookworm, lice or babesia (see Babesiosis).

Food poisoning, particularly with heavy metals like lead and zinc, can cause the condition, or a clotting defect (e.g. Von Willenbrand's disease, see page 237) may be to blame. Non-regenerative anemia is often the result of a dietary deficiency, in bone marrow diseases and in types of leukemia. The clinical signs of anemia are weakness and lethargy. The mucous membranes, just inside the mouth, look pale. If there is evidence of bleeding, an attempt should be made to stem the flow (see page 206).

Treatment depends upon the primary cause for the anemia. It should always be treated as an urgent condition.

ANAL ADENOMA (OR ADENOMATA)

These are tumors that occur underneath the tail or around the anus of older dogs. They can appear as multi-globular, firm, smooth and pale swellings.

The cause is unknown, but seems to be related to male hormones. Differential diagnosis includes anal gland abscesses, cysts and other types of cancerous growths.

Treatment involves removal of the tumor combined with castration, as these are more common in male dogs than female dogs. Other treatments can include the chemical use of estrogens.

ANAL FURUNCULOSIS

This skin condition is almost exclusively seen in German Shepherd Dogs and so there may be some hereditary predisposition. It is more commonly seen in dogs where the tail seems to be held tightly down over the anus, which may produce the correct microclimate in terms of temperature and bacteria to allow the furunculosis (ulcers) to develop. The cause is unknown, but it is probably related to the discharging of the anal gland into tissue around the rectum. The signs include straining (tenesmus), licking and rubbing of the area around the anus, an inflamed and eroded peri-anal skin, with areas of ulceration and holes (fistulae), developing. These may ooze pus.

Treatment is very difficult, but may include a course of antibiotics and painkillers. Removing the hair in the area to allow the air to come in and circulate can help, as does local cryo-surgery after removing infected areas. Removal of the anal glands may also improve the problem.

ANAL GLAND SACULITIS

The anal glands are a pair of glands situated either side of the anus at approximately four o'clock and eight o'clock positions. The glands are used by dogs for territorial marking. If the glands fail to empty, for instance when a dog has diarrhea, then the material within the gland can become impacted, leading to a bacterial infection of the gland. The signs are a classic 'scooting' along the ground causing local, self-inflicted injuries such as soreness around the anus. The dog may lick the area around the anus, or under the base of the tail, excessively, and he may experience pain on defecation.

If left untreated, abscessation of the anal gland can occur, together with a foul-smelling odor. Treatment includes emptying of the anal gland, which can be done at home after your being taught how to do it by a professional. In persistent cases, surgical removal of the anal gland may be required. Antibiotics and painkillers, or anti-inflammatories are sometimes required.

ARTHRITIS

Arthritis is inflammation of the tissues associated with a joint. It can be an acute arthritis, such as a sprained wrist or hock, or it can be a more chronic degenerative arthritis, such as the type found in old age. The causes can be due to excessive wear, poor joint conformation, or as a result of injury or infection. It can be immune-mediated, or it can be due to nutritional imbalance or deficiency.

The signs that are commonly seen are pain, possibly associated with lameness, stiffness when getting up, and a reluctance to go for a walk or to run around.

There are many different treatments depending on the cause. In younger animals, where the condition may be related to a development problem (see hip dysplasia and osteochondrosis dessicans or OCD), treatment may involve the use of glucosamines and chondroitin sulphates.

In older dogs, treatment may entail a change of lifestyle, usually less running and shorter walks – and it may involve a change in diet. It is better to try and keep the weight of the dog down. Medication may involve the use of non-steroidal anti-inflammatories. Acupuncture and homeopathy have a useful part to play in controlling arthritis.

ASPERGILLOSIS

Aspergillosis is a fungus that is present in the environment. Occasionally, the fungus may colonise the upper nasal tract of a dog, causing a chronic infection in the nose.

The signs include a copious pus and mucus discharge, and even nosebleeds (epistaxis). If the condition continues, it may lead to loss of weight, weakness and breathing problems. Differential diagnoses include foreign bodies up the nose, and other nasal problems leading to rhinitis, usually bacterial or viral. Cancer must also be eliminated. Specific tests include blood tests to look for antibodies for the aspergillus fungus, swabs taken for culture from the nose, radiography and possibly even MRI scans.

Treatment includes giving anti-bacterial antibiotics, anti-inflammatories, and some anti-fungal drugs have been developed. However, the prognosis without radical surgery is often not good.

BABESIOSIS (also known as piroplasmosis or infectious haemoglobinurea)

This is a disease caused by a parasite called Babesia canis. It is a blood-borne parasite transmitted by a tick called Ripicephalus sanguinus. The signs in the dog include a high temperature, anaemia and secondary jaundice (yellowing of the mucus membranes). In severe cases, it can be fatal. Specific diagnosis can be made by taking blood smears and having a look down the microscope where the small parasite can be seen. Prevention can be achieved by controlling the ectoparasite (the ticks) using a normal anti-parasiticide.

BALANITIS

Balanitis is the medical term given to a discharge from the prepuce of the penis. The signs include reddening or swelling of the prepuce. Discomfort can occur, with excessive licking of the penis. There may be a discharge which is sometimes pus-filled.

The causes can be a straightforward bacterial infection, a herpes viral infection, or overexcitement (hypersexuality). If a discharge is seen without any other obvious signs of inflammation or irritation, it can be considered normal.

BLINDNESS

There are many causes of blindness associated with all the different parts of the eye. The most common cause, as noticed by owners, is cataracts (see Cataracts, page 215).

The signs of blindness in a dog are often misleading, as dogs are highly capable of getting round the house by smell and sound alone. However, if the dog is stumbling or walking into objects, then blindness should be suspected and you should consult your veterinary surgeon.

BRONCHITIS

Bronchitis is inflammation of the bronchi and bronchioles – the small air passages that lead from the trachea to the lungs. The dog will usually suffer a chronic cough.

The causes can be bacterial or viral. However, irritants such as dust and smoke, or even excessive barking, can lead to chronic bronchitis.

Treatment includes anti-inflammatories and antibiotics as well as antitussives (drugs that will stop the dog from coughing). If the cause is parasitic (e.g. the lungworm filaroides), then endo-paraciticides are given. If the condition is caused by an inhaled foreign body, this might need to be removed either by using an endoscope or by surgery.

BRUCELLOSIS

Brucellosis, caused by the bacteria Brucella canis, is generally sexually transmitted.

The signs include the death of fetuses, leading to abortion, particularly round about the 50th day of pregnancy. If live puppies are born at full term, they may die soon afterwards. In the male, there may be inflammation of the testicle, infertility, or atrophy (shrinkage of the testicle). Treatment involves the use of antibiotics. However, in most countries there has been an attempt to eradicate this disease, and so treatment is not normally carried out.

BURSITIS

This can appear as soft or almost firm swellings (bursa) over the elbow. They are almost always painless except if they become infected. The skin over the area can become very thickened. They occur due to repetitive low-grade trauma, such as a heavy dog lying down repeatedly on a hard surface. The possible treatment can involve the removal of the fluid from the bursal sac. Painkillers can be given, as well as antibiotics. But most important is a change in lifestyle so that the dog avoids the repetitive trauma. In extreme cases, surgical removal of the bursa may be required.

CANINE DISTEMPER (HARD PAD)

This is caused by a Paramyxo virus, and often has secondary bacterial infections as complications.

Clinical signs include a high temperature, and the dog appears unwell and lethargic. He may have inflamed eyes (conjunctivitis); there may be respiratory or digestive tract or even nervous signs. For instance, there may be a rapid breathing rate, there may be vomiting or diarrhea, and there may be fits or even paralysis.

In chronic cases, there can be hyperkerotosis, which is an overgrowth of the hard pads in the feet and the nails – hence the name 'hard pad'.

Treatment involves treating the dog symptomatically (i.e. we treat the signs). For instance, if the dog has diarrhea, anti-diarrheal drugs would be needed. Good nursing is of critical importance, along with maintaining the vital functions of the dog. Medical help should be sought immediately. However, the prognosis or outlook is not good. There is a vaccine to prevent canine distemper (see page 202).

CANINE PARVOVIRUS (PARVO)

This is most commonly seen as a problem in young dogs, often in several puppies within the same litter. In young puppies, the signs might be a period of fast, difficult breathing with blueness of the mucus membranes and collapse. Death is often sudden.

In puppies and adults, infection can be characterized by vomiting and diarrhea. Often the diarrhea has a lot of blood in it, and it has an unmistakable smell. If the dog is untreated, he will dehydrate and die. Treatment is symptomatic. However, the outlook is poor, especially in younger animals. There is a vaccination available to prevent Parvovirus (see page 202).

CATARACTS

Cataracts are seen as a white, milky change in the lens of the eye. The causes can be inherited, or secondary to other inherited conditions, e.g. progressive retinal atrophy or glaucoma. They may also be caused by trauma to the eye. There is no specific medical treatment for cataracts. However, surgical removal (phaco-emulsification) is the best treatment. Under a general anaesthetic, a very small probe is put into the lens and it then sucks the cataract out.

CDRM (CHRONIC DEGENERATIVE RADICULO MYELOPATHY)

Also known as German Shepherd Syndrome, it is characterized as a progressive weakness of the hind legs with an inability to place the legs properly. There is desensitization of the limbs, so that, if the foot is knuckled over, the dog is unable to replace it. Worn toenails are often seen, as well as progressive muscle weakness on the back legs, and an inability of the dog to rise from a lying position. The cause is a failure of the nerves in the spinal cord that control the back legs. The condition is almost exclusively seen in large breeds, particularly in German Shepherd Dogs.

There is no specific treatment, apart from improving circulation to the back legs, and keeping the dog as fit and as strong as possible. The condition is often complicated by concurrent arthritis. The arthritis may well need to be treated so that the dog can continue with as active a life as possible.

CHOLANGIOHEPATITIS

This is an infection of the bile duct and of the liver. The clinical signs are a dull, depressed and quiet dog who is lethargic. There is often weight loss and poor appetite. The dog may vomit. As the condition progresses, a yellowing (or jaundice) of the mucus membranes in the mouth, and around the eyes, will be noticed.

Diagnosis is confirmed from blood samples. The causes are unknown, but are often related to infections from the small intestine spreading up the bile duct and into the liver. Treatment includes antibiotics, and often fluid-therapy in more severely affected cases. Vitamins may be given and sometimes anti-inflammatories, or steroids.

CHRONIC LIVER DISEASE OR CHRONIC LIVER FAILURE

Chronic liver failure can develop in older dogs as a result of numerous problems, most commonly infections, chemical-induced problems, cirrhosis or cancer.

The signs include a swollen abdomen (ascites), jaundice (yellowing around the eyes and in the mouth), weight loss and lethargy. Sometimes, behavioral changes will occur due to brain dysfunction, as a result of a build-up of breakdown product in the bloodstream. Diagnosis is made from blood tests, occasionally combined with radiography and ultrasonography. Biopsies of the liver may need to be taken.

Treatment includes specific symptomatic treatment, dietary changes and, possibly, long-term medication, including antibiotics, anabolic steroids and vitamins.

COLITIS

Colitis is a word for inflammation of the colon. The most common symptom of colitis is diarrhea, particularly with fresh blood in the feces, when it becomes called hemorrhagic colitis. The dog may be straining, passing small amounts of a mucus-covered and bloody diarrhoea.

The cause is multifactorial, but most commonly related to a dietary intolerance, either by eating a food that is too rich or by eating a food containing a toxin. However, some breeds of dogs are more prone to this (e.g. Histiocytic positive colitis is seen in Boxers). Stress can be a cause of colitis.

Treatment should involve starvation for 24-48 hours, and administering replacement fluids. Digestive tract calming drugs can be used, such as Kaolin; pro-biotics may also be helpful. If blood is present, you should consult your veterinarian. Antibiotics and anti-inflammatories may become necessary. If chronic colitis or irritable colon syndrome develop, then long-term dietary management is an important preventative measure. If in any doubt, seek expert help.

CONGESTIVE HEART FAILURE (CARDIAC INSUFFICIENCY)

This can occur due to congenital heart diseases, such as a puppy born with an arterial defect, e.g. patent ductus arteriosis. Or it might be an acquired heart disease, such as the progressive degeneration of the heart valves, which can start quite early in some dogs. This is known as endocardiosis.

The precise mechanism of the degeneration of these valves is uncertain. However, the prevalence and severity of the problem increases as the dog gets older. As the valves in the heart degenerate, they become less watertight, allowing congestion of blood in the major veins returning to the heart. This leads to congestion of fluid in the lungs, liver and abdomen. This condition is most frequently found in small breeds of dogs, particularly the Cavalier King Charles Spaniel, the Chihuahua, the Miniature Poodle, the Miniature Schnauzer and the Pekingese.

The symptoms include breathlessness, panting, exercise intolerance and a cough (known as the cardiac cough or heart cough), which occurs especially at night. The abdomen may become swollen with fluid (ascites), and the liver may become enlarged.

Treatment depends on the exact cause of the congestive heart failure, but includes cardiac drugs, plus changes in exercise and diet.

CONJUNCTIVITIS

Conjunctivitis is inflammation of the conjunctiva – the membranes around the eye. It is characterized by inflammation and reddening of these areas. There may be a discharge from the eye, which might contain pus. The eye may be swollen or partially shut, and the dog may rub his eye.

The causes are multiple, but include infection, presence of a foreign body, or trauma. Treatment depends upon the cause; veterinary assistance should always be sought.

CONSTIPATION

The signs of constipation in a dog are straining, irregular and painful passing of motions, or even the absence of motions. The feces may be hard or flattened. The dog may show pain around the anal area. The causes can be multifactorial, but the presence of a tumor or a foreign body, an enlarged prostate, a deformity of the pelvis, a hernia or a rupture are all possible.

Treatment depends on determining an exact cause of the problem. Laxatives, enemas, or even surgical treatments may be required.

COPROPHAGIA

This is the term given to dogs that eat their own feces. The causes can involve pancreatic problems, boredom, malnutrition, a low level of fiber in the diet, or possibly a high worm burden. Once deficiencies, parasites and disease have been eliminated, treatment should involve the regular removal of feces. The dog should also be encouraged to pass motions while exercising. The condition is quite commonly seen in bitches after whelping.

CORNEAL ULCERATION

This is where the outer layer at the front of the eye becomes ulcerated.

The signs include pain and closing of the eye. There may be a discharge from the eye, and there may be a local area of corneal opacity or cloudiness.

The causes include bacterial, viral and fungal infections, in-growing eyelashes or eyelids and, most commonly, trauma. Diagnosis is made using a small orange dye called Fluresceine that is retained in the ulcer after application.

Treatment includes topical antibiotics, and, in more complicated cases, surgery may be necessary. Sometimes contact lenses are placed over the ulcer to protect it while it heals.

CRANIAL MANDIBULAR OSTEOPATHY

This is a condition most commonly seen in the puppies of small-breed dogs, particularly West Highland White Terriers.

The signs include pain around the jaw, and the dog is hungry but unwilling to eat. The jaw may become swollen and, in the more extreme conditions, the dog may even have difficulty swallowing and breathing. Occasionally this can involve the bones of the legs and then the dog may show signs of lameness. The causes are unknown.

Diagnosis is confirmed using radiography. Treatment involves giving mild painkillers until the dog has matured. The condition is rarely seen in dogs over 12 months of age.

CYSTITIS

Cystitis is an infection of the bladder. The symptoms in the dog include frequent urination, straining when urinating, and producing very small quantities of urine. Blood may be found in the urine, and, occasionally, incontinence may occur.

The causes most commonly include an ascending bacterial infection or infections secondary to bladder stones, cancer, uterine infections or estrous (season).

Diagnosis is made from examination of the urine and determining what the underlying cause of the cystitis is. Treatment includes antibiotics, pain relief, and removing the underlying cause.

DEAFNESS

Deafness can be congenital, and is more common in some breeds such as Collies, Dalmatians, Cocker Spaniels, Boxers and Bull Terriers. Or the condition can be acquired, for instance, as a result of chronic ear infections or tumors.

Many older dogs become deaf without any obvious symptoms. An easy test is to stand behind the dog and clap your hands. Failure to respond often indicates deafness. A veterinary surgeon can carry out a more complex neurological test.

DEHYDRATION

The signs of dehydration include dry mucus membranes, a weak, lethargic dog, a rapid pulse, sunken eyes and loss of skin elasticity. When the skin is pulled up, it remains tented in an upright position rather than springing back to the normal flat skin.

If untreated, dehydration can become more severe, leading to collapse and death. The causes are multifactorial.

DEMODECTIC MANGE

This skin condition is caused by a mite called Demodex canis. It can occur as either localized skin lesions, particularly around the face and limbs, or it can be more generalized all over the body. A scaly, waxy skin condition, often associated with hair loss and some local itchiness (pruritis) and small spots, can develop.

Specific diagnosis is made from the appearance of the mange or by microscopic identification of the mite found in skin scrapings.

DERMATITIS (ECZEMA)

Dermatitis is the term used for skin inflammation and infection. It is characterized by reddening of the skin, heat, irritation and possibly thickening and dandruff. There might be production of an ooze and hair loss. Crusting may occur. The causes include parasitic infections, fungal infections, bacterial infections, food allergies, auto-immune skin diseases and self-inflicted trauma. Treatment is varied but may include creams, shampoos and antibiotics.

DERMATOPHYTOSIS

This is the correct name for ringworm. In dogs, this is most commonly caused by a fungus called Microsporum canis or by Trichophytum.

Often, patchy areas of thinning hair are seen, particularly on the head, feet and legs. Sometimes brown skin lesions, with a raised border, can be seen. Some ringworms fluoresce under ultraviolet light, otherwise diagnosis is made from skin scrapings and hair pluckings. The treatment involves the use of fungicides, which may be applied topically or given as tablets.

DIABETES

There are two kinds of diabetes:
1. Diabetes mellitus
2. Diabetes insipidus.

Diabetes mellitus occurs when cells in the pancreas are damaged, possibly from cancer or infection. These are the cells that produce insulin which controls levels of sugar in the blood. Failure to control these levels of sugar means that sugars are excreted from the kidney, causing an increase in urine production.

The signs include increased drinking and urination. There may be an increase in appetite without weight gain. Cataracts may develop rapidly, and, as the condition progresses, vomiting, depression and even dehydration can occur.

Treatment of diabetes mellitus involves insulin injections and dietary control. Feeding the dog on a higher-fiber, low-carbohydrate diet can be effective. Spaying will often help in bitches. Diabetes insipidus can appear similar, but the cause is different. It is due to a failure by the brain to produce a hormone called ADH, or a failure of the kidneys to respond to this hormone. Treatment of diabetes insipidus can require administration of ADH hormone by nose drops or injection.

DIARRHEA (SEE ALSO COLITIS)

Diarrhea in dogs can vary from watery to soft with an abnormal appearance. Dark/black feces may mean that digested blood is present. Diarrhea is often characterized by increased frequency of passing motions. The other signs often depend upon the specific cause. Treatment should involve withholding food, and seeking veterinary advice to investigate the causes.

DIROFILARIA IMMITANS

(See Heartworm, page 200.)

DYSPNOEA

Dyspnoea is the term used when a dog has difficulty in breathing. The breathing may be labored, rapid and painful. There are many different causes, but it can most often be attributed to heart failure, laryngeal collapse, respiratory conditions, including poisoning, and trauma, e.g. a road traffic accident.

ECLAMPSIA

This is a condition that is classically seen around whelping. It is caused by a decrease in blood calcium levels and may be related to blood sugar levels as well.

The signs are restlessness, panting, nervousness, difficulty in breathing, and a fast breathing rate. As the condition progresses, there may be muscle stiffness and muscle spasms, followed by collapse and death. Treatment involves reversing the deficiency in calcium and blood sugar levels, and treatment is invariably very fast in working. You should consult your veterinarian immediately.

ENDOCARDITIS

Endocarditis refers to inflammation of the inside of the heart. This could be caused by an infection, perhaps spreading via the blood from a wound or some other septic area.

The signs include a persistent or a recurrent fever, a lethargic, quiet dog, a fast heart rate, and, perhaps, weight loss. Diagnosis is gained from blood tests and culturing the blood to look for bacteria, and perhaps an ECG or ultrasonography.

Possible treatments include antibiotics, anabolic steroids and cardiac steroids.

ENTROPION

A condition where the eyelids turn inwards. There is an inherited tendency towards puppies being affected.

The eyelids run against the cornea which can lead to ulceration and ultimately to blindness. Surgery is usually needed to evert the eyelids.

EOSINOPHILIC ENTERITIS

Eosinophilic enteritis is a gut disorder, characterized by chronic diarrhea with large amounts of feces.

The dog has a ravenous appetite but is often losing weight. It is particularly common among young dogs, especially German Shepherds.

Diagnosis is gained from blood tests, fecal samples and, occasionally, from gut biopsy. Treatments can include corticosteroids, worming with anthelmintics, and dietary management.

EPILEPSY

Dogs can be epileptic in just the same way that humans can. The condition is characterized by collapse and loss of consciousness. Sometimes, convulsions may occur. The fits can last varying amounts of time, and may be preceded or followed by a period of confusion, depression and apparent unawareness.

The causes of the epilepsy can be congenital or inherited, or may be related to a poisoning, e.g. lead or a slug bait, such as metaldehyde.

Treatment involves determining the underlying cause. If true epilepsy is detected, the dog can be treated using specific anti-epileptics, such as the barbiturate phenobarbitone.

EPIPHORA

This is an over-production of tears, causing tear tracking to occur at the middle corner of the eye, running down over the nose. It can be related to eye infections, and is commonly seen where there are blocked tear ducts. You should consult your vet if you notice this.

EPISTAXIS

A nosebleed. This can occur from one or both nostrils and can often be seen together with a snotty discharge. If the nosebleed is from one nostril only, the problem must be in the nose. If the nosebleed comes from both nostrils, it may be coming from further back, such as in the throat.

The causes include the presence of foreign bodies, tumors, a trauma (such as a road traffic accident), or fungal infection, particularly aspergillosis.

In cases where a foreign body is involved, surgical removal may be necessary. Where cancer is involved, surgery or radiation therapy may be the treatment of choice. In the case of fungal infections, blood tests or swabs from the nose may indicate the presence of fungus, and then appropriate treatment can be given.

FADING PUPPY SYNDROME (also known as the fading puppy complex or neonatal mortality)

This is a condition that affects puppies of up to two weeks old. At birth, the pups are normally healthy and vigorous, and feed well for the first 24 hours.

After that, they begin to fade and they become progressively weaker. They stop suckling and they lose weight. They become restless, and cry almost continuously.

The cause is thought to be bacterial, particularly bacteria such as beta haemolytic streptococci and E.coli. However, viruses and other bacteria may also have a part to play in this. Treatment includes giving fluids, and possibly antibiotics. However, sadly, the outcome is often fatal.

FALSE PREGNANCY (PSEUDO-PREGNANCY)

This occurs as a natural phenomenon in bitches, six to nine weeks after the bitch has been in season. It is characterized by the production of milk, as well as by a distended abdomen in the bitch. There may be behavioral changes such as bed-making, nervousness or whining. It can mimic very closely a true pregnancy although, obviously, no puppies are born.

Although false pregnancy can be allowed to take its natural course, it can be prevented by using progesterone injections or estrone acetate tablets. (See Chapter 23, page 190.)

FLEA INFESTATION

Most commonly caused by the flea Ctenocephalides canis, although it can also be caused by the cat flea, Ctenocephalides felis. Occasionally, there are incidental passengers such as the hedgehog, rabbit or even human fleas.

The signs include scratching (pruritis), particularly along the back, from the base of the tail up towards the head.

Flea dirt is easy to find in the coat by rubbing the coat over with a piece of dampened, white kitchen towel.

The flea dirt is a characteristic comma shape and is made of blood. On the wet, white paper, it dissolves as a reddish-brown mark. This is known as the wet paper test. Alternatively, a flea comb can be used to find the fleas in the coat.

Treatment should involve using a household insecticide to treat the environment, and a parasiticide on the dog. There are a large number of products available, including the more modern spot-on treatments which act as a contact insecticide, or sprays, which effectively sterilize the flea by preventing the flea eggs from hatching out.

FURUNCULOSIS (ALSO KNOWN AS DEEP PYODERMA)

This is a severe bacterial infection of the skin that goes deep below the layer of the skin into tissues underlying it. (See also anal furunculosis).

The characteristic signs include patches of pustules which may coalesce, oozing blood and pus. The skin is thickened and inflamed and there is hair loss. The condition may be complicated by marked self-trauma. In chronic cases, it can result in scarring. Any area of the body may be affected, but it most frequently occurs at the end of the nose, and around and underneath the anus.

Treatment includes antibiotics, anti-inflammatories, plus finding methods of preventing the dog from self-traumatising. Prolonged treatment is often necessary, often necessitating up to six weeks of antibiotics. 'Elizabethan' collars are sometimes helpful to prevent self-mutilation.

GASTRIC TORSION/BLOAT

This is a condition that occurs most commonly in large-breed dogs soon after eating. The stomach can rotate, effectively blocking the entrance and exits. The food inside ferments and the dog rapidly develops a swollen abdomen. It is an emergency that may require surgical intervention. If you suspect this condition, seek veterinary assistance urgently.

GASTRITIS

Gastritis is inflammation of the stomach. It is characterized by vomiting and increased drinking, and occasionally a secondary diarrhea, plus depression and lethargy.

The causes can include presence of a foreign body, dietary changes, bacterial or viral infections, or it can be secondary to systemic disease, e.g. a pyometra or kidney failure.

Immediate treatment should include starvation for 24 hours, allowing the dog to drink only small amounts of water, little and often. This should be followed by feeding a bland diet, such as chicken and rice, for several days. If vomiting persists, you should consult your veterinary surgeon.

GINGIVITIS (PERIODONTAL DISEASE)

Gingivitis is characterized by reddened gums, and bleeding around the teeth. Painful ulcers may appear in the gums, and it can eventually lead to a lack of appetite and pain on eating. There is often a foul smell to the breath and increased salivation.

The causes tend to be secondary to dental calculus and bacterial infection, or secondary to a systemic disease such as chronic kidney failure.

The treatment depends on the underlying cause. In the case of dental calculus, teeth scaling and extraction of rotten teeth will help prevent the gingivitis, followed by a course of antibiotics to settle the infection down. In other cases, the underlying primary condition must be treated to allow the gingivitis to subside.

HEMATEMESIS

This is the term used when a dog is vomiting blood. It could be caused by a severe foreign body, acute poisoning, bleeding disorders, a gastric ulcer or stomach cancer.

HEMATUREA

Hematurea is the term used when a dog is passing blood in his urine. The causes include stones in the bladder, chronic infection, kidney disease, cancer or trauma of the urinary tract.

HEMORRHAGIC GASTROENTERITIS

Hemorrhagic gastroenteritis is one of the nastier complexes of vomiting and diarrhea. In HGE there is vomiting, and diarrhea with blood in it. It normally is of a sudden onset, and can lead to severe dehydration, and even death without treatment.

It is usually caused by an allergic or anaphylactic reaction to bacterial endotoxins. If your dog vomits blood, or passes blood in feces, you should seek immediate veterinary assistance.

HEATSTROKE

This is characterized by panting, a high temperature, dehydration, congestion of the membranes in the mouth, diarrhea, and, in extreme cases, stupor and even a coma. This condition normally occurs if the dog is confined in an environment of high temperature and poor ventilation. Immediate treatment includes cooling the dog, putting small amounts of water in his mouth and increasing ventilation.

HEPATIC ENCEPHALOPATHY

This is the condition that occurs when a dog has a liver disorder that leads to an increase in breakdown products in the bloodstream. These go round the circulation and end up affecting the brain, causing the dog to have neurological symptoms.

The symptoms include lethargy, apparent blindness, possibly even convulsions, and behavioral changes. The actual cause of these changes is high levels of blood ammonia.

Treatment involves determining the exact nature of the disruption to the liver, and rectifying the problem. The brain will then return to normal.

HEPATITIS

(See Infectious Canine Hepatitis, Chronic Liver Disease, Jaundice)
Hepatitis is the term given to inflammation of the liver. It comes in two forms. Acute hepatitis is characterized by vomiting and abdominal pain. The dog may go off his food and dehydrate. Sometimes there is yellowing (jaundice) of the mucous membranes in the mouth. Chronic hepatitis, the second form, is a slower, more insidious type of liver disease. The signs are often very vague, mainly that of a quieter, more lethargic dog,

who might have some good days and some bad days. There will be chronic weight loss, and yellowing of the mucous membranes in the mouth. A large pot-belly may develop, with fluid in the abdomen. Hepatic encephalopathy may develop.

The principal causes of both types include viral and bacterial agents, as well as chronic poisoning, cancer and trauma. Diagnosis involves blood tests to begin with, and then possibly radiography, ultrasonography, liver biopsies, or even an exploratory laparotomy.

Treatment is then determined by the cause, but may include antibiotics, anabolic steroids, vitamins, and, almost certainly, dietary changes.

HIP DYSPLASIA

This is an abnormal development of the hip. It is common in most large breeds of dog, except Greyhounds. It is a multifactorial condition in which genes (breeding), exercise, and feeding play a part. Treatment can be either surgical or medical. If caught early, then medical treatment with anti-inflammatories/supplements etc. can help in less severe cases. In severe cases, surgical intervention is often the only effective treatment.

HORNER'S SYNDROME

This is the name given to a very specialized condition that involves damage to one of the nerves that supply the area around the eye.

It tends to occur on only one side, and causes drooping of the upper and lower eyelids on that side. The third eyelid may then protrude across the eye. In time, the muscles above the eye may begin to shrink.

Treatment depends on locating and determining the primary cause. This may be trauma, a middle ear infection, a severe outer ear infection, or it may be brain or spinal cord damage.

HYPERADRENOCORTICISM (CUSHING'S SYNDROME)

This is a hormonal condition involving the adrenal glands. These glands sit just in front of the kidneys. They produce natural hormones, including the body's natural steroids. In Cushing's disease, there is an over-production of these chemicals. This may be due to a tumor of the adrenal gland itself, or it may be due to increased stimulation of the glands due to a disorder in the brain.

The classical presenting sign of Cushing's Disease is that of a dog that drinks a lot, passes lots of urine, has an immense appetite, and a large, pendulous abdomen with thinning of the skin. There may be an enlarged liver, and there may be hair loss. It can, in many cases, look very similar to an old dog with diabetes.

Specific diagnosis is gained from blood tests, and a test known as an ACTH stimulation test or a dexamethasone suppression test.

Some of the drugs used in human medicine are used for treating this condition, with relatively good success.

HYPERSEXUALITY

An excess of testosterone production leads to a dog that is over-sexed. The signs can include severe aggression, mounting of other dogs, or even attempting to mount humans or chairs. Excessive territorial marking, roaming, destruction, and excitability are all common signs. Treatment usually involves castration. Hormone treatment may also be used (see Chapter 23: The Question of Neutering).

HYPERTHYROIDISM

This term refers to an overactive thyroid gland. It is uncommon in dogs (far more common in cats). It is usually associated with an enlargement of the thyroid gland (a goitre). Excessive drinking is noticed, along with loss in weight despite a good appetite. Occasionally, diarrhea and weakness occur.

The cause could be cancer of the thyroid gland, or a tumor in the brain causing excessive stimulation of the thyroid gland.

Treatment involves anti-thyroid cancer drugs, after specific diagnosis has been made using blood tests.

HYPOADRENOCORTICISM (ADDISON'S DISEASE)

This refers to an underactive adrenal gland, characterized by vomiting, diarrhea, muscle weakness, a weak pulse, and sometimes collapse. The dog may have a very slow heart rate; he may tremble, and may even appear to be in shock. The dog will drink large amounts of water, and pass large amounts of urine.

Diagnosis is made from blood tests, and an ACTH stimulation test. Treatment involves giving steroids to replace the lack of naturally produced steroids.

HYPOTHYROIDISM

This is when a dog has an underactive thyroid. It is far more common than the opposite, hyperthyroidism. The signs include a quiet, lethargic dog who will have a thin and sparse coat. Sometimes there will be hair loss, particularly on the sides of the abdomen. The dog will tend to be overweight and, despite attempts to diet, will fail to lose weight. It is more commonly seen in middle-aged dogs.

Diagnosis is from blood tests, particularly looking at blood levels of the thyroid hormone, although it may require having a thyroid stimulation hormone test.

Treatment is relatively straightforward, giving the dog artificial thyroid hormones.

IMMUNE MEDIATED THROMBOCYTOPAENIA

This is an auto-immune or self-destruct disease in which the body begins to destroy itself. It may be due to some infection where the platelets begin to be destroyed.

It is characterized by small hemorrhages in the gums, and perhaps diarrhea and vomiting with blood in it. An increase in temperature, swollen lymph nodes, a swollen spleen, an enlarged liver and, occasionally, anemia are seen.

Specific diagnosis comes from blood tests, particularly looking at the platelet count and possibly even a bone marrow biopsy. Treatment is with high doses of steroids.

INFECTIOUS CANINE HEPATITIS (RUBARTS DISEASE)

This is caused by the canine adenovirus type 1, a virus that attacks the liver and the cells that line the inside of the blood vessels. Sufferers have a high temperature, with a poor color, and there may be vomiting and diarroea, with or without blood. The dog has abdominal pain, an enlarged liver and is occasionally jaundiced. As the condition progresses, nervous signs may develop. These signs may develop from being quite mild through to very acute. In the recovery phase, corneal edema can occur, which looks like a blue eye.

Diagnosis is from blood tests, and possibly even virus isolation. This is one of the diseases that can be vaccinated against along with parvovirus, distemper and leptospirosis (see page 202).

INFERTILITY

In male dogs, infertility can occur as a result of a lack of libido, or defects in the production of the sperm. This can be due to orchitis, inflammation of part of the testicle, which could be secondary to bacterial infection.

Tests on male dogs can be done by artificially inducing ejaculation, followed by examination of the semen.

Infertility in bitches can occur due to infections of the vagina or the uterus. They can also occur due to improper timing of mating, a faulty mating technique or even 'frigidity' in the bitch. Abortion may also be the cause, with fetal reabsorption or premature regression of the corpus luteum during pregnancy.

Sometimes, the vet may decide to take vaginal swabs, clitoral swabs or cervical swabs to determine what bacteria are present in the vagina prior to mating.

INTERDIGITAL PYODERMA (PODODERMATITIS)

This is an inflammation of the skin between the toes of the dog. The signs or symptoms include biting and chewing of the feet. The skin becomes reddened and thickened. In more acute cases, it can lead to a swelling of the interdigital glands.

A common cause is a penetrating grass seed, although other causes might be an allergic reaction, or a reaction to salt that might have been spread on the roads.

INTUSSUSCEPTION

This is when one piece of intestine telescopes into another piece of intestine, effectively causing a blockage of the intestines. It is most commonly seen in young puppies.

The causes can include excessive worm burdens or chronic enteritis. The signs include vomiting and diarrhea, straining, blood and mucus in the feces, and abdominal pain. The treatment is usually surgical, although, occasionally, external manipulation by the veterinary surgeon may be successful.

JAUNDICE (ICTERUS)

This is a condition in which excessive red blood cell breakdown, or failure to remove these breakdown products (bilirubin), leads to an increased build-up of them in the bloodstream. The color of these breakdown products is yellow, leading to a yellowing of the mucous membranes, particularly visible around the eyes, and in the mouth.

The causes include liver disease, and infections that might be causing excessive breakdown of red blood cells. Treatment depends on the underlying cause, but will often include fluid therapy, possible transfusions, antibiotics and possibly steroids.

KENNEL COUGH (INFECTIOUS CANINE TRACHEO-BRONCHITIS)

Kennel cough is caused by a bacteria (Bordetella bronchiseptica) and/or a virus, the canine parainfluenza virus or the canine adenovirus 2. The causal agent may be the bacteria on its own, or it may be combined with a virus.

The symptoms are a dry, hacking cough, particularly noticed at night-time. The cough is non-productive, i.e. no phlegm is coughed up. However, in severe fits of coughing, the dog can retch. It is most commonly picked up when dogs meet other dogs, especially in stressful circumstances, for instance when boarding at a kennels, hence the term kennel cough. Methods of treatment include antibiotics, anti-inflammatories, anti-tussives (agents that will stop the coughing) and cough suppressants, e.g. Benelyn. There is a vaccination to protect dogs from getting this condition (see page 203).

KERATO CONJUNCTIVITIS SICCA (DRY EYE)

This is an inadequate tear production. There is a predisposition with West Highland White Terriers. The signs include dryness of the outer layer of the eye, called the cornea. Occasionally, ulceration may occur. There is often a slightly pussy discharge from the medial corner of the eye.

Specific diagnosis is with a Shermer Tear Test, where a small piece of absorbable paper is used to measure the level of tear production.

LARYNGEAL PARALYSIS

When one part of the larynx fails to work, the windpipe (trachea) is partially blocked. This leads to difficulties in breathing and 'snoring'.

It is caused by damage to a nerve, the recurrent laryngeal nerve. Local infection, cancer or, occasionally, trauma, could lead to the nerve damage. This seems more common in large-breed dogs. Surgery may be necessary to restore an open airway.

LARYNGITIS

Laryngitis is an inflammation of the back of the throat. It may be caused by either a bacterial or a viral infection. It usually occurs as an extension of a respiratory disease or tonsillitis. Other causes may be trauma, e.g. due to a foreign body.

The signs include labored breathing, lack of appetite, breathlessness, a cough, and possibly a temperature. Treatment might include antibiotics and anti-inflammatories.

LEPTOSPIROSIS

There are two organisms associated with leptospirosis: Leptospira icterohaemorrhagica, which is usually associated with liver disease, and Leptospira canicula, usually associated with kidney disease – although the distinction is not absolute.

The symptoms of leptospirosis include a high temperature, thirst, vomiting, abdominal pain and a generally unwell dog. If the liver is infected, there can also be jaundice, small hemorrhages in the membranes in the mouth, and possibly even bloody diarrhea. If the kidneys are involved, there may be ulcers in the mouth, and foul-smelling breath. Jaundice may also occur. Diagnosis is made by detecting the organism in blood smears and/or in the urine.

Treatment is symptomatic, i.e. according to the symptoms displayed. Antibiotics are often used, particularly penicillin or streptomycin. This is one of the diseases against which dogs can be vaccinated (see page 202).

LICK GRANULOMA

This is a moist, red, thickening of the skin, particularly common on the top of the front legs, but it may also occur on the back legs. It is an area that a dog persistently licks or chews at. The condition is usually related to an underlying cause, such as arthritis in the joint, or else related to trauma, e.g. a splinter or thorn. However, boredom can also be a predisposing factor.

This is a self-inflicted problem, so treatment involves preventing the self-trauma. Other treatment may include the use of antibiotics and anti-inflammatories, or even an 'Elizabethan' collar to stop the dog being able to get at the granuloma. Occasionally, the legs may need bandaging.

MALABSORPTION SYNDROME (See Also Diarrhea)

The signs of this include a diarrhea which may be very bulky and smelly, containing some fat. The dog is usually very hungry but still loses weight.

It occurs due to failure of the pancreas to produce the correct enzymes necessary in digestion, or for the correct bacteria to be present in the digestive tract.

Treatment depends on the underlying cause but can include antibiotics, steroids, special diets and enzyme supplements.

MAMMARY NEOPLASIA OR BREAST CANCER

This is extremely common in entire female dogs. There is no specific chemotherapy for mammary neoplasis, but some drugs may bring about regression of some types of mammary tumors, e.g. carcinomas. However, the best treatment is surgical removal combined with spaying. (See Chapter 23: The Question of Neutering).

MASTITIS

This condition is manifested by the painful swelling of one or more mammary glands. The bitch will be off-color, not eating, and have a temperature. Occasionally, she may be sick. The cause is usually bacterial. The veterinary surgeon may decide to take a sample of fluid from the mammary gland for bacteriology to determine what type of bug is involved. Treatment involves antibiotics and anti-inflammatories, although hot fermentations are useful. A small towel, soaked in warm to hot water, is held over the swollen gland to help remove the infection. In severe cases, surgical excision may be necessary.

MEGAESOPHAGUS

This is a failure of the normal food pipe or esophagus, which runs from the mouth to the stomach, to work as a muscular tube. Instead, the muscle can be flaccid, leading to food getting stuck in the pipe. The condition can be inherited or developmental. Diagnosis is from radiography, particularly radiography where the dog is fed with a special meal containing barium.

Treatment is best achieved by feeding the food from a height, e.g. from a food-stand, so that gravity assists the food moving from the mouth into the stomach. Surgery can be helpful. Specialized foods, including liquidized diets, can be tried.

MENINGITIS

Meningitis is an inflammation or infection of the brain and/or spinal cord. The symptoms include stiffness of the neck, pain, and resentment of handling, especially of the neck or head. There might be some behavioral changes. The dog will almost certainly have a temperature, and may show unusual signs, such as apparent blindness.

The causes can be bacterial or viral. Diagnosis is made from blood tests, and sometimes from analysis of the fluid around the brain, the cerebrospinal fluid.

Treatment depends on the underlying cause, but includes painkillers, steroids, antibiotics and supportive therapy.

METRITIS (SEE ALSO PYOMETRA)

Metritis is a bacterial infection of the uterus, most commonly occurring after whelping. The signs include a blood-stained vaginal discharge. There may, or may not, be pus in the discharge. The dog is depressed and has a high temperature and, if she has been feeding puppies, the milk soon dries up. Treatment is with antibiotics.

MISALLIANCE

This is the term given to an accidental mating between a dog and a bitch. A 'morning after' injection can be given to prevent an unwanted pregnancy.

MYIASIS (FLY STRIKE)

Fly larvae, carried on the coat of the dog as eggs, hatch and invade the flesh. There is normally an area of traumatized or dirty skin that allows the maggots to burrow into the skin. If left untreated, the maggots eat the flesh and can cause a severe area of skin loss.

Treatment involves removal of the maggots and eggs, cleaning the wound, antibiotics and painkillers. In bad cases, repair of the wound under anesthesia may be necessary.

NASAL DISCHARGE (SEE ASPERGILLOSIS)

When a nasal discharge is coming from only one nostril, then invariably the problem is in the nose. If the discharge is coming from two nostrils, then it is more likely that the problem is further back, possibly in the throat or even in the windpipe.

NEOPLASIA

This is the medical term for cancer.

OBESITY (OVERWEIGHT)

On average, about 30-40 per cent of dogs presented to a veterinary surgery are overweight. The classical signs include the obvious increase in weight but also secondary lethargy. The causes can include excessive food intake or inadequate exercise. Occasionally, it is due to hormonal imbalances, particularly hypothyroidism.

OSTEOCHONDRITIS DISSECANS (OCD)

This is a developmental condition, particularly of large-breed dogs. It is a disturbance of the growth plate leading to a disruption of the cartilage in the joint.

It is related to a fast growth rate, and, occasionally, to dietary problems, and is made worse by too much exercise at a young age. It most commonly occurs in the elbows, shoulders and knees.

The signs include lameness, abnormal posture, and possibly pain on feeling or palpating the bones or joints. It can occur bilaterally (on both sides), in which case lameness may not be apparent at an early stage.

Diagnosis is by radiography, and treatment can include the use of glucosamines, non-steroidal anti-inflammatories, rest and, in extreme cases, surgery.

OSTEOMYELITIS

This is a bacterial infection of bone resulting from either trauma, or from infection spread by the blood. The signs are a local swelling, pain, a high temperature, and possibly even development of an abscess. Treatment is with antibiotics, particularly with antibiotics that attack anaerobic bacteria.

OSTEOSARCOMA

This is a tumor of the bone. It is most commonly seen in large-breed dogs, especially Irish Wolfhounds and Great Danes. It particularly affects the long bones, such as the humerus, radius, ulna and femur. Diagnosis is made by radiography.

There is no direct medical treatment. Surgery, particularly radical amputation of the limb, followed by chemotherapy, is the only available treatment.

OTITIS EXTERNA

This is an infection of the outer part of the ear. It is most common in those breeds of dogs that have floppy ears or narrow ear canals, e.g. Springer Spaniels.

The cause is multifactorial, including mites, bacteria, fungi and yeasts, although occasionally there are underlying problems, e.g. presence of a grass seed.

The signs include an unpleasant discharge from the ear, head-shaking and head-rubbing, scratching and a noticeably foul smell from the ear.

Treatment includes eliminating any underlying cause. Bacterial swabs may need to be taken to determine what bacteria are present, and then a specific ear ointment applied. Occasionally, surgery is required to open out the ear canal.

PANCREATIC INSUFFICIENCY (See Also Diarrhea)

The pancreas fails to produce sufficient enzymes, possibly because it is degenerating and shrinking, or because there is a chronic infection. The signs include weight loss, with diarrhea; the dog may even start to eat his own feces (coprophagia).

Treatment can be simple, involving just dietary alterations and adding supplementary pancreatic enzymes.

PANOSTEITIS

This is a developmental condition, particularly of large breeds of dog. It is the equivalent of dogs' 'growing pains'.

The symptoms include lameness that seems to shift from one leg to the other, and the dog seems uneasy in himself. The pain is associated with the long bones.

Diagnosis is made by radiography, and treatment includes using painkillers until the dog has reached maturity.

PARONYCHIA

This is inflammation and infection of the nail bed of the toes. There is a brown, occasionally cheesy or even pussy, discharge from the nail beds. The dog may, or may not, be in pain. The causes include chronic infections.

Treatment involves bathing the feet in shampoo, antibiotics and anti-inflammatories.

PATELLA LUXATION

This is a condition where the kneecap dislocates, and it is more often found in smaller breeds, such as Shih Tzus and Yorkshire Terriers.

It is usually seen in young dogs and is caused by a malformation of the stifle joint, which may be hereditary.

The signs are hindleg lameness, which may appear quite suddenly and disappear when the patella goes back in place. In severe cases, surgery is required.

PERICARDIAL INFUSION

This is the term given to a build-up of fluid in the sac that surrounds the heart, the pericardium. The causes can be infection, especially bacterial or even fungal.

The clinical signs include difficulty in breathing, lethargy and a lack of exercise tolerance. The veterinary surgeon would notice muffled heart sounds when he listened to the heart.

Specific diagnostic tests that might be used include radiography, echocardiography and ultrasound.

Treatment will often involve draining off the fluid under anesthesia, and then giving medication to prevent its return.

PERITONITIS

This is an infection of the abdomen characterized by abdominal pain, with possible abdominal distension due to a build-up of free fluid in the abdomen. The dog will have a high temperature and will be off his food. There may also be vomiting, and, as the condition progresses, it may lead to collapse.

Peritonitis is a serious condition that can be fatal. Treatment includes anti-inflammatories, painkillers, antibiotics, and washing the inside of the abdomen with fluids to assist removing the infection.

POLYDIPSIA

This is term used for excessive drinking.

POLYPHAGIA

An abnormally increased appetite.

POLYURIA

An increase in passing urine.

PROGRESSIVE RETINAL ATROPHY

There are two forms of this eye condition. Generalized PRA is inherited, and takes the form of night blindness. Irish Setters are particularly prone to this condition, which is caused by a degeneration of the light receptors. There is no treatment.

Central PRA takes the form of daytime blindness, and Collies, Retrievers and Spaniels are the breeds most commonly affected. It is caused by the center of the retina (where the cones of light receptors are most closely packed), becoming damaged. The onset of blindness does not occur until dogs are two to three years of age. There is no known treatment.

PROSTATIC HYPERPLASIA

An enlarged prostate gland, possibly secondary to hormonal changes, or it could be an age-related change. The signs include straining, apparent constipation, and motions that may be thin and ribbon-like.

It can be a cause of perineal hernia developing, or it may be related to cancer of the prostate. Diagnosis is by rectal palpation, radiography, possibly even biopsy and blood tests. One of the main methods of treatment is castration, as the removal of testosterone will diminish the hormone that stimulates the prostate.

PROSTATITIS

This is an infection of the prostate gland.

PRURITUS

A medical term for scratching and itching. The most common causes are ectoparasites, particularly fleas or mites. Other causes include allergies, such as allergies to food or to environmental factors, fungal infections, bacterial infections, or autoimmune diseases.

Treatment involves determining the specific underlying cause and treating that.

PYOMETRA (SEE ALSO METRITIS)

Pyometra is an accumulation of uterine secretions, bacteria and pus in the uterus. It can be either an open or a closed pyometra.

In an open pyometra, the cervix opens and the secretions and fluid are discharged by the vagina. In these cases, a white, creamy discharge can be seen.

In a closed pyometra, the cervix stays shut. There are, therefore, no external symptoms. A closed pyometra is often an acute emergency.

The signs include an increased thirst, a loss of appetite, occasionally a swollen abdomen, vomiting and, in an open pyometra, a vulval discharge.

Pyometra most commonly occurs about four to eight weeks after a bitch has been in season. Diagnosis can be made from examination of the dog, blood samples and, occasionally, radiography. Treatment is antibiotic therapy and, commonly, spaying.

RABIES

Rabies is caused by a virus, the rhabdovirus. The clinical signs include a change in temperament, particularly aggression. The dog will have a temperature, and may be very itchy at the site of the actual infection.

As the disease progresses, the dog will become more excitable, restless and may even begin to salivate. There is an excessively large appetite. Later in the course of the disease, the dog has difficulty in swallowing. Convulsions and paralysis may develop, followed by coma and death. The course of the disease is normally less than about two weeks. There is also a 'dumb' form, but this is unusual in dogs.

Diagnosis is normally from clinical signs and post mortem. There is a vaccine available (see page 203).

SALIVARY CYST (OR SALIVARY MUCOCOELE)

This is a swelling that can occur at the angle below the jaw and the neck. It can be as large as a grapefruit. It is caused by a blockage in the salivary duct, leading to a build-up of saliva in the salivary gland. Diagnosis is either by radiography, or by removing a small amount of fluid from the cyst. Many cure themselves, although surgical treatment is often necessary.

SARCOPTIC MANGE (CANINE SCABIES)

This skin condition is caused by the mite Sarcoptes scabii canis. Dogs often pick up the skin condition from wild foxes.

It causes a localized redness of the skin, with small pus-filled spots. It is most commonly seen around the ear, the elbows, the back legs and along the chest. As it progresses, it can become more generalized, causing severe itchiness and thus self-trauma.

The diagnosis is made by the microscopic observation of the parasite, or its eggs, in a skin scraping. Treatment involves using an ectoparasitic shampoo. It should be noted that this is a zoonotic disease that can spread to man.

SEBORRHEA

This is a skin condition characterized by either a dry or greasy-feeling coat. It can be a primary skin condition in its own right, or secondary to other problems. It is a dog's equivalent of having dandruff.

Treatment involves treating the underlying causes (liver disease, skin infections, dietary insufficiencies, and allergies), possibly antibiotics, fatty acid supplements, or using shampoos that break down the abnormal secretions and remove the excessive skin bacteria.

SKIN FOLD DERMATITIS (Lip Fold Pyoderma)

This is a skin condition commonly seen in dogs with drooping skin, e.g. Spaniels. The fold in the skin allows a build-up of moisture that acts as a nice, warm, wet environment in which bacteria can multiply. This is very commonly seen in the area around the vulva, or the lower lips. As the bacteria multiply and cause a local infection, the skin swells, exacerbating the fold and creating a vicious circle of infection and irritation.

Treatment involves cleaning the area and allowing ventilation. This may require surgical intervention. Antibiotics are also often used.

SYNCOPY

This is an episode of sudden loss of consciousness. These episodes are normally brief and caused by heart failure, or a reduction in blood supply to the brain because of an underlying reason. The condition is often confused with epileptic fits. Treatment depends upon the underlying cause.

TENESMUS

This is the medical term for straining. It can involve fecal tenesmus, i.e. constipation, or urinary tenesmus, for instance straining to urinate due to cystitis.

TRACHEITIS

An inflamation of the trachea. This can be caused by dust inhalation or by infection (see Kennel cough).

TRAVEL SICKNESS

This can be treated with mild sedatives. Ask your vet for advice.

TUMORS

This term is used as an equivalent to cancer. In fact, any swelling can be referred to as a tumor. Tumors may be benign, or they may be malignant, meaning they can spread into adjacent structures.

URINARY INCONTINENCE

This is a common problem in older bitches. It can also occur as a post-operative problem due to spaying. It is most commonly seen as a damp patch left behind in the bed of the bitch after she gets up.

The causes include bacterial infection, or trauma, e.g. from bladder stones. It can also occur in young dogs due to congenital abnormalities, such as ectopic ureters. Treatment depends on the underlying cause, but the condition can often be successfully managed.

UROLITHIASIS

The medical condition where stones develop in the bladder. There are a number of different types of stones. The most common are phosphate calculi; the second most common are cystine calculi. Dalmatians are very prone to developing urate calculi.

Whatever the type of bladder stones, the clinical symptoms are similar: difficulty in passing urine. Occasionally, there is blood present in the urine, and pain in passing urine. With secondary cystitis, there may be an arching of the back and straining. The dog may be depressed and lack appetite.

Diagnosis is made by testing the urine, from radiographs, ultrasonography, and even by exploratory laparotomy to remove the stones, followed by chemical analysis of the stones.

UTERINE INERTIA

This is when a whelping bitch is unable to push out the puppies. It may be due to physical exhaustion, a hormonal imbalance, or psychological stress, which is particularly common in small-breed dogs. Treatment involves emergency examination by a veterinary surgeon, plus possible injections of hormones, particularly oxytocin. If that fails to create uterine contractions, an emergency cesarean may be necessary.

VOMITING

A reflex action which results in the expulsion of the stomach contents. It may be caused by eating grass or scavenging, or it may be a sign of a more serious condition, e.g. kidney failure or abdominal cancer.

Short-term vomiting can be treated by withdrawing food for 12-24 hours, and making sure that the dog is allowed to drink very small quantities of water. If the condition persists, consult your vet who will carry out tests, which may entail blood testing, X-rays, or endoscope examinations.

VON WILLENBRANDS DISEASE

This is a clotting disorder, where a particular clotting factor is missing. It is an inherited disease in dogs, particularly in Irish Wolfhounds. The clotting factor that is missing, or low, is clotting factor No. 8. It is possible for dogs to be carriers of this genetic disorder.

WARTS

Warts are commonly seen, especially in older dogs. They may be caused by a virus, in which case they are really viral papillomas. Unless the wart is causing a problem, e.g. the dog has rubbed it and made it bleed, then it is sensible to leave it alone. Treatment can be by surgical removal.

Chapter 28

Alternative Therapies

The holistic approach; Homeopathy; Acupuncture; Physiotherapy and massage; Chiropractic

Alternative medicine and complementary medicine are all-embracing titles, which imply many separate disciplines, usually involving two common themes:

- Natural medicines
- Holistic principles.

There are three major 'systems' of medicine included under this heading and two supportive therapies:

- Homeopathy
- Chinese medicine (incorporating acupuncture)
- Herbal medicine
- Chiropractic
- Physiotherapy/massage.

An overview of these will be provided in very brief detail below. Broadly speaking, homeopathy and acupuncture act as stimulants or triggers to the body's healing powers. Herbal medicine, however, the true forebear of modern conventional medicine, is a holistically-based therapy which uses blends of natural substances directly to alter the body's way of operating.

Other therapies such as bach flowers, radionics, color therapy, tissue salts, anthroposophy, osteopathy, etc. are not described here, but do attach themselves to the 'alternative medicine' tag.

Physiotherapy, a worthwhile system of helping the body to rehabilitate, for instance after injury, is not a system of medicine in its own right, neither stimulating healing nor directly altering biochemistry, although it has often been put forward under the 'alternative medicine' banner. While it has little 'stand-alone' therapeutic value in disease, it is, in fact, a very useful and often invaluable physical adjunct and logical support to any system of medicine and can act as a 'health maintenance' tool.

A study of nutrition, and the necessary understanding to formulate natural diets, which are wholesome, as free as possible from pollution by modern chemicals and which are compatible with the special evolved needs of each species, are fundamental requirements of any medicine which purports to be holistic.

For instance, dogs need to chew bones and raw flesh, in order to maintain gum and teeth health. This is one of the disease areas least well prevented in our modern management. While dogs can become 'vegetarian', this is not to be considered wholly desirable. When advocating a more natural approach, the preference must be to feed fresh food to dogs, rather than the processed canned or bagged foods, in the same way that it is wiser to feed ourselves on fresh food.

Since diet is a common thread through all the 'systems' of natural medicine, when properly applied as opposed to a medical practice in its own right, it is not the subject of this chapter, vitally important though it is to health and to healing.

VETERINARY HOMEOPATHY

Veterinary homeopathy is based on the same principles as its human medical counterpart, i.e. the principles discovered and worked out by Samuel Hahnemann in Germany in 1790 (over 200 years ago!). The earliest references to veterinary homeopathy are found in a little-known manuscript of a lecture by Dr Hahnemann, given in Leipzig in, or about, 1813.

Homeopathy is the science of medicine based on the principle 'similia similibus curentur' (let likes be cured by likes). Samuel Hahnemann discovered that Peruvian bark (or cinchona which gives us the drug Quinine) was able to produce signs and symptoms in a healthy body (his own), which were quite indistinguishable from those of malaria, a disease which it is singularly able to cure. This apparently paradoxical effect he named 'homeopathy', which means (from the Greek) 'similar to the suffering'.

An analogous phenomenon is observable for an infinite variety of substances, whether plant, animal or mineral in origin. In other words, in order to cure a disease syndrome, we must select a substance most able to produce similar signs and symptoms in a healthy body. The substances used are commonly known as remedies. Their properties are listed in books called 'Homeopathic Materia Medica'.

THEORY OF DILUTION

Hahnemann found, in addition to this startling discovery, that if he serially diluted his curative substances (and succussed or violently agitated the solution at each stage), they were less and less able to produce any harmful effects and became (paradoxically again) more and more powerful curatively. We now know, from molecular and atomic physics, that his common dilutions were beyond the point at which we would mathematically expect the last molecule or atom to remain.

This 'sub-molecular' nature of the remedies means that we are using energy, not drug material, as a curative force. This rules out any chance of 'side effects', and hence rules out any damage that ensues from such side effects. We call these dilutions 'potencies'. The level of potency is denoted by a number, written after the remedy name, and representing the number and scale of dilution undergone by the solution (e.g. 30c denotes a dilution of one-in-one-hundred, repeated thirty times, i.e. 10^{-60}!).

TAKING A CASE HISTORY

Homeopathy treats the animal as an 'energetic whole', not as a collection of symptoms or signs with a specific 'scientific' disease name. For this reason, since we are treating the animal itself, not the disease, we need to know a great deal of information about the patient and about his medical history, his background, and his home environment. This entails asking seemingly strange questions, which appear often to be quite unrelated to the specific problem for which the animal is presented. We then need to identify and remove those factors in the life of the patient which may impede healing, since we must reduce or remove these to achieve health.

POWERS OF HEALING

Homeopathy is a force for good in the animal world, since it is able to treat so many diseases, ranging from simple to serious and acute to chronic, without the risk of side effects and without the need for laboratory animal experimentation. Humans have already volunteered as 'guinea pigs' and have done the work of determining the effects of the substances in healthy bodies!

Since the prescription is so 'individualized', for any named disease, in a conventional sense, many different homeopathic medicines may be required for the different patients. Conversely, a single homeopathic medicine may be able to treat many different named diseases, if the symptom-picture in a particular patient fits that of the remedy. This apparent paradox is not easily comprehended by the conventionally-trained mind.

Homeopathy works in the body by stimulating the body's own powers of healing. The final outcome of treatment by homeopathy depends both upon the prescriber's ability to select the correct remedy, and upon the animal's ability to respond. We do not necessarily need to know the 'name' of the disease and, in many cases, diseases may be undiagnozable, in a conventional sense. If no mechanism exists in the body to heal the disease effects, then, necessarily, no cure can result (e.g. in kidney degeneration). The best we can hope for in such diseases is an improvement in quality of life, cessation of the degenerative process, and a stimulation of remaining healthy tissue to function better. Even so, many so-called 'incurable' diseases can respond.

WHO CAN BE HELPED?

The range of diseases which can respond to homeopathy is very wide, but it is particularly useful in skin disorders, allergies, digestive disturbances, viral diseases (for which conventional medicine has no answer), behavioral disorders (since we are treating mind and body together), cardiac support and acute conditions such as injuries.

Patients suffering from cancer are presented regularly. There are opportunities of success, even with these, but only if the disease has not gone too far, if the body has sufficient ability to fight the disease (with help), and if diet and other external factors are optimized. While individual successes are wonderful news, the overall statistical success rate is not high.

VETERINARY ACUPUNCTURE

Veterinary acupuncture is based on the ancient Chinese art of acupuncture in humans, which started to evolve anything up to 4,000 years ago. It is part of traditional Chinese medicine (TCM), which also includes Chinese herbal medicine, dietary wisdom and moxibustion.

Acupuncture, properly applied, treats the animal as an 'energetic whole', rather than as a body presenting with a specific named disease. As such, it constitutes much more than a method of pain relief. This is especially true when it is used, as originally intended, with dietary work and internal medicine. Many of the disappointments of modern veterinary acupuncture are probably attributable to the modern tendency to short-cuts – applying needles alone, without the full dietary and medical support which is part of the tradition.

ENERGY FLOWS

Disease is considered to be a result of disordered energy flow in the body. The normal energy patterns in humans were charted in China, several thousand years ago, in the shape of meridians or channels, of which there are twenty-six major ones. Health depends upon the regular, rhythmic flow of energy within these channels, and upon the balance between *yin* and *yang*, 'the eternal opposites'.

When the energy flow is interrupted, disturbed or wrongly distributed, symptoms of disease are seen. Cure of this disease situation depends upon rebalancing the disturbance, and this is done by the stimulation of precisely identified points on the body surface.

These points can be stimulated in various ways, for example needles, finger massage, heat (moxibustion), laser, electrical impulse, implant or injection. Herbs and diet are also brought to bear, by the wise practitioner, in order to aid return to a proper energetic balance.

The mechanisms involved in the working of acupuncture, based as it is on oriental philosophy, are obscure to modern Western minds, which use linear thinking. Each living creature is thought to be endowed at birth with life energy (qi or ch'i). This energy is consumed by the body in the business of living, and is replenished by eating and breathing. Imbalance in the flow of this energy through the meridians is caused by internal or external factors (pernicious influences, which the good practitioner must identify and minimize), and is the fundamental process of disease.

The acupuncturist will attempt to correct this imbalance by stimulation of specific points as described above. These points are often far removed from the site of apparent trouble, since points are found, relating to various organs and functions, over the whole body.

The primary purpose of acupuncture treatment is to stimulate the body's own healing powers and its own ability to maintain the equilibrium of its internal environment. The acupuncturist is therefore less concerned with the specific 'scientific' name of the disease from which the animal is suffering than with the nature of the general energy imbalance caused, and the causative factors themselves.

WHO CAN BE HELPED?

Diseases which can respond are not merely painful conditions such as injury, lameness (arthritis) or back problems, but also many serious or non-serious internal diseases. The success depends upon the body's stimulated ability to heal, and therefore upon whether or not mechanisms exist within the body which, if appropriately stimulated, can resolve the problem.

There are, therefore, many spectacular successes, some major disappointments and a proportion of cases in which palliation, or temporary relief only, is achieved. A notable area of success is in the treatment of nerve dysfunction or paralysis. Consistent success has been seen in spinal disc prolapse, and the impairment of hind leg function or paralysis, which usually follow such a lesion.

Treatment is generally non-painful. Some sensation, transitional between pain and pleasure, can be felt by humans at the site of needling, so it is reasonable to assume that animals feel this effect similarly. There is often a relaxing effect during treatment and an immense sleepiness for 24 hours following treatment.

Treatment lasts for varying periods from 5 to 30 minutes, generally averaging at 15-20 minutes. We usually repeat the treatment at between 2- and 14-day intervals and, if no response is seen after three or four such treatments, the likelihood of a response is much reduced. Dogs tolerate acupuncture well. They often go to sleep during treatment.

VETERINARY HERBAL MEDICINE

Herbal medicine is as old as human civilization itself. Records go back as far as the oldest medical textbooks known; the *Huang Ti Nei Ching Su Wên* and the *Pen T'sao*

Ching, which are foundation books for Traditional Chinese Medicine, and which reputedly date back as far as 4,000 years, according to some sources.

All cultures have deep traditions of herbal medicine, and a study of these in different civilizations makes not only for fascinating reading but also provides a wealth of medical lore. African tribes, Amazonian Indians, Native North Americans, Middle Eastern and Near Eastern cultures, the Indian subcontinent, the Far East including of course China, Australian Aborigines, Maoris and many others all show understanding of the wisdom of herbal medicine.

They have a rich and diverse plant medicine culture, deeply integrated within their societies. Only the poor Eskimo would have had difficulty in building up a large herbal pharmacopœia, so widespread and varied are the botanical gifts bestowed upon us by nature! It is hard to imagine anyone in Britain living more than 100 yards from at least one plant species with known medicinal properties, even in urban centers.

It is not surprising that our forefathers mingled religion, mystique, folklore and superstition with their medicine. Shamanism, and its counterparts, were very much linked with reputed medical knowledge. Witch doctors, druids, tribal medicine men and, later, in medieval Europe, the Christian church, took on the role of traditional medical continuity.

Astrology also became entangled with herbal medicine, a tradition epitomized by Nicholas Culpeper in the mid-17th century. Herbal medicine, however, still holds its validity without the strong mystical and religious connotations handed down to us from ancient works.

FIGHT FOR SURVIVAL

Sadly, however, many traditions of herbal medicine were unwritten and many formulas, which were enshrined in oral tradition, will have been lost over the centuries, as a result of the conquest of civilizations and the destruction of cultures.

Many of these will inevitably remain hidden to our modern world. Even when records were properly kept, wars and clashes of culture often combined to destroy them. For instance, 700,000 or more books, amassed in the medical school in Alexandria (incorporating information from conquered territories such as India and the Middle East), were destroyed by Christian fanatics in 391 AD. The pictogram records of the Aztecs, encoding great culture and lore, were destroyed by the Conquistadors, in an act of mindless vandalism so often enacted by conquering armies throughout history. Victory brings on a form of intoxication, fuelled by adrenaline and by the perceived need to subjugate by destruction of culture.

Even in modern times, systematic efforts at eliminating herbal competitors to the modern drug industry have been seen. The massive profits to be obtained from drugs, so often directly derived from the very plant medicine the industry professes to despise, are a powerful magnet and anesthetic to conscience.

PLANT POWER

Our western herbal medicine culture dates back to Greek and Roman traditions, oversown with lore from Saxon and medieval scholars from all over Europe. Names such as Hippocrates, Pliny, Dioscorides, Galen, Paracelsus, Gerard and Culpeper crop up again and again in writings.

The rationale behind herbal medicine has changed and evolved through these times, astrological and religious beliefs being intertwined with medical experience. However, one recurring theme which dates back to Paracelsus and probably much earlier, is the *Doctrine of Signatures*, or the *Cosmic Principle of Signatures*.

According to this principle, a plant could give a clue to its medical uses via its habit, habitat, morphology and appearance. Chelidonium (the greater celandine), for instance, is a remarkable remedy for jaundice. It led ancient prescribers to this idea via its bright yellow sap, which, when it comes into contact with skin, turns it a bright orangey-yellow color – exactly as if the person were suffering from jaundice. Turmeric was similarly adopted in the ancient East, showing this 'theory' to be widespread among independent peoples.

Nowadays, however, herbal medicines are selected more according to their known medicinal action, which is mediated via their analyzed ingredients. Active chemicals in plants, in unique combinations, have known medical effects which are supported by modern science, eg: alkaloids, glycosides, saponins, flavones. Herbs can also be grouped according to their general action, eg: alteratives, aperients, astringents, bitters, demulcents, diuretics, expectorants, nervines, vulneraries.

A surprisingly large proportion of modern, conventional drug medicines are either prepared from herbal material or owe their origins to herbs. For example, vincristine started from the Madagascar periwinkle, aspirin (salicylic acid) from willow or meadowsweet, digoxin from the foxglove, morphine derivatives from the opium poppy, and so on. Many other drugs have originated from fungi; for example, penicillin from moulds, ivermectin (a powerful modern anthelmintic and parasiticide) from a Japanese soil fungus.

HOLISTIC PRINCIPLE

One major difference between modern chemical medicine and properly applied traditional herbalism, however, is the holistic principle. This is applied both to the patient (i.e. treating the patient as a whole rather than just trying to counteract the symptoms), and to the medicine (using the whole plant with its 'drugs' and many essential natural synergists, as opposed to a single supposed 'active ingredient').

Herbs can also be combined in a formula, which is tailored to the individual, in order to achieve a balancing effect within the body. It is these properties which render herbal medicine so safe, when properly applied by adequately qualified people, avoiding harmful side effects of some conventional medicines.

WHOM CAN IT HELP?

Herbal medicine is well suited to animals too. Dogs will often seek out their own herbal medicines. You may well have seen your own dog eating 'goose grass', 'pellitory of the wall' etc.

Herbal remedies have proven useful for the majority of disease conditions from which animals suffer, either on their own or co-ordinated and integrated with other therapies such as homeopathy or acupuncture. Nutrition is also vital. Lung allergies, rheumatism and arthritis, hyper-excitability, digestive problems and many others respond well.

Treatment with herbs is safe and without side effects, as long as it is used carefully, with due regard to formulas and doses. It can be given in fresh form, chopped leaves, dried form, capsules, powders, tablets, tinctures, infusions, oils, creams, ointments, etc. but instructions must always be carefully followed. All species of animals respond to this most natural of therapies.

> ### WARNING
> It is important to watch out for products with inadequate labeling and those formulated by manufacturers who may not have the appropriate tradition, knowledge or understanding of the subject. The marketing of such products owes more to commercial intentions than to good or safe medicine.
>
> Off-the-shelf formulas show no pretence at individualization for a given patient, so stand little chance of being ideal – and some chance of being downright dangerous. The naming of such products often contains a cunningly worded and quasi-legal allusion to a specific disease syndrome, in order to encourage sales.

CHIROPRACTIC

This form of manipulative therapy literally means 'done by hand'. The McTimoney training for animal chiropractors teaches very gentle techniques. Some other forms of chiropractic have a tendency to be a little 'heroic'.

Since the innervation for the organs and muscles of the body (whether conscious or autonomic) comes from the spine, it stands to reason that body function can be directly affected by spinal alignment. Many canine patients show some degree of misalignment, and correction produces immediate evidence of relaxation and comfort. There is particularly an effect on the jumping ability and co-ordination of hind limb movement by pelvic misalignment, which many dogs show.

It is recommended that only suitably qualified animal chiropractors are visited, unless your veterinary surgeon has the necessary skills. Chiropractors can only operate on your vet's recommendation, and under your vet's supervision.

PHYSIOTHERAPY & MASSAGE

As mentioned before, this is not a 'stand-alone' therapy, but a means of health maintenance or of encouraging healing, by gentle massage and active movement. It has great wellbeing benefits, if gently and sympathetically performed. Correct movement provides the body with the necessary challenge for correct healing of locomotor structures. If the dog does not like it, then it is not being done correctly for that patient.

There is a plethora of technological instruments, designed to enhance the capability of the practitioner. These have advantages and disadvantages, and their safety or efficacy depends greatly upon the skills and sensitivity of the practitioner.

As with chiropractic, physiotherapists can only operate on your vet's recommendation, and under your vet's supervision.

SUMMARY

There is a huge wealth of knowledge and understanding, accumulated over many centuries of human civilization, which can be brought to the aid of ailing or disabled animals. This lore is supported by some good modern research work and by a continuous thread of clinical reports and experiences, leading down the ages to the present day.

There are also training courses for vets in the major therapies. The safety of natural medicine, in the right hands, is unrivalled, having been tested 'in the field' for so long. The quality and quality control of natural medicines, if purchased from properly-licensed manufacturers, are on a par with the best that modern pharmacies can offer.

If natural medicine help is needed for an animal, then it is best to seek out those organizations which can provide a list of properly trained veterinary surgeons. Those vets will be able either to provide the best possible care or to refer the patient to a colleague, who is well versed in the appropriate techniques. In the UK, the Royal College of Veterinary Surgeons is the central body, and can point inquirers in the correct direction. In the US, each state is governed by a State Board of Veterinary Examiners; there is also an American Association of Veterinary State Boards (see Appendix I: Useful Addresses).

In both the UK and the USA, it is illegal for any medicines to be prescribed or acupuncture to be given to animals, except by a qualified veterinarian; manipulation therapies alone are permitted for non-vets.

I: Useful Addresses

KENNEL CLUBS

Your national Kennel Club will be able to give you contact details for breeders and clubs in your area, as well as show listings.

KENNEL CLUB (UK)
1, Clarges Street,
London, W1Y 8AB, UK.
Tel: 0870 6066751
Fax: 020 7518 1058
E-mail: info@the-kennel-club.org.uk
Website: www.the-kennel-club.org.uk

AMERICAN KENNEL CLUB (USA)
260 Madison Avenue,
New York, NY 10016, USA.
Tel: 919 233-9767
Fax: 919 816-3627
E-mail: info@akc.org
Website: www.akc.org

UNITED KENNEL CLUB (USA)
100 East Kilgore Road,
Kalamazoo,
MI 49002-5584,USA.
Tel: 616 343 9020
Fax: 616 3437037
Website: www.ukcdogs.com

CANADIAN KENNEL CLUB (CANADA)
89 Skyway Avenue,
Suite 100, Etobicoke, Ontario, Canada.

Tel: 800 250 8040 or 416 675 5511
Fax: 416 675 6506
E-mail: information@ckc.ca
Website: www.ckc.ca

FCI (INTERNATIONAL KENNEL CLUB)
Secrétariat Général de la FCI,
Place Albert 1er, 13,
B-6530,
Thuin, France.
Tel: 715 91238
Fax: 715 92229
Website: www.fci.be

CANINE PRESS/WEBSITES

DOG FANCY (US MAGAZINE)
Fancy Publications Inc, 3, Burroughs,
Irvine, CA 92618, USA.
Tel: 949 855 8822
Fax: (949) 855 0442
Website and online magazine:
www.animalnetwork.com/dogs/default.asp

DOG WORLD (US MAGAZINE)
260 Madison Avenue, 8th Floor,
New York, NY 10016, USA.
Tel: 917 256 2305
Fax: 917 256 2304
E-mail: dogworld@primediasi.com
Website and online magazine:
www.dogworldmag.com

THE AKC GAZETTE
The American Kennel Club, Inc.
260 Madison Avenue, New York,
NY 10016, USA.
E-mail: gazette@akc.org

DOGS TODAY (UK MAGAZINE)
Pet Subjects Ltd,
Pankhurst Farm, Bagshot Road,
West End, Woking, Surrey,
GU24 9QR, UK.
Tel: 01276 858880
Fax: 01276 858860
E-mail: dogstoday@dial.pipex.com

DOG WORLD (UK NEWSPAPER)
Somerfield House, Wotton Road,
Ashford, Kent.
TN23 6LW, UK.
Tel: 01233 621877
Fax: 01233 645669
E-mail: editorial@dogworld.co.uk
Website: www.dogworld.co.uk

OUR DOGS (UK NEWSPAPER)
5, Oxford Road, Station Approach,
Manchester, M60 1SX, UK.
Tel: 0161 228 1984
Fax: 0161 236 0892
E-mail: ourdogsedit@lineone.net

YOUR DOG (UK MAGAZINE)
Roebuck House, 33, Broad Street,
Stamford, Lincs, PE9 1RB, UK.
Tel: 01780 766199
Fax: 01780 766416
E-mail: lisabpgroup@talk21.com

DOGS ONLINE
A website featuring breed information, lists for
breeders and merchandise.
Website: www.hoflin.com/Default.com

WORKING DOG WEB
News and stories about all types of dogs,
referral lists, advice on health and care, plus
merchandise.
Website: www.workingdogweb.com

DOGOMANIA
A fully comprehensive website devoted to all
aspects of dogs and dog ownership.
Website: www.dogomania.com

RESCUE/CHARITIES

AMERICAN SOCIETY FOR THE
PREVENTION OF CRUELTY TO
ANIMALS (ASPCA)
424, East 92nd Street,
New York, NY 10128, USA.
Tel: 212 876 7700
E-mail: website@aspca.org
Website: www.aspca.org

THE HUMANE SOCIETY OF THE
UNITED STATES (HSUS)
2100, L Street, NW,
Washington, DC 20037, USA.
Tel: 202 452 1100
Website: www.hsus.org

ANIMAL PROTECTION INSTITUTE
(USA)
P.O. Box 22505, Sacramento, CA 95822, USA.
Tel: 916 447 3085
Fax: 916 447 3070
E-mail: info@api4animals.org
Website: www.api4animals.org

ROYAL SOCIETY FOR THE
PREVENTION OF CRUELTY TO
ANIMALS (RSPCA)
Wilberforce Way, Southwater, Horsham,
West Sussex, RH13 7WN, UK.
Tel: 0870 333 5999 (UK calls) +44 707 533
5999 (outside UK)
Fax: 0870 753 0048 (UK Calls) +44 707
553 0048 (outside UK)
Website: www.rspca.org.uk

BLUE CROSS
Shilton Road, Burford, Oxfordshire,
OX18 4PF, UK.
Tel: 01993 822651
Fax: 01993 823083
E-mail: info@bluecross.org.uk
Website: www.bluecross.org.uk

LOW-COST NEUTERING AND ADVICE

SPAY USA
North Shore Animal League International,
14, Vanderventer Avenue, Suite L-1,
Port Washington, NY 10050, USA.
Tel: 800 248 SPAY
Website: www.spayusa.org

CELIA HAMMOND ANIMAL TRUST
Head Office, High Street,
Wadhurst, East Sussex, TN5 6AG, UK.
Tel: 01892 783820
Fax: 01892 784882
E-mail: info@celiahammond.org
Website: www.celiahammond.org

PEOPLE'S DISPENSARY FOR SICK
ANIMALS (PDSA)
Whitechapel Way, Priorslee, Telford,
Shropshire, TF2 9PQ, UK.
Tel: 01952 290999
Fax: 01952 291035
Website: www.pdsa.org.uk

TRAINING

Your national Kennel Club will be able to give
you a list of affiliated training clubs for all
sports and activities.

If the increasingly popular method of clicker
training appeals to you, try visiting:
www.clickertraining.com (US) or
www.clickertraining.co.uk (UK).

BEHAVIOR COUNSELING

Trainers specialising in overcoming problem
behaviours can be found through the following
organisations.

ASSOCIATION OF PET BEHAVIOR
COUNSELING (APBC)
Although this is a UK-based organization, it
holds details of APBC-approved counselors
and trainers in all countries.
APBC, PO Box 46, Worcester,
WR8 9YS, UK.
Tel: 01386 751151
Fax: 01386 750743
E-mail: apbc@petbcent.demon.co.uk
Website: www.apbc.org.uk

AMERICAN DOG TRAINERS NETWORK
An online information website, holding details
of ADTN-approved trainers and behaviour
counselors all over the USA.
Website: www.inch.com/~dogs/training.html

DERBYSHIRE DOG AGILITY CLUB
This website gives out trainer details for all
types of canine sports and problem behaviors,
throughout the UK.
Website:www.derbyshiredogagilityclub.co.uk/
DDAC/dogtraining.html

GENERAL ADVICE WEBSITES

DOG FRIENDLY.COM (US)
Gives a list of dog-friendly places to stay as
well as links to other websites containing
information about caring for your dog.
Website: www.dogfriendly.com

DOG.COM (US)
A website all about caring for dogs, with links
to related sites.
Website: www.dog.com

GENERAL DOG (UK)
A website providing information on all aspects of dog ownership as well as selling merchandise.
Website:
www.cofc.edu/~huntc/gendogpage.html

PROVET (UK)
The Provet website devoted to the health of dogs.
Website:
www.provet.co.uk/online/dogs/dogshome.htm

THERAPY DOGS

CANINE COMPANIONS FOR
INDEPENDENCE INC (USA)
HQ: 2965, Dutton Avenue,
PO Box 446, Santa Rosa,
CA 95402-0446, USA.
Tel: 707 577 1700
E-mail: info@caninecompanions.org
Website: www.caninecompanions.org

PAWS WITH A CAUSE (USA)
4646, South Division, Wayland,
MI 49348, USA.
Tel: 616 877 7297
Fax: 616 877 0248
E-mail: paws@ionline.com
Website: www.pawswithacause.org

PETS AS THERAPY (UK)
4, New Road, Ditton, Maidstone, Kent,
ME20 6AD, UK.
Tel: 01732 872222
Fax: 01732 842175
E-mail: info@pat-prodog.org.uk
Website: www.pat-prodog.org.uk

THERAPY DOGS INTERNATIONAL
88, Bartley Road, Flanders, NJ 07836, USA.
Fax: 973 252 7171

E-mail: tdi@gti.net
Website: www.tdi-dog.org

PET LOSS

ASSOCIATION FOR PET LOSS AND
BEREAVEMENT (US)
PO Box 106, Brooklyn, New York,
NY 11230, USA.
Tel: 718 382 0690
E-mail: aplb@aplb.org
Website: www.aplb.org

SOCIETY OF COMPANION ANIMAL
STUDIES (SCAS) (UK)
SCAS organises a befriender service, where people can talk to a trained pet-loss counselor.
SCAS, 10b, Leny Road, Callander,
Scotland, FK17 8BA, UK.
Tel: 01877 330996 or 0800 096 6606
Website: www.scas.org.uk/pbss.htm

PET LOSS SUPPORT (INTERNATIONAL)
A first-class website, with lots of advice and support for those who have just lost a much-loved pet. Website: www.petloss.com

VETERINARY BODIES

ROYAL COLLEGE OF VETERINARY
SURGEONS (RCVS)
Belgravia House, 62-64 Horseferry Rd,
London, SW1P 2AF, UK
Tel: 020 7222 2001

AMERICAN ASSOCIATION OF
VETERINARY STATE BOARDS
3100 Main St., Suite 208, Kansas City,
M0 64111.
Tel: 861 931 1504
Fax: 816 931 1604
E-mail: info@aavsb.org
Website: www.aavsb.org

II: Classification Of Breeds

The American Kennel Club and the English Kennel Club follow the same general group classifications for dog breeds. Individual differences are noted

SPORTING/GUNDOG
American Water Spaniel
Bracco Italiano
Brittany
Italian Spinone
Kooikerhondje
Large Munsterlander
Pointer
Pointer – German Shorthaired
Pointer – German Wirehaired
Pointer – German Longhaired
Setter – English
Setter – Gordon
Setter – Irish
Setter – Irish Red and White (UK only)
Spaniel – Clumber
Spaniel – American Cocker
Spaniel – English Cocker
Spaniel – English Springer
Spaniel – Field
Spaniel – Irish Water
Spaniel – Sussex
Spaniel – Welsh Springer
Spanish Water Dog
Retriever – Chesapeake Bay
Retriever – Curly-Coated
Retriever – Flat-Coated
Retriever – Golden
Retriever – Labrador
Retriever – Nova Scotia Duck Tolling
Vizsla – Hungarian
Vizsla – Hungarian Wirehaired
Weimaraner
Wirehaired Pointing Griffon

HOUNDS
Afghan Hound
Basenji
Basset Bleu De Gascogne
Basset Fauve De Bretagne
Basset Griffon Vendeen (Grand)
Basset Griffon Vendeen (Petit)
Basset Hound
Beagle
Black and Tan Coonhound
Bloodhound
Borzoi
Dachshund
Deerhound – Scottish
Elkhound
Finnish Spitz
Foxhound – American
Foxhound – English
Grand Bleu de Gascogne
Greyhound
Hamiltonstovare
Harrier
Ibizan Hound
Irish Wolfhound
Norwegian Elkhound

Otterhound
Pharoah Hound
Rhodesian Ridgeback
Saluki
Segugio Italiano
Sloughi
Whippet

WORKING
Akita (UK Utility Group)
Alaskan Malamute
Anatolian Shepherd (UK Pastoral Group)
Beauceron
Bernese Mountain Dog
Boxer
Bullmastiff
Canadian Eskimo Dog
Dogue de Bordeaux
Doberman Pinscher
Giant Schnauzer
Great Dane
Great Pyrenees (Pyrenean Mountain Dog – UK Pastoral Group)
Greater Swiss Mountain Dog
Greenland Dog
Hovawart
Komondor (UK Pastoral Group)
Kuvasz (UK Pastoral Group)
Leonberger
Mastiff
Mastiff – Neapolitan
Mastiff – Tibetan
Newfoundland
Portuguese Water Dog
Rottweiler
Saint Bernard
Samoyed (UK Pastoral Group)
Siberian Husky
Standard Schnauzer (UK Utility Group)

TERRIERS
Airedale Terrier
American Staffordshire Bull Terrier
Australian Terrier
Bedlington Terrier
Black Russian Terrier
Border Terrier
Bull Terrier

Cairn Terrier
Cesky Terrier
Dandie Dinmont Terrier
Fox Terrier (Smooth)
Fox Terrier (Wire)
Glen of Imaal Terrier
Irish Terrier
Jack Russell Terrier (UK Parson Russell Terrier)
Kerry Blue Terrier
Lakeland Terrier
Manchester Terrier (Standard)
Miniature Bull Terrier
Miniature Schnauzer (UK Utility Group)
Norfolk Terrier
Norwich Terrier
Scottish Terrier
Sealyham Terrier
Skye Terrier
Soft-Coated Wheaten Terrier
Staffordshire Bull Terrier
Welsh Terrier
West Highland White Terrier

TOY GROUP
Affenpinscher
Australian Silky Terrier
Brussels Griffon
Bolognese
Cavalier King Charles Spaniel
Chihuahua
Chinese Crested
Coton de Tulear
English Toy Spaniel (UK King Charles Spaniel)
English Toy Terrier
Griffon Bruxellois
Havanese
Italian Greyhound
Japanese Chin
Maltese
Manchester Terrier (Toy)
Miniature Pinscher
Papillon
Pekingese
Pomeranian
Poodle – Toy (UK Utility Group)
Pug
Shih Tzu (UK Utility Group)
Yorkshire Terrier

NON-SPORTING/UTILITY

American Eskimo Dog
Bichon Frise (UK Toy Group)
Boston Terrier
Bulldog
Chinese Shar Pei
Chow Chow
Dalmatian
Finnish Spitz
French Bulldog
German Spitz
Japanese Spitz
Keeshond
Lhasa Apso
Löwchen (UK Toy Group)
Poodle – Miniature, Standard (UK Utility Group)
Schipperke
Shiba Inu
Tibetan Spaniel
Tibetan Terrier

HERDING /PASTORAL

Australian Cattle Dog
Australian Shepherd

Bearded Collie
Belgian Groenendael
Belgian Lakenois
Belgian Malinois
Belgian Tervuren
Border Collie
Bouvier des Flandres (UK Working Group)
Briard
Canaan Dog (UK Utility Group)
Collie – Rough
Collie – Smooth
Estrela Mountain Dog
Finnish Lapphund
German Shepherd Dog
Lancashire Heeler
Maremma Sheepdog
Norwegian Buhund
Old English Sheepdog
Polish Lowland Sheepdog
Puli – Hungarian
Shetland Sheepdog
Swedish Lapphund
Swedish Vallhund
Welsh Corgi (Cardigan)
Welsh Corgi (Pembroke)

III: Index